THE MARIAN
CONSPIRACY

THE MARIAN
CONSPIRACY

*The Hidden Truth About the
Holy Grail, the Real Father of Christ
and the Tomb of the Virgin Mary*

GRAHAM PHILLIPS

SIDGWICK
& JACKSON

First published 2000 by Sidgwick & Jackson
an imprint of Macmillan Publishers Ltd
25 Eccleston Place, London SW1W 9NF
Basingstoke and Oxford
Associated companies throughout the world
www.macmillan.co.uk

ISBN 0 283 06341 6

3 5 7 9 8 6 4 2

A CIP catalogue record for this book is available from
the British Library.

Phototypeset by Intype London Ltd
Printed and bound in Great Britain by
Mackays of Chatham plc, Chatham, Kent

CONTENTS

Acknowledgments

The author would like to thank the following people for their invaluable help.

Father Michael Rinsonelli for showing me the Secret Archives and inspiring the project. Dr David Deissmann and Carole Snyder for their help and hospitality during my stay in Israel. Edna Bowen, Margaret Timmings and Steve Jowett for providing me with invaluable information during my research in England and Barry Davis, Tom Ellis, Graham Russell and Jodi Russell for their special help in Wales. Ann Smith for rediscovering the Pabo poem. Tara Gildea for solving the mystery of the *Ave Maria*. Andrew Collins for his work into the origin of the Fool in British mythology. The Edwards family for permitting the survey of Trevail's Acre and Sheila Lea for allowing us access to Berth Hill. Anglesey Highways and Technical Services Department for allowing the geophysics scan of the area around the well. Martin Keatman for co-authoring *King Arthur: The True Story.* Charlie Mounter, Ann Cooke and Sue Philpott for all their hard work. Kellie Knights and Louise Simkiss for working so efficiently as my researchers and Lorraine Evans, whose remarkable discoveries concerning the origins of Judaism helped make this book possible.

I would also like to thank the following people for contributing their valuable expertise. Dark Age military history: Dan and Susanna Shadrake of Britannia. Geophysics survey of the Berth: John Gater, Dr Susan Ovenden, Dr Clare Adam and Clare Stephens of Geophysics of Bradford. Shropshire archaeology: Dr Roger White. History of Shropshire and the kingdom of Powys: Mike Stokes, curator of Rowley's House Museum, Shrewsbury. The Dark Age history of Anglesey: John Smith, the technical services officer of Oriel Ynys Môn, Llangefni. Geophysics survey of the Llanerchymedd well: Helen and Simon Bourne. French literature: Lisa Rooney. French translations: Jane Parker. Welsh translations: Dave Griffiths and Helen Jones. German translations: Peter Gärtner. Hebrew translations: Pam Kritz. Latin translations: Dr Toby Deler.

Finally, a special thanks to my agent Simon Trewin and my commissioning editor Gordon Wise.

Graham Phillips. London, 1999

I

THE SECRET ARCHIVES

THE SOFT BLUE eyes of the Madonna stared serenely down at me from the gilt-framed painting hanging above the desk of the man in the billowy striped costume. By contrast, the man eyed me up and down suspiciously as he picked up the phone and dialled. Attired in sixteenth-century dress – baggy breeches and jacket, starched white neck ruff and floppy black beret – he might easily have been manning a stand at a Renaissance fair. However, this man was no dreamy re-enactor of bygone times, but a sergeant in the Swiss Guard: a soldier of the smallest yet, arguably, one of the most influential countries in the world – the Vatican City State. I was standing in the Constantine Portico, the pedestrian entrance to the Apostolic Palace on the north side of St Peter's Square, awaiting an appointment with Father Michael Rinsonelli.

Father Rinsonelli had written to me a few months earlier, following the Italian publication of my book *The Search for the Grail*. I had investigated the historicity behind the Grail legend and had arrived at a controversial conclusion. Today, most people think of the Holy Grail as the cup used by Jesus at the Last Supper, but I had argued that the term

'Grail' was originally applied to any holy relic that was thought to have been associated with Christ. In fact, I discovered that a whole variety of receptacles were depicted as the Grail in medieval times: everything ranging from cauldrons to dishes to cups. One such artefact was even an ointment jar, said to have been used by Mary Magdalene to collect drops of Christ's blood when he appeared to her after he rose from the tomb.

The ointment jar disappeared in Britain during the Middle Ages but it was claimed to have been found by a Midland businessman in the 1920s. The discovery received no recognition at the time and the forgotten relic remained stored away in an attic in the English town of Rugby until I managed to trace it in 1995. When the story of the jar's discovery broke in the Italian press in the August of that year it ignited immediate controversy. It began with Rocco Zingaro di Ferdinando, the grand master of a secret society claiming descent from the ancient Crusaders, the Knights Templar, holding a press conference in Rome. Zingaro claimed to possess the true Grail and produced an ornate stone cup as proof. So much did the story of the two Grails dominate the Italian media that it sparked a rumpus within the Church itself. The Italian cathedrals at Genoa and Lucca also came forward with their conflicting claims to possess the real Holy Grail, and the squabbling even became international when the Spanish cathedral of Valencia joined in with its claim to house the sacred relic.

I was considering a follow-up book and came across a reference to the so-called Secret Archives – supposedly Vatican records to which very few Church officials have access. They were said to contain all sorts of ancient documents concerning events in Church history that the Vatican kept secret. Just out of interest, I wrote to the Vatican Library asking if they could confirm or deny the existence of the archives. I did not really expect to hear back; it came as a complete surprise when Father Rinsonelli – a priest who actually worked in the Vatican Library – wrote me a very friendly reply. He knew of me from the recent publicity and had actually read my book. Father Rinsonelli had trained as an historian at Oxford University before he was ordained and had long been fascinated by the Grail legend. He not only wanted to meet me if ever I was in Rome, he even offered to show me the Secret Archives.

The sergeant replaced the receiver and told me in a polite but clipped Germanic accent that Father Rinsonelli would be down in a few minutes. As I waited, I paced across the portico, my footsteps echoing along the column-flanked corridor that led to the grand stairway which swept upwards into the heart of the Holy See. I stopped and looked up at Bernini's famous seventeenth-century statue of the person responsible for founding the Vatican and establishing the Roman Catholic Church: the Roman emperor Constantine the Great. It always seemed to me a peculiar irony that Christianity and its message of peace and goodwill should have been so furthered by a man whom history records as a tyrant and a murderer.

In the second decade of the fourth century the Roman empire was in a state of civil war between two would-be emperors, Maxentius and Constantine. Constantine held much of the western empire, but Maxentius still held the city of Rome. On 28 October AD 312 Constantine was ready to lay siege to the capital. Legend has it that on the night before the battle he experienced a vision which converted him to Christianity and he accordingly triumphed. Whatever kind of Christianity the emperor imagined he had embraced, it had little to do with the teachings of Jesus. Years after his so-called conversion, Constantine murdered his own son and had his wife boiled alive in her bath.

Historians surmise that Constantine made Christianity the state religion of the Roman empire as an act of political expediency. He needed something to unite the empire and as his domineering mother, the empress Helena, had already embraced the widespread religion, it was Christianity he chose to adopt. However, he first needed to unify the Christians, and that was easier said than done. There was a wide variety of Christian movements throughout the empire, with greatly differing views and practices. There were the Gnostics of southern Egypt who practised mystical meditation, the Ebionites of Decapolis who lived in communes, the Docetists of Alexandria who believed in the spiritual omnipresence of Jesus, and a myriad others.

In AD 325 Constantine summoned all the Christian leaders to his palace at Nicaea, in what is now Turkey, for a council to agree on the foundations of a unified Church. The emperor faced an almost impossible task. Eventually, after weeks of wrangling, Constantine appointed his political ally Eusebius, the head of the Church at Caesarea in Palestine, to draft a compromise settlement. What Eusebius came up with were, in essence, the religious dogmas which still remain the central pillars of the established Church. Nearly everyone present objected to something or other, and Constantine lost patience. He decreed that anyone who refused to sign the agreement would be banished from the empire. And he enforced his ruling: those who dissented were never heard from again and those who conceded became the hierarchy of the Universal or Catholic Church. To commemorate his conversion, Constantine built a splendid church in Rome, on the site thought to be that of St Peter's tomb. So began the Vatican, now a sprawl of gigantic High Renaissance buildings spreading over forty-four hectares.

'Mr Phillips!' came a voice from behind me. I turned to face a tall, slim, almost completely bald man in his mid-fifties. 'Father Rinsonelli,' he said cordially, holding out a hand. Father Rinsonelli spoke perfect English with hardly a trace of accent, which was due, I later learned, from his having spent much of his early life in England. He had been born in Rome, but his parents had moved to England after the war. He had been brought up in London and only after studying history at Oxford had returned to Italy to train for the priesthood.

'I thought I'd take you to the library by the scenic route,' he said, as he led me along the corridor towards the wide stone staircase. This was my first time inside the Vatican and the initial effect was breathtaking: because of both the incredible architecture and the arduous climb. As we made our way up the seemingly endless Scala Regia, two long flights of marble steps separated by a corridor, I became aware that the pilasters supporting the vaulted ceiling were placed at gradually diminishing intervals. Apparently the design was a deliberate attempt by the architect Bernini to leave the visitor with the impression that he was approaching ever closer to the holiest of holies. As indeed we were, Father Rinsonelli informed me when we neared the top. The Pope's private apartments were just off to the right, behind a doorway flanked by two Swiss Guard.

'The Sala Regia,' he said as we reached the head of the great stairway. 'The ceremonial centre of the Apostolic Palace.' We were in a huge barrel-vaulted hall, so vast and empty that it made me feel somewhat exposed as I walked across its marble floor, ever in the gaze of the Swiss Guard who stood in pairs at their posts beside the various doorways that led off in different directions. Father Rinsonelli pointed to the last and most impressive exit. 'The Sistine Chapel,' he said, leading the way.

The word 'chapel' I had always associated with humble little buildings. The Sistine Chapel, however, was a enormous single chamber, large enough to contain a modest English cathedral, every inch of its walls and ceiling covered with incredible works of art. Directly facing me as we entered was one of the largest paintings in the world. Covering the entire wall above the high altar was Michelangelo's *Last Judgement*, some eighteen metres high and twelve wide. To either side were other priceless works of art – frescos by Botticelli, Luca Signorelli, Rosselli and Perugino.

Scattered around the hall, groups of tourists were awkwardly craning their necks to get a view of what is arguably the world's most famous work of art: Michelangelo's painting of the Creation on the Sistine Chapel ceiling. I did likewise, and immediately felt dizzy. It was not so much the awe inspired by Michelangelo's workmanship as the fact that I could not work out what was holding up the roof. Even in the corridors there had been columns and pillars to either side to support the ceiling. Here the huge concave expanse appeared just to hang there. It seemed as though the whole edifice would come crashing down on top of us at any moment.

Suddenly the throng of tourists in front of us parted as a stream of black-clad clergy made their way from one door, across the hall and out through another. By the scarlet braiding on his cassock, the elderly gentleman leading the party was a cardinal and the priests that followed him, with their briefcases and leather-bound folders, seemed more like an entourage of business executives following their chairman into a board meeting. One of the trailing priests, a young man who was hurrying to catch up, was almost knocked over by a tourist who backed into him while still gazing up at the ceiling. The tourist apologized profusely, but the priest just glared at him and hurried on.

'It can be pretty difficult trying to work here sometimes,' said Father Rinsonelli. 'We welcome visitors, but they can get in the way. The Vatican oversees the faith of almost a billion Catholics – that's over three times the number of people who live in the United States. Imagine the US government trying to conduct its day-to-day business with sightseers wandering freely around the corridors of power.'

As we made our way to the Vatican Museum, where the library was situated, Father Rinsonelli told me the history of the Secret Archives. The Archives of the Apostolic See, to use their real name, were basically a record of all that ever went on in the Vatican. They included everything from the minutes of daily meetings to the thinking behind Church dogma and papal decrees – thousands of folders containing briefs, letters and accounts spanning the history of the Vatican. They were, in fact, the working documents of the Curia, the two-thousand-strong Vatican bureaucracy. Father Rinsonelli, however, was far more than a filing clerk. Archivists such as he were members of the Amministrazioni Palatine, a select Vatican department answering directly to the Pope.

My guided tour of the magnificent galleries of the Vatican Museum ended above the Apostolic Library in a dull, white-washed storeroom some nine metres square.

'The Secret Archives,' Father Rinsonelli announced casually, motioning to the bundles of manila folders stacked all over the floor. I looked at the priest incredulously as he led me on through a series of further dull-looking rooms filled with filing cabinets and endless stacks of loosely bound papers and documents. Here were none other than the infamous Secret Archives – the records of everything that has gone on behind the Vatican walls for centuries.

'I'm afraid the term "Secret Archives" is rather misleading,' continued the priest. 'The archives were secret once, and that's how they got their name, but in 1883 Pope Leo XIII declared that the papacy had nothing to fear from history and opened the archives to secular scholars. The real secret about the archives is that they are a complete shambles.'

Father Rinsonelli explained how most of the documents had remained unbound and uncatalogued for centuries. In 1980 the Pope had inaugurated a project to house the archives in a new underground facility beneath the Cortile della Pigna, and the library staff had since spent much of their time binding and cataloguing everything as the work proceeded. A few years before, one cardinal-librarian tried to initiate a similar project but abandoned the idea when his staff confidently informed him that the project would take a hundred years.

'Sadly, we have less than twenty staff at any time,' the priest complained. 'The work has been going on for almost two decades and we've hardly made a start. Some say the archives will eventually take up fifty kilometres of shelves, so I think the original estimate of a hundred years may be optimistic.'

Intrigued, I listened as Father Rinsonelli told me about

some of the fascinating documents that had been redis-covered during the move: the momentous papal bulls that pronounced the excommunication of Martin Luther and Henry VIII; letters written by Michelangelo and the infam-ous Lucrezia Borgia; even the signed testimony of Galileo.

'Unfortunately, most of it makes pretty dull reading,' he concluded, bending down to examine one of the folders. 'Stationery requisitions for August 1961.'

'Why are you showing me all this?' I asked eventually.

'You wrote that you thought the Church is in the business of concealing its history. I wanted you to realize that today that simply isn't true. If there is any particular document you want to see, just ask and I'm sure I can arrange it.'

I didn't quite know how to respond to Father Rinsonelli's invitation. If there were secret documents in the Vatican archives, how would I know what they were so as to be able to ask for them?

'I'm not quite sure what I'll be working on next,' I said after a few moments' thought.

'Have you considered a possible link between the Holy Grail and the Holy Mother?'

'The Virgin Mary! Why?'

'I found a rather interesting reference concerning the Grail in the archives.' Father Rinsonelli began by describing a fascinating episode of Vatican intrigue concerning modern Church teachings regarding the Assumption – the Virgin Mary's ascension into heaven.

Even though the Bible makes no reference to the event, an old Church tradition holds that the Virgin Mary ascended bodily into heaven. More progressive members of the Church considered the story a myth, and that Mary's mortal remains would have been interred according to contemporary custom. The Catholic world remained divided on the issue and until recently it was left up to individual churchgoers to make up their own minds. In 1950, however, the Assumption was declared dogma by Pope Pius XII. From then on Mary's bodily ascension into heaven became official Church doctrine.

The new doctrine meant that, unlike other saints, Mary's mortal remains were not to be found anywhere on earth. This left the Church with a problem. Just to the east of Jerusalem in the Valley of Jehosaphat is a dark underground shrine which for centuries had been regarded as the Virgin's tomb. It is now empty, but when it was discovered in AD 517 by Severus, the bishop of Antioch, it did contain a number of bodies, one of which was said to be Mary's. Since the sixteenth century the parish church of Calcata in Italy has made claim to possessing some of these bones, which were credited with miraculous healing properties, and every year thousands of Catholics made a pilgrimage to visit the shrine were the relics where housed.

Fearing that the shrine might be used by critics of the Church to undermine the credibility of the papacy, cardinal-advisers to the Pope set up an official investigation into the authenticity of the relics. Giovanni Benedetti, an archaeologist attached to the Vatican Museum, was sent to examine the relics, presumably in the hope of proving them a fake. Although, much to the relief of the Vatican, the relics turned out to be sheep bones, Benedetti inadvertently opened up a completely new can of worms. While he was waiting to examine the bones, he had investigated the authenticity of the Jerusalem tomb. He concluded, like most historians, that there was no evidence that the tomb in the Valley of Jehosaphat was really Mary's tomb. (Severus himself even admitted that he learned that it was Mary's tomb in a dream.) However, during this investigation Benedetti had come across what he considered to be evidence for an altogether different tomb of the Virgin Mary.

When he reported back on his findings, he was summoned to appear before one of the most powerful departments in the Vatican – the Holy Inquisition. Although it was renamed the Holy Office in 1908, this High Court of orthodoxy is still, even today, very much in the business of ferreting out heretics, and something of its sinister reputation still clings to its offices in St Peter's Square. The Inquisition may no longer have the power to burn dissenters at the stake, but it does wield the authority to censor Church writings and to excommunicate any Catholic who it deems to have offended the faith. On pain of excommunication, Benedetti was instructed to discontinue his work and was forbidden to publish or speak publicly about his research. A good Catholic and an employee of the Vatican, he complied.

Father Rinsonelli had found the minutes of Benedetti's appearance before the Holy Office. They apparently made no specific reference to the evidence for a second tomb, but they did make the Holy Office position clear. Although it was evidently their informed opinion that the second tomb was simply a Dark Age legend, they considered that any further investigations into the subject by a Vatican official would appear divisive.

Like the Holy Office, Father Rinsonelli accepted the doctrine of the Assumption and considered the second tomb to be a myth. However, he had found something in the report which had intrigued him. It seems that Benedetti had spoken to someone about his theory because the minutes showed that he had been specifically instructed to clarify a remark that he had made. Father Rinsonelli took a notebook from his pocket and read his translation of the relevant reference: ' "His [Benedetti's] statement that the Holy Mother was the Holy Grail should be properly clarified so that no improper inference should be made. Namely, that the Grail was merely an artistic representation of the Holy Mother." '

This was a concept new to Father Rinsonelli, and he wanted to know if I had ever come across any evidence of a link between Mary and the Grail legend.

'Mary Magdalene, yes,' I replied, 'but not the Virgin Mary. But even that, I'm certain, was a medieval legend.' It was indeed an interesting concept: a sacred chalice which contained the holy blood of Jesus – an early Christian symbol for Christ's mother. 'I wouldn't disagree, though,' I said. 'As you know, I think the Grail became different things to different people. As for the Virgin Mary, I don't know much about her.'

'Nor does anyone,' said Father Rinsonelli, turning and staring out through the window across the jumbled rooftops of the Vatican City. 'Our Lady is the most important woman who ever lived, yet the Bible tells us almost nothing about her.'

From the Catholic perspective Farther Rinsonelli was right. According to the Dogmatic Constitution of the Church, 'Mary has by grace been exalted above all angels and men to a place second only to her Son.' The Virgin Mary is by far the most venerated of saints. Most saints have only one annual feast or holy day, while St Mary has one every few weeks, and all Catholic churches, abbeys and cathedrals have a Lady chapel dedicated to her, regardless of which saint the building itself is dedicated to. Moreover, most daily prayers are offered exclusively to the Virgin. Of the 180 prayers of the rosary, required to be recited by Catholics as part of the confessional process, 150 are the 'Ave Maria' – the 'Hail Mary'.

The Bible, on the other hand, is strangely silent concerning most of her life. It gives Mary great importance as the mother of Christ; it tells how she conceived by direct intervention of the Holy Ghost and gave birth to Jesus in Bethlehem. But apart from her presence at the foot of the cross during the Crucifixion, she appears in only a few brief episodes during Jesus' ministry and then only as a peripheral character. After the Crucifixion the gospels tell us nothing of where she lived or died: neither is there a single reference either to her burial or to the Assumption.

Giovanni Benedetti's investigations concerning the tomb of the Virgin Mary were only one of the many topics Father Rinsonelli and I discussed before parting company that day, but the story had intrigued me far more than the priest knew or intended. It had me thinking about the whole question of the Virgin Mary. Marian devotion – the veneration of the Virgin Mary – is a central theme of Catholic theology. To almost a billion Catholics, Mary is the most important woman who ever lived. However, her life on earth is almost a complete mystery. She appears only briefly in a few biblical verses, and no contemporary records concerning her have ever been found. There and then I decided on my next historical investigation. I was determined to discover the truth about the mother of Christ. Who was she, really? What was she like as a person? Where did she live out her life and where did she die? And then there was the most compelling question of all – where was she buried?

As I left St Peter's Square later that afternoon, I glanced

over at the High Renaissance building directly opposite the Constantine Portico – the Holy Office. Bound by the doctrine of the Assumption, Father Rinsonelli had not given a second thought to Benedetti's notion that there might be a real tomb of the Virgin Mary. I, however, could not help feeling that there was more to the Holy Office muzzling Benedetti than the report revealed. Had he discovered convincing evidence that there really was a second tomb? Although I did not know it at the time, I was about to embark upon the search to uncover one of the greatest secrets in Christian history – the tomb of the Virgin Mary.

Summary

- The Bible is silent concerning most of the Virgin Mary's life. It gives her great importance as the mother of Christ; it tells how she conceived by direct intervention of the Holy Ghost and gave birth to Jesus in Bethlehem. However, apart from her presence at the foot of the cross during the Crucifixion, she appears in only a few brief episodes during Jesus' ministry and then only as a peripheral character. After the Crucifixion the gospels tell us nothing of where she lived or died, and there is not a single reference to her place of burial.

- Even though the Bible makes no reference to the event, an old Church tradition holds that the Virgin Mary ascended bodily into heaven. More progressive members of the Church considered the story a myth. The Catholic world remained divided on the issue and until recently it was left up to individual churchgoers to make up their own minds. In 1950, however, Mary's bodily ascension into heaven – the Assumption – was made official Church doctrine by Pope Pius XII.

- The new doctrine meant that, unlike other saints, Mary's mortal remains were not to be found anywhere on earth. This left the Church with a problem. Just to the east of Jerusalem in the valley of Jehosaphat is a dark underground shrine which for centuries had been regarded as the Virgin's tomb. Fearing that the shrine might be used by critics of the Church to undermine the credibility of the papacy, cardinal-advisers to the Pope set up an official investigation into its authenticity.

- Giovanni Benedetti, the archaeologist attached to the Vatican Museum who was sent to examine the tomb, concluded that there was no evidence that it was really Mary's final resting place. However, during this investigation he had come across what he considered to be evidence for an altogether different tomb of the Virgin Mary.

- When Benedetti reported back on his findings, he was summoned to appear before one of the most powerful departments in the Vatican – the Holy Office. On pain of excommunication, he was instructed to discontinue his work and was forbidden to publish or speak publicly about his research. The location of the second tomb that Benedetti discovered was never made public.

II

CITY OF GOD

MY EARS POPPED as the plane swept down over the diamond-blue waters of the Mediterranean, as smooth as glass and sparkling in the morning sun. We were beginning our descent into Ben Gurion International Airport at Tel Aviv. I was somewhat disappointed by my first view of the Holy Land. The coastline looked like a Spanish holiday resort: luxury hotels lining the seafront, with rows of extruded office blocks and apartment buildings beyond – all shrouded in a brown haze.

Once I was on the bus and heading for Jerusalem, however, everything changed: the parched land, the sun-baked palms and the crumbling hills all seemed far more familiar as the land of Jesus Christ. It was here, two thousand years ago, that Mary had raised a son who would change the world for ever. I took out the pocket-size copy of *The Living Faith*, a Catholic handbook that Father Rinsonelli had given me, and glanced at the introduction to the chapter on the Virgin Mary:

Mary is the Mother of God and Queen of Heaven. She is the co-redeemer of the universe, part of the trinity, and the

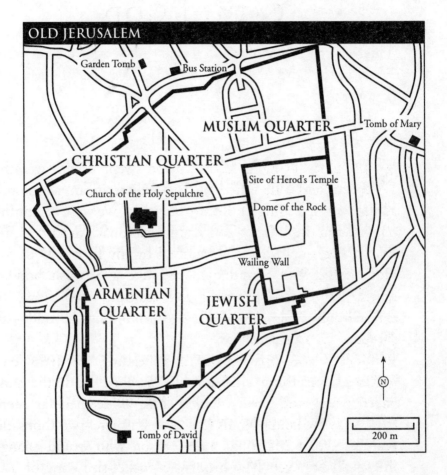

OLD JERUSALEM

Garden Tomb • Bus Station

MUSLIM QUARTER Tomb of Mary

CHRISTIAN QUARTER

Site of Herod's Temple

Church of the Holy Sepulchre

Dome of the Rock

Wailing Wall

ARMENIAN QUARTER

JEWISH QUARTER

N

Tomb of David

200 m

only human being who is the theme of an article of faith. She is the Immaculate Conception, born exempt from original sin. She is the model of faith and charity. She is the most superior and wholly unique member of the Church. She is forever Virgin.

This was the Mary of Church doctrine – the Mary of faith. Here, in the land of Israel, I hoped to discover the Mary of history.

Late that afternoon I stood on the balcony of the Sheraton Plaza hotel looking out over the city of Jerusalem. To the west was the New City, like any modern metropolis with its high-rise blocks, department stores and streams of traffic; but to the east was the Old City with its great stone walls, the Church of the Holy Sepulchre and the golden Dome of the Rock. This was the capital of ancient Palestine where Jesus had preached and died.

After showering and changing I wandered back on to the balcony and looked again over the holy city. The sun had set but the sky was still red with twilight and a full moon hung just above the distant mountains. Somewhere out there, I wondered, was there really a forgotten tomb of the Virgin Mary: a secret that had died with Giovanni Benedetti? True to his word, he never published anything on his investigations into Mary's tomb. As far as I could discover, he never even mentioned the episode again before his death in 1961. I would have to start at the beginning. Try to discover as much as I could about Mary's life. But there was nothing I could do that evening. I decided that I would sample the Jerusalem night life; find out what the average Israeli did on a Friday night.

Suddenly I became aware of something strange. Lights

were twinkling in the houses below but an eerie silence had settled over everything. I leant over the parapet and looked down at the streets. They were completely empty. The fuming traffic and rushing pedestrians of only an hour before were all gone. For some minutes I stood there mystified until the deathly calm was broken when a single taxi raced past the front of the hotel and disappeared into a side street.

Suddenly, my heart was pounding. The most famous image of the Gulf War came flooding into my mind. The CNN reporter looking out of his Tel Aviv hotel window as the camera shakily zoomed in on a fiery glow somewhere across the city. The first of Saddam Hussein's Scud missiles had fallen on Israel and no one yet knew if its payload was nerve gas. An anxious voice from the studio implored the reporter to close the windows and put on his respirator.

Only a few weeks earlier the West had again come within a whisper of launching air raids on Baghdad when the Iraqis had obstructed the UN weapons inspectors. Israel had been on high alert in preparation for expected Iraqi reprisals. Had hostilities finally broken out? Had the noise of the shower drowned out the sound of the air raid sirens? Had everyone fled for cover? Was a Scud attack imminent? I quickly left the balcony, slammed shut the sliding glass door, grabbed the phone and dialled reception.

'What's going on?' I asked nervously. 'Outside, the streets, they're empty.'

A pause and then a laugh.

'It's *shabat*, the Sabbath, sir.'

Of course; the Sabbath. From sundown Friday to sundown Saturday, no work and no travel. Sighing with relief, I flopped back on the bed.

Having absolutely no idea what non-Jews were expected

to do or not to do on the Sabbath day, I decided to play safe. Accordingly, I spent that evening and the following day in my hotel room going over all the information I had on the Virgin Mary's background.

Nazareth was a small Jewish community about a hundred kilometres north of Jerusalem, and it is here that Mary makes her first appearance in the Bible story. When she was born, just over two thousand years ago, Palestine was a province of the Roman empire – the mightiest empire the world had known, encompassing the Mediterranean and stretching throughout much of western Europe, the Near East and northern Africa. Although the Jews were Roman subjects, overseen by the Roman military presence, their way of life continued pretty much as it had before the Romans annexed the country in 63 BC. Jewish religion was permitted and remained under the jurisdiction of the Sanhedrin, the priesthood at the great temple in Jerusalem. The Jews even had their own king, albeit a puppet king – Herod the Great – who exercised considerable authority from his palace at Herodium, some twenty-five kilometres south of Jerusalem.

Each year on 25 March, the modern Church celebrates the Feast of the Annunciation, commemorating the day when, according to the Bible, Mary was visited in Nazareth by the angel Gabriel and told that she had conceived a divine child – Jesus. According to the narrative, Mary is perplexed by the news as she and her husband Joseph have not yet consummated their marriage. The angel, however, tells Mary that the child is not Joseph's, but the son of God. Through the miraculous intervention of the Holy Ghost, Mary has conceived as a virgin. She has been chosen to bear Christ: the Hebrew Messiah.

Although the name Christ is now used specifically in reference to Jesus, it originally came from the Latin *Christus*, which came in turn from the Greek *Khristos*, meaning 'anointed one'. For the early Christians, it was the nearest translation of the Hebrew term *Messiah*. Although the word itself, roughly translated, does mean 'anointed one', *the* Messiah to the ancient Jews was a unique individual. To understand Mary's role, it is first necessary to understand the concept of Messiah.

The ancient Hebrews believed that it was their destiny to settle in Canaan, a fertile strip of land stretching around a hundred kilometres inland from the southern coast of the eastern Mediterranean – specifically, Palestine, southernmost Canaan, between and around Lake Galilee and the Dead Sea. Culturally, the Hebrews were exceptional for their time in that they believed in one, nameless god who was known only by such titles as *Adoni* – 'Lord' – or *Jehovah* – 'I am that I am.' They were originally twelve separate tribes who settled in Palestine during the thirteenth century BC but were eventually unified into one kingdom, the kingdom of Israel, by David around 1000 BC. Within a century, however, the country had split into two separate kingdoms.

The schism resulted in numerous squabbling sects, leaving Israel prey to foreign aggression, and both kingdoms were conquered by a succession of invaders including the Babylonians, the Greeks and ultimately the Romans. The ancient Hebrew prophets, such as Isaiah and Zechariah, had warned the Hebrews of their folly. They predicted that God would turn his back on Israel until the kingdom again came together as one nation, united by a common religious cause. The man foretold to unite Israel was a royal son of God – a priest-king – the Messiah. He would, like David before him, unify the Hebrews into a new kingdom of Israel. By Mary's time the Hebrews were collectively called the Jews and so the Messiah would be king of the Jews.

So who was this remarkable woman, chosen by God to bear the saviour of Israel? Strangely, the Bible itself does not say anything about Mary's background. It does not name her parents; it does not say where she was born or even how she came to be with Joseph. Her story simply starts with the Annunciation.

Church tradition, however, does reveal something of Mary's childhood. Her father, the tradition holds, was a pious Jew called Joachim and her mother was a devoutly religious woman named Anna. For many years the couple remained childless until an angel appeared to Anna and told her that she was to bear a very special daughter. Today's Church celebrates the appearance of the angel to Anna on 8 December as the Feast of the Immaculate Conception, because Mary's conception was considered immaculate or divine. According to modern Church doctrine, as the future Mother of God, Mary was conceived free from original sin – the vices and immorality which corrupt the rest of humanity.

Mary's birth is celebrated every year on 8 September and, according to the same Church tradition, Mary was born a remarkable girl. She was a beautiful and gifted child who could even walk at the age of six months. When she was three her parents took her to the temple in Jerusalem, where she promptly danced on the steps of the temple portico. The high priest saw this as a sign from God, and Mary was accepted as a temple maiden; for many years she served the Lord as an altar girl in the holy precinct. According to the law, on reaching puberty she was compelled to leave and the high priest found her a guardian: an old widower named Joseph, whom she ultimately married. Mary lived her life as a modest Jewish woman, praying diligently, never losing her virginity to the elderly Joseph.

Although this story has been told by the established Church for centuries, there is not actually one word of it anywhere in the Bible. In fact, there is not even anything in the biblical narrative to suggest that Mary herself was an immaculate conception. Where, then, did the story originate?

The oldest surviving reference to this popular account of Mary's childhood is found in the *Protevangelium*, a book attributed to the second-century Christian leader James of Ephesus. Although no original copy survives, it still exists, partly transcribed, in the works of the third-century Christian writers Origen and Clement of Alexandria. Even within the Church itself there were those who treated the story with suspicion and it was not until 1854 that the account was fully endorsed by Pope Pius IX, who made the concept of the Immaculate Conception official dogma.

Pope Pius based his judgement on faith. Did the mysterious James who wrote the *Protevangelium*, sometime around AD 180, draw upon any historical sources, or was he too inspired by faith alone? James firmly associates Mary with the Jerusalem temple, so do any records of her time as a temple maiden still exist? Could I discover anything about her childhood at the temple of Jerusalem?

Before leaving England I had spoken on the phone with David Deissmann, an archaeologist from the Hebrew University who was involved in excavations of the Jerusalem temple. He had agreed to meet with me on the Monday morning and suggested the most appropriate place – the famous Wailing Wall. So here I was, on the fourth day of my visit to Israel, the only Gentile standing on the wide plaza at the foot of the sacred wall. I was flanked on each side by dozens of Jewish worshippers, who almost mesmerized me with their rhythmic rocking before the ancient weathered stones. Bowing repeatedly, they dutifully recited from prayer books that were cupped devoutly in their hands. Others came and bowed just once or twice before slipping a piece of paper, a written prayer, into cracks in the crumbling façade. This fifty-metre rampart, the site of pilgrimage for Jews from around the world, is all that now remains of the temple of Jerusalem.

Almost a thousand years before Mary was born, David's son Solomon built the first temple in the Israelite capital of Jerusalem, and it soon became the holiest shrine for all Hebrews. Although, following the fragmentation of the country after Solomon's death, northern Israel made its capital at Samaria, it was still Jerusalem, now the capital of the southern kingdom of Judah, that all Hebrews continued to venerate as the holy city. It was in this kingdom, later called Judea by the Romans, that the Hebrew faith continued to develop and, accordingly, the kingdom ultimately lent its name to the Israelite religion and its adherents as a whole: namely, Judaism and the Jews. For almost half a millennium the Jerusalem temple remained the centre of the Jewish faith, until the city was invaded by the Babylonians in 587 BC. Thousands of Jews were enslaved and carted off to exile in the city of Babylon when the Babylonian king Nebuchadnezzar ordered the temple sacked and razed to the ground. Then, in 515 BC, when the Persians defeated the Babylonians, the Jews were allowed to return to Jerusalem. The temple was partly repaired but this too was plundered by the Greeks in

169 BC. By the time the Roman general Pompey took the city in 63 BC, the once great temple was little more than a highly venerated pile of rubble.

Paradoxically, the Roman occupation of Palestine actually brought greater prosperity to the area than it had known for centuries. When Herod was installed as king by the Romans, he used this new-found wealth to reconstruct the temple on an even grander scale than the original. Work began about 19 BC, and by the time it was completed the new temple was one of the largest and most impressive structures in the Near East.

The Jewish historian Josephus, writing around AD 90, tells of the astonishing magnitude of the project. Built on a flat-topped hill at the edge of the city, the outer walls measured 240 by 1,000 metres: an incredible two-and-a-half-kilometre walk. They were 50 metres high in places and made from stones weighing as much as 50 tonnes. At the grand entrance to the south end of the town-sized complex, broad flights of steps led upward to the gateways of the Royal Portico: a great columned hall, opening on to the vast outer courtyard beyond. According to Josephus, the pillars that supported the portico roof were so massive that three men standing with arms outstretched could not encircle them.

The outer courtyard was large enough to fit thirteen modern football pitches and was surrounded on all sides by colonnades. Beneath these covered walkways, which provided shade from the blistering sun, visitors could meet and teachers and students could debate religious issues. Glistening in the middle of the courtyard was the inner temple complex, built on top of a gigantic stone platform over a metre high. Its castellated walls measured some 300 by 150 metres and were about 30 metres in height, with defensive turrets at strategic points. At various intervals steps led up the platform to eight huge doors covered with gold and silver plating. The main entrance, the Corinthian Gate, was on the eastern side. Over fifteen metres high, its double bronze doors were so heavy, Josephus tells us, that twenty men were needed to push them shut.

Anyone could enter the Royal Portico and the outer courtyard but only Jews were allowed inside the central complex. Notices written in Greek and Latin warned everyone who was not Jewish to keep out. Any foreigner who ignored the warning was likely to find himself lynched. Through the Corinthian Gate, worshippers entered another court, some 67 metres square, again surrounded by covered walkways. This was known as the Women's Court, as beyond this point women could not venture. Only men were allowed to climb a further flight of steps and pass through a final gate, to stand in the inner court before the temple itself – an exact replica of Solomon's temple as described in the ancient scriptures. It was around 50 metres high and some 300 metres square, its walls flanked by columns and its roof surrounded by gilded spikes to prevent birds from perching along its edge. Inside there was an outer sanctuary, housing braziers for the animal sacrifices required by contemporary Judaic law, and the high altar bearing the *menorah*, the golden seven-branched candlestick which symbolized the presence of God. Finally, beyond this, the innermost sanctuary, the 'holy of holies', was left empty. In the original temple the Ark of the Covenant had rested here, but mysteriously it had disappeared centuries before. Herod's new temple again became the focus of pilgrimage for Jews throughout the world. There may have been many synagogues but there was only one temple of God.

Unfortunately, I could learn nothing of Mary's childhood service at the temple from its historical records, for it long ago all but vanished. The destruction of the temple was apparently foretold by Christ himself. The ancient Hebrew prophets predicted that the Messiah would enter the holy city of Jerusalem and challenge the corruption of the temple. According to the Bible, this is exactly what Mary's son Jesus eventually did.

Religious law compelled every Jew to pay temple tax once a year, and it could only be paid in silver shekels. For this reason there were money-changers stationed in the Royal Portico to exchange travellers' coins. In fact, the portico became a hive of industry as there were also lines of stalls selling sacrificial animals, such as birds, sheep and goats. Many of the traders charged extortionate commission and unfairly high prices, taking advantage of the pilgrims, many of whom had spent their savings travelling from far afield to worship at the temple. The traders had to pay for permission to have their stalls in this area, and the priesthood was growing rich off the profits. Finding the entire procedure abhorrent:

> Jesus went into the temple, and began to cast out them that sold and bought in the temple, and overthrew the tables of the money-changers, and the seats of them that sold doves. (Mark 11:15)

Jesus was so appalled at the corruption of the temple that he even foretold its destruction:

> Seest thou these great buildings? There shall not be left one stone upon another, that shall not be thrown down. (Mark 13:2)

Jesus' prophecy came true after the Jewish revolt against Rome late in the seventh decade. In AD 70 the magnificent temple was reduced to rubble when the Romans looted it of its treasures and burnt it to the ground. The emperor even ordered the entire complex to be demolished stone by stone. Only one section of wall still remains – the Wailing Wall. The several courses of stones which now rise above the modern pavement of Old Jerusalem were once part of the western wall of the Royal Portico.

David Deissmann arrived on time and after we had exchanged pleasantries he led me to a nearby setting with an altogether different ambience – a broad flight of steps swarming with tourists.

'This is the staircase that once led up to the Royal Portico,' he said. 'The very steps on which the child Mary is said to have danced. Sadly, however, the story is a myth.'

'I suspect so myself,' I said. 'But, like most ancient traditions, it can't be proved one way or the other.'

'It can,' he said, handing me a monochrome photograph. It showed two Roman coins. 'They were found beneath the stones down there.' He pointed to the lower steps where a party of Japanese sightseers were being videoed by a tour guide.

I looked at the photograph again and David's meaning became clear. The coins bore the head of the emperor Tiberius.

The discovery completely undermined the story written by James of Ephesus in the second century. The temple steps might still have been visible surrounding the rubble of the desecrated temple in James's time, but they would not have been there at all when Mary was a child. From Josephus we know that the work on the temple complex began, firstly, on the inner temple, and moved progressively outwards until finally the Royal Portico was built sometime before Jesus' ministry around AD 30. The Roman coins had been discovered beneath the lowest level of the steps. Whether they were deliberately placed there for some reason or were accidentally dropped will never be known. What *is* certain is that they found their way under the steps when the work began. As Tiberius did not become emperor until AD 14, the steps must postdate this time. Consequently, they were not even there when Mary was supposed to have danced on them some three decades earlier.

David went on to explain that even the story of Mary's service as a temple maiden, serving at the high altar, fails to withstand historical scrutiny. Not only were all females, young and old, forbidden to enter the inner temple, let alone go anywhere near the high altar, but there was no such thing as a temple maiden in contemporary Judaism. In fact, the entire concept is Roman. James came from Ephesus, a seaport city in what is now Turkey, and in the late second century there was a thriving Christian community there. Ephesus was also a huge cultic centre for the Roman goddess Diana. At Diana's temple in the city, it was one of the highest honours for a young girl to be chosen as a temple maiden to serve the goddess until she reached puberty. It seems to have been this pagan custom that James transposed, out of time and cultural context, to the Jewish Palestine of two centuries earlier.

With the entire story of Mary's birth and childhood in question, I was left with the Bible itself from which to ascertain anything concerning her early life.

We may not be told of Mary's parentage in the biblical narrative, but we are told of her cousin. According to the Bible, after Mary learns that she is to bear the Christ Child she goes to stay with her cousin Elizabeth, who the angel tells her will also bear a son – although seemingly not as a virgin. This child is to be John the Baptist, the preacher who will one day prepare the way for Christ's ministry. In the modern Church calendar Mary's stay with Elizabeth, the Feast of the Visitation, is commemorated each year on 31 May. In the Bible story Mary actually stays with her cousin for three months, before returning home to Nazareth. Soon after, however, she is again compelled to travel – this time to Bethlehem. Bethlehem was to be my next port of call.

David kindly offered to drive me to see the very place where Jesus is said to have been born. We would probably have been better off walking to Bethlehem like the pilgrims traditionally do, as a massive tailback had formed on the Hebron Road. Israeli soldiers were searching cars at a checkpoint on the outskirts of Jerusalem. It seemed that they were looking for a suspected terrorist who was expected to try to pass into the semi-autonomous Palestinian region in which Bethlehem was located.

'Once, in Royal David's City . . .' – the opening words of the famous children's carol – go on to tell of Jesus' birth in Bethlehem. The contemporary Jews believed that Bethlehem was King David's town of origin and the ancient prophets had foretold that the Messiah would arise from David's line. The Messiah, it seemed, would be born in Bethlehem and it is there, the Bible tells us, that Joseph and Mary had travelled when Jesus was born. Bethlehem was not, however, a city as the carol asserts. It was, and still is, a small town about ten kilometres south of Jerusalem.

When we eventually made it into Bethlehem our car was parked for us by an Arab official and searched again, this time by armed Palestinian police. Finally, though, we were in Manger Square, the heart of town, surrounded by cafés and souvenir shops. Much of the twenty thousand Arab population, half Christian and half Muslim, David informed me, make their money from the tourist trade – in particular the manufacture and sale of images of the holy family. It was certainly a lucrative business – the square was bustling with sightseers and parties of pilgrims being shown around by nuns from the town's Sisters of St Joseph's Convent and monks from the nearby Franciscan monastery. Despite the reverent atmosphere, the scene could not have been more in contrast to the sanctity of the Vatican's St Peter's Square. Instead of the colourful Swiss Guard with their gleaming pikes, Manger Square was ringed by Israeli soldiers with sub-machine-guns slung over their shoulders. Despite the policy of self-determination for the Palestinians, the Israelis still retained a military presence in the area. The whole thing seemed incredibly precarious: I could not help worrying that if someone got trigger-happy then we would all find ourselves massacred in the cross-fire.

Dominating the east end of the square was the Church of the Nativity, standing over the shrine of Christ's birth. It actually looked more like a fortress than a church as the present structure, built by the Roman emperor Justinian in the sixth century, was fortified by Crusaders in medieval times. Justinian was not responsible for the very original church; that was down to the emperor Constantine in the late 320s. Evidently, he built it over a cave that his mother Helena confidently informed him was the site of the Nativity. She had been told of it by a local Christian hermit, it appeared.

Bowing our way through the single low entrance into the church, we found ourselves at the back of a long queue expectantly waiting to file through the grotto itself, situated beneath the high altar. All around us the church attendants were busy lighting incense and candles and seeing to flowers: the Greek Orthodox priests in their black robes, the Armenian priests in their cream and purple robes and the Franciscan monks with their hooded brown habits. All three denominations tend the church but, incredibly, so far as I could discover, no one was in overall charge.

About an hour later we had reached the altar and the flight of narrow stone steps that led down into the cave of Jesus' birth. 'This is the actual manger where Jesus was born,' an American woman in front of us was telling her little girl. I had to smile: this was one of the two popular misconceptions about the Nativity story. The manger was not the stable but the animal feeding-trough that was used as a bed for the baby Jesus. 'The three kings stood over there,' she continued, pointing to the Altar of the Three Kings in the corner of the church. And this was the second: the Bible does not refer to them as kings at all – they are simply called 'wise men'.

Finally we were in the grotto itself, dimly lit and reeking with the incense smoke that belched from overhanging burners. This was the actual place where Jesus may have been born, the precise spot marked with a silver star on the floor, bearing the Latin inscription: *Hic de virgine Maria*

Jesus Christus natus est – 'Here Jesus Christ was born of the Virgin Mary.'

The little cave looked nothing like the familiar hut of the children's Nativity play – the tale that most people recognize as the story of Jesus' birth. In the familiar pageant Joseph and Mary are depicted travelling from Nazareth to Joseph's home town of Bethlehem to register for a tax census decreed by the emperor Augustus. When they arrive the inn is full and the couple can only find shelter in a stable. When the holy child is born he is laid in the humble manger, yet angels appear bringing shepherds to worship him. A miraculous star – the star of Bethlehem – shines brightly overhead, guiding the three wise men from the east who come to pay homage to the infant with gifts of gold, frankincense and myrrh.

Strictly speaking, this particular scenario is not the Bible story at all. There are four separate accounts of Jesus' life in the Bible: in the gospels of Matthew, Mark, Luke and John. Only two of them mention the Nativity, Matthew and Luke, and they each give a completely different version of events.

In Luke's version Jesus is born in Bethlehem when his parents are compelled to travel there to be taxed. Because there is no room in the inn the baby has to be laid in a manger. A host of angels then appear to shepherds in a nearby field and tell them to pay homage to the Christ Child. In this version there is no star or wise men: they appear in Matthew's account. Matthew gives no circumstances of Jesus' actual birth. There is no manger, no angels and no shepherds. We are simply told that Christ is born in Bethlehem. The wise men from the east then follow the wondrous star that portends the birth, leading them ultimately to the holy family. In this version we are specifically told that when the wise men arrive Mary and the baby Jesus are not in a stable but in a house.

So the familiar Nativity scene is in fact a conflation of two separate accounts – firstly, the stable scene with angels and shepherds and, secondly, a house scene with a star and wise men. Some biblical commentators address these apparent discrepancies in the two accounts by suggesting that each writer has concentrated on a different period of the Nativity: Luke focuses on the actual birth, while Matthew focuses on events shortly after, when the wise men arrive. Unfortunately, this does not address the fact that there are other glaring discrepancies which are completely contradictory.

According to Matthew, when the wise men first arrive in Judea they visit King Herod, assuming he knows where the holy child is to be found. Hearing of the divine birth, Herod fears that Christ will usurp his throne and, learning that the baby has been born somewhere in Bethlehem, he conspires to kill Jesus. After the visit by the wise men, an angel appears to Joseph and tells him of Herod's plan. Mary and Joseph accordingly flee with the infant into Egypt, where they stay until Herod's death. Strangely, Luke fails to mention this crucial episode at all. On the contrary, he has Judea so safe for the Christ Child that Mary can even take him to visit the Jerusalem temple. After the visit the family return to Nazareth, without incident, where they appear to live peacefully for years.

There are further, even more conspicuous inconsistencies between Matthew's and Luke's versions of events. In Luke's familiar version the angel foretells the birth of Jesus to Mary (Luke 1:28), whereas in Matthew the angel leaves Mary out altogether and announces the coming birth to Joseph (Matt.

1:20). Also, oddly, both give Joseph a completely different lineage (Matt. 1:6–17, Luke 3:23–38): even his father has a different name – in Matthew he is called Jacob and in Luke he is called Heli. Perhaps the most serious inconsistency of all, however, is that the two authors disagree as to the time that the Nativity occurred by at least ten years.

In the mid-sixth century the Church decided to begin the Christian era at Christ's birth and, according to the calculations of a Russian monk, Dionysius Exiguus, this was worked out to be the twenty-seventh year of the emperor Augustus' reign. From then on this particular year became the year AD – *Anno Domini* ('in the year of the Lord') – 1. (Confusingly, there is no year 0 in the Christian calendar.) This dating is still used throughout the western world today and, surprisingly, when we apply it to the gospels, neither Luke nor Matthew actually has Jesus being born in the year AD 1. Luke tells us that the tax census that occurred when Jesus was born happened 'when Quirinius was governor of Syria' (Luke 2:2). This particular tax census is recorded by the Romans in AD 6 so, according to Luke, Jesus' birth occurred in that year. Matthew, on the other hand, has Herod the Great still alive. As both Roman and contemporary Jewish records show that Herod died in 4 BC, according to Matthew, Jesus was born in or before that year.

From a purely historical perspective, the Nativity story was beginning to look as suspect as James's story of Mary's childhood. From my background reading I already knew that few modern biblical scholars accept the gospel accounts as 'gospel truth'. Just after the Second World War, some even began to question whether Jesus existed at all. The controversy all began in 1947 with the discovery of the Dead

Sea Scrolls, so on my return to Jerusalem the next day I decided to see these ancient manuscripts for myself.

Hailing a cab, I crossed the New City to the cultural capital of Israel, the Valley of the Cross. Here, in the far south-west of Jerusalem, were the National Library, the Hebrew University, the Israel Museum and the Shrine of the Book: the home of the Dead Sea Scrolls. Paradoxically, though the shrine was purpose-built to contain one of the oldest manuscript collections in the world, its design is strangely futuristic. The main gallery is more like the inside of a flying saucer: a huge, round, windowless room covered by a great ringed dome and bathed in an orange luminescence that seems to radiate from the very walls. At the centre of the room are the most precious of the scrolls, contained inside a circle of illuminated panels that looks like the control console for an alien vessel.

When the scrolls where discovered in a cave overlooking the Dead Sea in 1947 there was excitement throughout the Christian world. Amongst the ancient rolls of parchment were dozens of first-hand documents dating from the very time that Christ is said to have lived. They had been written by the Essenes, a Jewish sect to which many believed John the Baptist had belonged – perhaps even Christ himself. However, far from shedding new light on the historical Jesus, the scrolls had the opposite effect. Although everyone expected them to make reference to a contemporary religious leader as influential as Jesus is said to have been, they made absolutely no mention of him. Some scholars began to argue that this was clear evidence that Jesus never existed at all.

But if Jesus never existed, then neither did his mother. Was there reason for me to continue my search? Looking at the faded brown lettering on the yellowed strips of parchment in the display case before me, I realized that I had to carefully consider other ancient documents – the literary evidence for Jesus' life – before continuing with my investigation into the Virgin Mary.

The story of Jesus' life is contained solely in the New Testament of the Bible: in the four gospels which, in essence, tell the same story. Here, we learn that Jesus was a carpenter from Nazareth who, around the age of thirty, began his ministry. With his twelve closest followers, known as disciples or apostles, he spent two or three years travelling around Palestine spreading God's word of love, fellowship and salvation. After performing numerous miracles and gaining a considerable following, he eventually entered the holy city of Jerusalem where he was proclaimed King of the Jews by his followers. Arrested for subversion by the Jewish elders, he stood trial before the Roman governor Pontius Pilate and was condemned to die on the cross. On the third day he rose from the dead and appeared to his disciples, before ascending bodily into heaven. The New Testament story is then taken up by the Acts of the Apostles, which tell how Jesus' disciples continued to spread his teachings after his departure from the world.

For centuries the gospels were assumed to be eyewitness accounts, and their four authors – collectively called the Evangelists – were thought to have been Christ's disciples. However, numerous contradictions, such as exist in the Nativity story, made modern historians seriously challenge their authenticity. It began in 1835 when German theologian David Friedrich Strauss published his *Life of Jesus Critically Examined*. The work opened up the entire debate on biblical authenticity and, slowly but surely, even mainstream biblical scholars began to doubt that the gospel writers were really eyewitnesses to the events they were describing.

Firstly, they discovered numerous geographical errors in the biblical narrative. For example, the topography of Galilee, Jesus' home province, is all wrong. Mark has Jesus passing through Sidon on his way from Tyre to the Sea of Galilee (Mark 7:31), when Sidon is in fact in the opposite direction, and he places Gadarenes on the shore of Lake Galilee when, in reality, it was almost fifty kilometres to the south-east (Mark 5:1). Incredibly, Galilee's capital, Sepphoris, only six kilometres from Nazareth, goes completely unmentioned in all four gospels. From such errors and omissions it became clear that the gospel writers were not familiar with the map of early first-century Palestine.

Close inspection of the New Testament accounts also revealed that the authors actually disagreed on the locations where events occurred. Take the Ascension, for instance: Luke tells us that Jesus ascended to heaven from the town of Bethany (Luke 24:50–1), Matthew suggests it was from a mount in Galilee, a hundred kilometres to the north (Matt. 28:16–20), and Mark says it was from a room in a house seemingly in Jerusalem (Mark 16:14–19). The famous version of the Ascension from the Mount of Olives just outside Jerusalem comes from the Acts of the Apostles (Acts 1:4–12). The gospel of John, however, makes no mention of the episode at all.

There were equally serious historical errors. For example, the gospel writers seemed ignorant of many aspects of con-temporary Judaism. John talks of the Jewish priesthood electing to stone an adulteress to death (John 8:5), when the Great Sanhedrin – the Jewish Supreme Court – had long before abolished the death penalty for adultery. Mark has

Jesus appearing before the Sanhedrin on the night of the Passover Feast at the palace of the high priest (Mark 14:53), when historically the Sanhedrin met at the Beth Din, a part of the Jerusalem temple, and it was sacrilegious for them to convene at night or during a religious festival. Mark also talks of a woman divorcing her husband (Mark 10:12), although in the Jewish world of the time a woman had no rights of divorce. It therefore became clear that the gospel writers were equally unfamiliar with contemporary Jewish law.

By the 1920s another German theologian, Rudolf Bultmann, widely acclaimed as one of the century's greatest New Testament scholars, drew attention to further indications of late authorship in the gospels. They lacked, he argued, the kind of descriptive detail one would expect to find in first-hand accounts. For instance, they fail to describe any of the people who appear in their narratives – even Christ himself. It is a popular misconception that Jesus' appearance is described in the Bible – the tall Caucasian figure with soft blue eyes, long dark hair and a beard is a medieval conception. In fact, none of the gospel writers offer any description of the man they considered the most important individual who ever lived. The same is true of the Virgin Mary: the beautiful, serene young woman dressed like a nun in a long blue gown and pure white wimple was an invention of much later Christian artists. In fact, unlike Jesus, we are not even told how old Mary is at any point in the biblical narrative.

Critical analysis of the Bible by modern scholars made it altogether evident that the gospels were not contemporary accounts. So when were they written, and by whom?

The Bible, as we now know it, did not come into

existence until the early fourth century – three hundred years after Jesus had lived. There were many early gospels, accounts of Christ's life, referenced by Christian scribes before this time, such as the gospel of Thomas, the gospel of Philip and the gospel of Mary (Magdalene). There were also numerous regional gospels used by different communities, such as the gospel of the Hebrews, the gospel of the Ebionites and the gospel of the Egyptians. Matthew, Mark, Luke and John, therefore, were merely four of many such gospels used by various Christian sects. For at least twenty years after the emperor Constantine formed the Roman Catholic Church at the Council of Nicaea in AD 325, Bishop Eusebius of Caesarea was effectively in charge of sanctioning the religious writings of the newly unified faith. He gathered together all these various gospels and other early Christian writings, chose those that best fitted the new Church's purpose and, from them, compiled what we now know as the New Testament.

Apart from the gospels of Matthew, Mark, Luke and John – now called the canonical gospels – Eusebius included the anonymously compiled Acts of the Apostles, the letters of St Paul and a few other short letters ascribed to other early Christians (Peter, James, John and Jude), and finally added a series of mystical visions ascribed to St John: the Book of Revelation. This New Testament was eventually added to the Torah and a collection of other Hebrew scriptures – now collectively known as the Old Testament – in order to place Jesus in an historical context, and a composite Christian holy book was created. It was called the Bible, from the Greek word *biblia*, meaning simply 'The Book'. Accordingly, the Old Testament contains a collection of texts concerning the history of the Jewish religion prior to Jesus' time and the New Testament takes up the story with the various accounts of Christ's life. Constantine decreed that the Bible was the only true word of God, and all other gospels – the non-canonical gospels – were ordered to be destroyed. The programme was extremely efficient: of the many non-canonical gospels referenced by early Christian authors, only one complete copy has ever been rediscovered.

Although references to these gospels did survive, the Church continued to deny that they ever existed. With no ancient text to contradict it, the Vatican's word went unchallenged until 1945 when an entire library of non-canonical gospels was discovered buried in a cave in Nag-Hamadi in Egypt. Dating from the mid-fourth century, the texts seem to have been hidden by a Christian community in Egypt at the very time of Constantine's gospel purge. The cache included a complete copy of the gospel of Thomas and lengthy passages from the gospel of Philip, the gospel of the Egyptians and the gospel of Mary (Magdalene). Interestingly, they all contain merely a collection of Jesus' sayings, with no details of his life. Whether or not these gospels were actually written by those who had followed Jesus during his earthly life is impossible to tell. However, they do show that Christians outside the Catholic mainstream had numerous texts with just as much claim to historical authenticity as the canonical gospels.

The oldest surviving copy of the New Testament is in the *Codex Sinaiticus*. Now preserved in the British Museum, it is a Greek translation dating only from around AD 350. So how old are the canonical gospels? Only a few tiny papyrus fragments of them have been discovered that predate the mid-fourth century. Of this small handful of verses, the oldest from Luke's gospel dates from the early third century and the oldest from Matthew's dates from the late second. There is a hotly disputed piece of papyrus known as 7Q5, containing two verses from Mark, which some scholars believe to date from as early as AD 50, although most authorities place it a century later. This leaves the earliest dated fragment of any part of the New Testament as the Rylands Fragment. Now in Manchester University, it bears a few verses from John's gospel penned around AD 125.

Biblical scholars are divided between Matthew and Mark as to which gospel came first. However, most agree that they could not have been written before AD 52, as the authors make reference to Roman laws that were not introduced until Claudius Felix became governor of Judea at that time. Similarly, Luke and John could not have been compiled before AD 70 because they make reference to the destruction of the Jerusalem temple by the Romans in that year. Accordingly, at the very earliest, the first of the gospels was not written until around two decades after Jesus' death.

The old notion that the Evangelists were Christ's disciples – such as Matthew being the apostle Matthew, the tax collector – is now dismissed by all but the most fundamentalist Christian scholars. As the oldest reference to the four gospels by their present names does not appear until the second-century writer Irenaeus mentions them around AD 170, it seems that the original narratives were anonymously compiled during the Roman persecutions of the late first century and were later accredited to the disciples by early Christian scribes.

As the New Testament is neither contemporary with the life of Jesus nor does it contain any eyewitness testimony to the events, we must turn to external historical sources. What does history tell us of Christ?

Unfortunately, no contemporary records from Palestine, Rome or anywhere else in the world have yet been discovered to confirm anything the Bible tells us about Jesus. In fact, there is not even a casual mention of him. The man we now call Jesus would not have been known by that name while he was alive, however. The name Jesus comes from the Greek version of the New Testament, which was subsequently translated into Latin and modern languages. 'Jesus' was the Latin rendering of *Iesos*, which in turn was the Greek rendering of *Yeshua*, a common name amongst the first-century Hebrews. There are a number of Yeshuas referenced in first-century Jewish writings, but only one would appear to have been Yeshua of Nazareth, the preacher who was apparently crucified during the governorship of Pontius Pilate. The source, though, has become the subject of bitter controversy.

Towards the end of the first century, the Jewish historian Josephus wrote twenty-eight volumes on his people's history. Two short passages mention Yeshua. In the second, Josephus refers to the execution of James, the brother of Yeshua, and in the first he says:

> About this time lived Yeshua, a wise man, if indeed one should call him a man. For he was a performer of astonishing deeds, a teacher of men who are happy to accept the truth. He won over many Jews, and indeed also many Greeks. He was the Messiah.

Josephus' work only survives in a copy made by Christian monks in the Middle Ages and the controversy concerns whether or not this passage was a medieval addition. Josephus, by his own admission, was a pious Jew. If he really did believe that Jesus was the long-awaited Hebrew Messiah, it seems highly unlikely that he would casually mention the fact, then move on to a completely different subject. It is now generally agreed amongst historians that the passages were the interpolations of a medieval Christian copyist.

The gospels, therefore, would appear to be the only evidence that survives concerning the life of Jesus. So just how reliable are they as historical texts?

There are, in fact, many contradictions between the gospels other than those concerning the Nativity. Indeed, there are literally dozens. For example: Matthew has the famous 'Sermon on the Mount' delivered on a mountain (Matt. 5:1), whereas Luke has it delivered on a plain (Luke 6:17); Luke has Jesus performing the miracle of the Miraculous Catch (the net full of fish) when he first meets Simon Peter (Luke 5:1–10), while John has him perform it when they last part company (John 21:3–8); and Matthew, Mark and Luke relate that Jesus cast the money-changers out of the temple just before the Crucifixion (Matt. 21:12, Mark 11:15, Luke 19:45), whereas John places the event early in Jesus' ministry (John 2:13–16).

After a few decades one might expect certain geographical or chronological deviations to have occurred in the narratives as the story is passed on by word of mouth. All the same, if, as conventional thinking has it, the gospels were all written within one or two generations of the events, we should still expect the important details of the most significant events to tally. They don't. The details of the Crucifixion, for instance, are completely different in each gospel. All four gospels give a different version of the Superscription – the words written on the plaque attached to the cross above Jesus' head (Matt. 27:37, Mark 15:26, Luke 23:38, John 19:19) – and they give three completely different renderings of Jesus' last words (Matt. 27:46, Mark 15:34, Luke 23:46, John 19:30). They don't even agree on the day the Cruci- fixion occurred. This is nothing, though, compared with the conflicting accounts of the most significant religious event in Christian history – the Resurrection.

Later that Tuesday I decided to pay a visit to the site where many believe the Resurrection really occurred – Christ's tomb. It seemed the most appropriate place to make a working decision about the historical existence of Jesus.

The Catholic and Orthodox Churches believe that the Church of the Holy Sepulchre in the north-west corner of the Old City marks the site of Christ's tomb. It was first built by the emperor Constantine over a small cavern in which his mother Helena believed Jesus had been buried when she visited the Holy Land in AD 327. (Evidently, she had been told of the cave by local Christians.) Most Prot- estants, on the other hand, prefer the simplicity of the Garden Tomb, just to the north of the Old City. They point out that, being outside the city walls, it fits better with known history. Jewish law did not allow for burials inside the city, yet the Holy Sepulchre was built well within the city walls. The present walls, however, date from the mid- sixteenth century and the course of the ancient city walls is still far from clear. Either tomb might have been inside or outside the walls in the early first century.

Of the two, the Garden Tomb seemed the most fitting. Regardless of its authenticity, it was in its original setting, out in the open rather than in a candle-lit vault beneath an incense-filled basilica. When I arrived at the little garden at the end of an alley off the Nablus Road, I was surprised to find such a tranquil setting so close to the bustling East Jerusalem bus station. Shaded from the burning sun by dusty olive trees, the garden was surrounded by rockeries of colourful flowers and shrubs, well tended by the Christian caretakers who looked after the tomb. To one end of the central pavement was a vertical rock face hewn into a craggy little hill. Here the tiny single tomb was entered by a doorway cut into the rock.

Historically, the tomb has even less claim to authenticity than the Holy Sepulchre. It was found by the British general Gordon when he was staying in East Jerusalem in 1882. One morning he looked out of his window and, on seeing the craggy hill, decided that it looked like a skull. According to the New Testament the place where Jesus was crucified was outside the city on a hill called Golgotha – 'the place of the skull'. When Gordon went down to investigate he discovered the little tomb cut in the rocks below the hill and decided that this must have been where Christ was buried. Even though Gordon may have found Golgotha, there is no evidence whatsoever that this particular tomb ever contained Jesus' body. Such reasoning, however, would have made no difference to the beliefs of the party of Evangelical Americans who were being shown the tomb by an impassioned caretaker on the day when I visited.

'The Bible tells us that on the third day Christ rose from the tomb,' he was saying. 'When the disciples visited the tomb they found it empty. There was no body in it.' A broad smile lit up his face. 'And you know, the wonderful thing about this tomb is that there is no-*body* in it.' Gasps, murmurs and a few Amens echoed from the chamber as the party followed the man inside.

When they eventually emerged I took my chance to enter the tomb alone. I found myself in a small rectangular anteroom with an opening to the right, leading into the burial chamber itself. It seemed originally to have been intended for a twin burial as there were two niches for the bodies, one to either side. The one to the right was roughly cut and unfinished, and it was the second niche where Christ's body is said to have been laid.

Regardless of whoever was really laid to rest in this sepulchre, it seems to date from the right time and would have been similar to the one portrayed in the gospels. It was at a tomb such as this that Mary Magdalene is said to have arrived on the first Easter morning to learn that Jesus had risen from the dead. To the non-Christian such a story is hard enough to believe, but to anyone objectively reading the gospel accounts the episode becomes highly suspect. Once more, the Evangelists each give a totally different description of events.

Mark tells us that Mary Magdalene, Salome and Mary, mother of James, were the first to discover the already opened tomb, in which a lone man in a white garment informed them that Christ was risen (Mark 16:1–6); Luke tells us that a woman called Joanna and a number of other women were also present and that the news of Christ's Resurrection was conveyed by two men in shining garments (Luke 24:1–10); John has Mary Magdalene alone when she finds the already open tomb and the news is conveyed to her by two angels (John 20:1–13); and Matthew tells us that the two Marys actually witnessed the opening of the tomb and saw an angel descend from the skies and roll away the stone that sealed the entrance (Matt. 28:1–6).

As I left the tomb another party, this time English teenagers with Army of God stickers on their rucksacks, were being given the same speech by a different guide. ' . . . there is no-*body* in it,' I heard him declare jubilantly as I emerged into the sunlight. At that moment I realized just how far apart the Jesus of faith and the Jesus of history really were.

Despite the sensational claims they make, the biblical gospels must have been compiled many years after Jesus is said to have lived – far longer than a couple of generations, as is generally thought. As even the most essential religious aspects of the story – such as the Nativity, the Resurrection and the Ascension – have altered so dramatically, a considerable period of time must have elapsed between Jesus' day and the completion of the gospels. Perhaps almost as much as a century.

Sitting on a stone shelf in the corner of the Tomb Garden I decided to make my decision. Was I wasting my time trying to discover the truth about a woman who may never have existed? Applying a common-sense approach to the gospel accounts of Jesus' life, rather than to blindly accept conflicting versions of events on faith alone, I was left sceptical. I took out my notebook and examined the list I had made of the pros and cons concerning Christ's existence. Heading the list of pros I had written the words 'Jesus' Teachings'.

In the gospel accounts it is the events portrayed in Jesus' life that are so erroneous and contradictory. It is these that make the texts so unreliable as historical evidence for Christ's existence. Jesus' teachings, however, seem far more authentic. Although the gospel accounts vary concerning his exploits and the miraculous episodes in his life, they do agree on his teachings. In many places they are repeated word for word for several verses. The serious divergences in the various narratives as they now exist certainly show that the gospel writers must have been from separate Christian communities where *some* original story had become independently embellished. Was this original source, like the Nag-Hamadi texts, primarily a collection of Jesus' teachings? Remarkably, there survives early historical evidence that it was just that. An original copy of one of the gospels – Matthew's – was obtained by the Christian missionary Papias of Phrygia in AD 120. In his surviving work he does not tell us precisely what was in the gospel, but he does make the enlightening comment:

> Matthew compiled the sayings [of Jesus] in the Aramaic language and others translated them as best they could.

Papias' reference to 'sayings' clearly implies that Matthew's original gospel was indeed simply a collection of Jesus' sermons and parables.

Matthew's gospel, as it existed in the second century, was written in Greek for a readership outside the Jewish world. But Papias tells us that the original was compiled in Aramaic. This was the everyday dialect of first-century Palestine – the very language that Jesus and his followers would have spoken. If Papias is right and 'the sayings' were originally written in Aramaic, it would go a long way towards demonstrating that they were transcribed during or very close to Jesus' time. It would accordingly constitute compelling evidence that Jesus, at least as a preacher, was a genuine historical figure.

Remarkably, evidence that Jesus' teachings were originally written down in Aramaic is still preserved in the Bible. In 1984, British author Ian Wilson, in his book *Jesus: The Evidence*, drew scholarly attention to passages in the gospels which still retained evidence of an original Aramaic source. The Evangelists seem to have mistranslated certain Aramaic words. For example, Luke in chapter 11, verse 41, uses the term 'give alms', whereas a parallel passage in Matthew chapter 23, verse 26, uses in its place the word 'cleanse'. Since in Aramaic the word for giving alms is *zakkau* and the word for cleansing is the very similar *dakkau*, it is obvious that both authors have translated an Aramaic text and one of them has made an understandable error. Moreover, Wilson pointed out, when Jesus' words are translated back into Aramaic poetical characteristics occur. For instance, in Matthew's 'Sermon on the Mount' verses flow melodically and lines rhyme. This suggests that they were original words spoken by a teacher which were set in a mnemonic form so that they could be easily remembered by followers – the teacher, it seems, being Jesus himself.

Hearing yet another guide making the 'nobody in it' speech, I decided to make my own leap of faith. There was, I concluded, enough evidence for Jesus' historical existence. I would continue my search to discover the truth about his mother and the role she really played in the advent of a religion that changed the world. I decided that the next day I would leave Jerusalem and go back to where it all began – to the town of Nazareth.

Summary

- The only documentary evidence for the existence of the Virgin Mary written within a hundred years of the time she is said to have lived is to be found in the Bible. This, however, provides no details of her family or background.

- The oldest surviving reference to Mary's childhood is found in the *Protevangelium*, a book attributed to the second-century Christian leader, James of Ephesus. James's account, however, is likely to have been based largely on legend. For example, it refers to Mary's childhood service as an altar girl in the Jerusalem temple at a time when women were not allowed into the inner sanctum.

- Modern literary analysis of the biblical gospels has revealed that in their present form they were not compiled until at least a generation after the events they describe. As the only historical evidence for Mary's existence, just how accurate is the New Testament?

- In AD 120 the Christian missionary Papias of Phrygia claimed that the original gospel accounts were compiled in Aramaic, the everyday dialect of first-century Palestine. Evidence that the gospel accounts were originally compiled in this tongue would go a long way towards demonstrating that they were based to some degree on eyewitness testimony.

- Remarkably, evidence that Jesus' teachings were originally written down in Aramaic is still preserved in the Bible. When Jesus' words are translated back into Aramaic poetical characteristics occur. For instance, in Matthew's 'Sermon on the Mount' verses flow melodically and lines rhyme. This suggests that they were original words spoken by a teacher which were set in a mnemonic form so that they could be remembered by followers.

- From such evidence it seems that at least some aspects of the story of Jesus' life come from original, first-hand sources. There therefore seems no serious reason to doubt that his mother Mary was an historical figure.

III

BEHOLD A VIRGIN

THE ROAD WOUND upwards from the stark Jezreel Plain
and into the rolling Galilean hills. Having the week off,
David Deissmann had kindly offered to drive me up to
Nazareth and show me the sites of the ancient town. Now,
here it was before me, clinging to the inside of a vast bowl
of dusty rock, its row after row of white, flat-topped houses
tiered like the seats of a Roman amphitheatre. I had expected to find a quiet little village, with archaic buildings,
palm-lined streets and sandy, cobbled squares: an isolated
community where traditional Jewish life had continued
almost unchanged from the time of Christ. I could not have
been more wrong. Nazareth was a thoroughly twentieth-
century town – nothing less than a religious holiday resort
with prefabricated structures run up using high-speed
building methods, streets overloaded with traffic and an
eighty-thousand population massively swollen by tourists.
Even its forty or so churches, convents and monasteries were,
for the most part, recent constructions, hardly any dating
back more than a hundred years. As for Jewish life – except
for the presence of Israeli police, Nazareth must be about

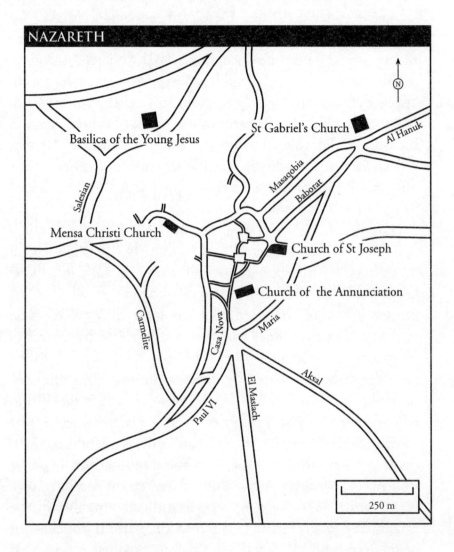

the least Jewish town in all Israel. Most of its population are Arab and nearly all its visitors are Christian.

Having decided that there was enough evidence for Mary's historical existence, I needed to determine the extent of her true role at the inception of Christianity. I had to decide between three possible Marys: Mary visited by an angel, the woman divinely foretold to bear the son of God; Mary a misguided visionary, whose beliefs inspired her son to assume the role of Messiah; Mary an historical patsy, whose part in the scheme was the invention of others, years after Jesus was proclaimed the Christ. Just how influential was the historical Mary?

For the historian examining the New Testament it is a matter of trying to separate fact from early Christian legend or, at best, misinterpretation. Even the most fundamentalist Christian is left with a dilemma, for the four gospel accounts cannot be, word for word, the absolute truth. Were there two angels in the empty tomb, or one? Did Jesus ascend to heaven from Bethany or the Mount of Olives? Did he rampage through the temple at the beginning of his ministry, or at the end? Unfortunately, the event in which the Virgin Mary features most prominently, the Nativity, seems the most spurious episode of all. Not only is it riddled with contradiction but, from the scientific standpoint, it is pretty unbelievable: angels, a miraculous star, to say nothing of a virgin birth. Was there *anything* historically credible in the account of Jesus' birth? I had read the various conclusions of modern biblical scholars, but before making up my mind I wanted to reflect on them in their pertinent surroundings.

At the end of the café- and hotel-flanked Casa Nova Street was the Church of the Annunciation, the basilica built over the very site where the angel Gabriel is said to have appeared to the Virgin Mary. I had at least expected this church to be old, but no. Like so many other religious buildings in the town it was modern, dating from as recently as 1966. The huge edifice, built over the foundations of a Franciscan monastery demolished in the 1950s, was unlike a usual Catholic shrine. It more resembled a Mormon tabernacle or an Evangelical church, with its postmodernist architecture and thirty-seven-metre dome shaped like an upturned ice-cream cone with what looked like the lamp-turret of a lighthouse on top.

Like the Church of the Holy Sepulchre in Jerusalem and the Church of the Nativity in Bethlehem, the site was, once again, discovered by the emperor Constantine's mother Helena in the early fourth century. Although Constantine himself had been responsible for establishing Christianity as the state religion of the Roman empire, it was Helena who founded the myriad Christian shrines in Palestine. Many scholars have surmised that she had far more influence in the establishment of the Catholic Church than history records. The emperor was a nominal Christian who needed the religion to unify his empire; his mother, however, was a fervent Christian who spent months travelling around the Holy Land hoping to rediscover the various sites associated with Jesus' life. Apart from Christ's tomb and the cave of the Nativity, she apparently found the house of the Last Supper, the Garden of Gethsemane, the hill where Jesus was crucified and many more locations. She even claimed to have discovered the cross on which Jesus was crucified and the very tree from which the wood was cut. Visiting Nazareth, the empress found a cave which she decided was the very spot where Mary had been when she miraculously conceived Jesus. The original church Helena ordered to be built over the site was destroyed by the Persians when they invaded the area in AD 614, and a second church, built by the Crusaders in the twelfth century, was also destroyed within a hundred years. The Franciscan monastery, built in 1730, was pulled down in 1955 to make way for the present structure.

The levelling of the Franciscan buildings made possible a full-scale archaeological excavation, and although the dig did not reveal anything new concerning the lives of Mary, Joseph or Jesus, it did unearth evidence that the site was continuously occupied from around 1000 BC. Nazareth, however, does not seem to have been a town of any religious importance to the Jews of pre-Christian times, as it is not mentioned anywhere in the Old Testament or in any other early Hebrew writings. Conversely, it was not the kind of pastoral backwater we might imagine today, inhabited by rustic peasants, shepherds and subsistence farmers. Recent archaeology at the ruins of the Galilean capital of Sepphoris, only six kilometres to the north-west, has shown that the city was being massively rebuilt by the Romans at exactly the time Jesus was born. This brought great prosperity to the province, and Nazareth, lying within a couple of hours' walk – literally commuting distance – from Sepphoris, would have benefited economically. Mary's family, in particular, would have benefited from the reconstruction of Sepphoris. According to the gospels Joseph was a carpenter, someone whose skills would have been in constant demand as the new city grew up over a period spanning two decades. Accordingly, the popular image of Joseph as a humble tradesman, eking out a meagre living fixing the occasional broken cart, is in all probability wrong. The real Mary and Joseph were more likely a well-to-do middle-class couple living in the 'stockbroker belt' of a thriving cosmopolitan city.

The Grotto, the cave where Helena believed the angel Gabriel appeared to Mary, can still be seen in the Church of the Annunciation. At the heart of the bustling basilica, surrounded by modern architecture, with sculptures and frescos depicting episodes from the Virgin's life, are the incongruous remains of an old stone wall and archway. Looking like the quiet ruins of a medieval chapel that would be more at home in a leafy corner of an English meadow, this is all that remains of the Crusader church that stands above the cave. It is now encompassed by ornate black railings and covered by a huge copper canopy bearing the Latin declaration: *Verbum hic caro factum est* – 'Here the word was made flesh.' The inscription refers to a passage from the gospel of John concerning Jesus as the incarnation of God's message – 'And the word was made flesh, and dwelt amongst us' – a strange verse to choose, I thought, since John's gospel fails to mention the Nativity or the Annunciation at all.

Whether or not this was the real site Luke had in mind when he described the Annunciation, the author certainly believed that Gabriel appeared to Mary somewhere in Nazareth. The Roman Catholic Church holds that the angel visited Mary in person, whereas Protestants tend to believe that she experienced a vision, divinely inspired by the Holy Spirit. Whatever their denomination, the awe-struck visitors who crowded the vast chamber that echoed with whispered prayers, firmly believed that the word of God was made flesh in Nazareth two thousand years ago. Historically, there can be little doubt that, even before the gospels were written, the earliest Christians believed that Mary had conceived God's son. The Roman historian Suetonius, writing around

AD 115, refers to the Christians in Rome during the reign of the emperor Claudius (AD 41–54). He tells us that they were followers of 'Christus'. As this was the Latin rendering of the Hebrew 'Messiah', it demonstrates quite clearly that within only a couple of decades of his death Jesus was already believed to have been the son of God.

The authors of the four canonical gospels were certainly in no doubt that Jesus was the Hebrew Messiah, and two of them, Matthew and Luke, were equally convinced that Mary was an essential element in the divine plan. Although neither author actually uses the word 'Christ' or 'Messiah' during the Nativity story, this is clearly what is being implied. According to Luke the angel tells Mary about her future son:

> He shall be great, and shall be called the Son of the Highest: and the Lord God shall give unto him the throne of his father David. (Luke 1:32)

This is a direct reference to the Messiah found in Isaiah's prophecy:

> For unto us a child is born, unto us a son is given . . . and his name shall be called Wonderful . . . upon the throne of David. (Isa. 9:6–7)

Even calling the child Jesus was in accordance with the name of the Messiah as foretold by the ancient Hebrew prophets. In Luke's account the angel tells Mary:

> And, behold, thou shalt conceive in thy womb, and bring forth a son, and shalt call his name Jesus. (Luke 1:31)

The Luke gospel that now survives comes from the New Testament of the Roman Church. Here 'Jesus' is the Latin rendering of the Hebrew *Yeshua*. Jesus, however, is not the only Yeshua to be found in the Hebrew Bible. There are many, such as Yeshua the son of Nun (I Kings 16:34), Yeshua the son of Josedech (Haggai 1:1), and the most famous, Yeshua the conqueror of Jericho. When the books of the Old Testament were translated into Greek in the second century the name was transliterated as Joshua. As the earlier translators of the New Testament gospels had opted to render Christ's name as *Iesos* – Jesus – this name stuck as a way to clearly distinguish Yeshua of Nazareth from any other Yeshua in the Bible. In keeping with the transliteration of the name in the Old Testament, therefore, the angel's words in Luke's gospel should read, 'call his name Joshua'. It is under the name Joshua that the Old Testament prophet Zechariah refers to the Messiah:

> And he showed me Joshua the high priest standing before the angel of the Lord, and Satan standing at his right hand to resist him. (Zech. 3:1)

To Zechariah the Messiah would be both a priest *and* a king:

> Rejoice greatly, O daughter of Zion; shout, O daughter of Jerusalem: behold, thy King cometh unto thee. (Zech. 9:9)

The passage also shows the importance of the Messiah's mother in the prophecy, for she is the daughter of Zion, the daughter of Jerusalem – a descendant of King David. This makes sense of an otherwise mysterious passage that appears in both Luke's and Matthew's gospels, where they both give,

name for name, the genealogy of Jesus right back to King
David (Matt. 1:6–16, Luke 3:23–31). They tell us that this
is Joseph's lineage. However, this makes no sense in the
context of the story which portrays Mary as a virgin.
According to the gospel writers God was Jesus' father, not
Joseph. Why then include Joseph's genealogy to show that
Jesus was descended from David? The genealogy in the
original source must surely have been Mary's, and confusion
must have arisen amongst early Christian copyists. Indeed,
the Isaiah prophecy makes it very clear that it is the Messiah's
mother – and not his earthly father – who is of the royal
line:

> Listen, O isles, unto me; and harken, ye people, from far;
> the Lord hath called me from the womb; from the bowels
> of my mother hath he made mention of my name.
> (Isa. 49:1)

It is from Isaiah's prophecy regarding the Messiah's mother
that the very concept arose concerning Mary as a virgin.
Isaiah when foretelling the Messiah's birth says:

> Behold, a virgin shall conceive, and bear a son, and shall
> call his name Immanuel. (Isa. 7:14).

(Immanuel means 'God is with us'.) It is the virgin theme
that Matthew takes up in his account of Jesus' birth when
the reader is reminded of Isaiah's prophecy:

> Behold, a virgin shall be with child, and shall bring forth
> a son, and they shall call his name Emmanuel. (Matt.
> 1:23)

As I looked around me at the Roman Catholics who knelt to recite the rosary, the Anglicans who held their palms together in prayer and the born-again Christians who raised up their hands to feel the power of the Holy Spirit, I wondered if they knew just how much controversy had surrounded this one verse.

In the Bible story, as it now survives, God is portrayed as Jesus' true father by direct intervention of the Holy Ghost; Joseph merely acts as Jesus' guardian. Mary, we are told, was a virgin when she conceived and bore Christ. When we examine the New Testament it is strange, considering the enormity of the claim, that the virgin birth is not even mentioned in two of the gospels, nor in the Acts of the Apostles or any of the letters of St Paul. This was something that concerned the theologian Rudolf Bultmann when he began to question the authenticity of the gospels in the 1920s. Nothing, however, could have prepared him for what he would discover. Examining the Hebrew version of the Old Testament he found something so damning that it haunted him until his death in 1976. What he uncovered was clear evidence that the virgin birth was one theme that certainly could not have been in the original narratives. In fact, it seemed that the entire concept was not added to the gospels until around a century after Jesus' birth.

Incredibly, the idea of the virgin birth appeared to have arisen from a simple mistranslation of the Isaiah prophecy. Until the second century, the Jewish texts that were later to be brought together to form the Old Testament were only available in Hebrew. Sometime around AD 130 the growing Christian movement gradually began to translate them into Greek and ultimately Latin. This led to numerous mistranslations, some of which are still retained in the modern Bible.

One such example is found in the name of the stretch of water which parted to allow the Israelites to flee Egypt. In the original Torah – the Jewish work that now makes up the first five books of the Old Testament – the Hebrew name was *Yam Suph*. In Hebrew, *Yam Suph* means 'Reed Sea' or 'Sea of Reeds', and appears to have referred to a lake in the north-east of Egypt. It was mistranslated as 'Red Sea' and the erroneous notion of the parting of the 'Red Sea' became part of Christian tradition.

Bultmann discovered that a similar mistake had been made when the early Christians had translated the passage from Isaiah – namely the word now rendered as 'virgin'. The original text did not employ the Hebrew word for 'virgin' – *betulah*; it used the word *almah* – 'a young woman'. The original Hebrew passage had predicted that a 'young woman' – not a 'virgin' – would conceive and give birth to the Messiah. The essential theme of the prophecy was that the mother of the Messiah was more important than the father: she would be of David's line, not he. The passage, it seemed, had nothing whatsoever to do with a virgin birth. Someone had quite clearly interpolated the concept into the narrative after they discovered the Greek or Latin version of the Isaiah verse in order to better fit Mary into the mistranslated prophecy. The original Matthew narrative may have included the Nativity story and it may have included the episode where Mary learns she will bear the Messiah, but the virgin birth must have been tagged on around a hundred years after Jesus' time.

In the original gospel accounts, Jesus could still have been considered God's chosen son, without the necessity of a virgin birth. In fact, this fits precisely with Jewish belief concerning the Messiah. The Hebrew texts that make up the

Old Testament show that, although they believed that he would be the spiritual son of God, the Jews expected the Messiah to have an earthly father – just like David before him.

As we left the Church of the Annunciation that morning I reckoned I knew what the devout Christians, queuing expectantly to file past the Grotto, would think about Bultmann's revelation. Like the Vatican theologians who responded to him in the 1920s, they would probably believe that the mistake had itself been divinely inspired to reveal the true nature of Christ's birth. Like Bultmann, however, I was left wondering whether the entire Annunciation story was an invention. Had Mary really been visited by an angel? Had she just thought she had? Or had the whole episode been interpolated by the gospel writers?

David and I made our way through the narrow streets of central Nazareth, towards the Church of St Joseph. It was here, according to the empress Helena, that Mary and Joseph had lived and worked. The busy lanes were stiflingly hot, filled with the noise of sightseers haggling with local traders over the price of everything from cans of Cola to straw hats. All along the claustrophobic little streets, restaurants and cafés were crowded with hungry tourists, while row after row of narrow-fronted shops sold a stunning array of religious memorabilia: everything from pictures of the Pope to bottles of holy water moulded in the image of the Virgin Mary. Despite the centuries of strife and warfare that have plagued the area, Nazareth has emerged as a tourist resort to rival Miami or the Costa del Sol. By contrast, Sepphoris, the ancient capital of Galilee, has all but faded from the map. All that now remains of the once splendid city are a few broken stones of the Roman town, the ruins of a Crusader castle and an abandoned Arab village. I was quite sure that

Nazareth would have been forgotten to history altogether had Mary and Joseph not made it their home.

As we escaped the crowds and neared the Church of St Joseph, I tried to imagine what Christ's childhood home was really like. A white mud-brick house, perhaps two storeys high; stairs on the outside leading to a flat-topped roof where Mary hung out the washing. Next door, a series of wattle-and-daub outhouses: Joseph's workshop, where the child Jesus eagerly helped his father toil.

'Here we are,' said David, pointing to the gleaming lime-stone cathedral that stood before us – the Church of St Joseph, erected in 1914 on the site of an original Roman church built in the early fourth century. Thankfully, the church was not so crowded as the Church of the Annunciation and it did not take long for us to file into the crypt and peer into a dank little cavern, festooned with flickering candles and glistening images of the holy family.

'Helena certainly had a thing for caves,' said David, when the party moved on. 'According to the empress, Mary conceived in a cave, gave birth in a cave and eventually settled down to raise a family in a cave.' When Helena visited Palestine in AD 327, he went on to explain, she found many Christian mystics living as hermits in hillside caves. Many of them believed that their particular cave was in some way associated with an episode from the gospel stories. It seems that those who had the most convincing tale to tell found themselves thrown out and had a church built over their home.

I had thought that by visiting the very place where Christianity began I would find myself close to Mary's world. Here I could build up a picture of the real woman behind her image as a holy-water phial or a marble statuette. I had imagined archaeological digs where the foundations of first-century dwellings had been uncovered. I had imagined museums displaying artefacts from the time: pots, lamps and household utensils; brooches, rings and other jewellery; ornaments, statues and reliefs – all helping to reconstruct a picture of Mary's day-to-day life. Instead, I found myself in the world shaped by a Roman empress who had lived three centuries later. Aptly, like the gospels themselves, Nazareth was founded in history but evolved through faith. I had still to discover the Mary who lay beneath the wrappings of faith. Like the truth about Helena and her cave shrines, it would only be by placing Mary into an historical context that her real story might emerge.

Jesus was apparently hailed as the Messiah once he began preaching – it was certainly happening within a few years of his death. Despite what the Bible tells us, though, did anyone actually believe Jesus was the Messiah when he was born? Did Mary herself, virgin or not, consider that she had conceived the Christ? Did Herod, the wise men, the shepherds or anyone else in Palestine really think that the child born in Bethlehem was the saviour of mankind? In short, was there any truth at all in the Nativity story?

It seems as though the original Aramaic source for the gospels may only have concerned Jesus' teachings, and the details of his life were added later by the authors now called Matthew, Mark, Luke and John. How accurate was their information concerning these events? First I had to ascertain exactly when the events were supposed to have occurred. Was I to accept Luke, that Jesus was born in AD 6? Or Matthew, that he was born in or before 4 BC?

Besides the tax census, Luke provides another datable reference. He tells us that Jesus began his ministry by being baptized by John the Baptist 'in the fifteenth year of the reign of Tiberius Caesar' (Luke 3:1–2). Luke (3:23) also tells us that when Jesus was baptized he was 'about thirty years of age'. Tiberius is known to have become emperor in AD 14, which would mean that the fifteenth year of his reign would have been in AD 28/9. If Jesus was born in AD 6, as Luke's Quirinius reference suggests (see page 35), then he would only have been twenty-two or twenty-three at the time. There is clearly some confusion here. If Luke is right about Jesus' age, his ministry did not begin until around AD 36. From the gospels we can gather that Jesus' ministry lasted between two and three years, which would mean that – according to Luke – he was crucified after AD 38. This dating has to be wrong. As Roman records show that Pontius Pilate ceased to be governor in AD 36, he would not have been in Judea for Jesus to appear before him at his trial as all four gospels relate.

Matthew's dating fares far better. According to him, Herod the Great was still alive when Jesus was born. Herod died in 4 BC, and if we go with this latest date for Jesus' birth then he would have been thirty-one or thirty-two in year fifteen of Tiberius' reign. This more closely fits with Luke's assertion concerning Jesus' age. This dating also fits with Pilate's governorship. If Jesus was born around 4 BC, he would have died around AD 30, a time when Pilate was indeed still governor. (He was appointed in AD 26.) From this assorted evidence, historians now consider the true date of Jesus' birth to have been around 4 BC, shortly before the death of Herod.

In 1977 support for this date came from the most unlikely quarter. Remarkably, it also seemed to confirm the historicity of one of the Nativity marvels. An article in the *Quarterly Journal of the Royal Astronomical Society* by British astronomers David Clark, John Parkinson and Richard Stephenson suggested that the star of Bethlehem might have been a genuine, but rare, astronomical event that occurred in 5 BC. In the contemporary records of Chinese astronomers of the Han dynasty, they found reference to a brilliant star, brighter than any other star or planet in the heavens, that appeared from nowhere and remained visible for three months. The astronomers of the Han dynasty kept meticulous records of celestial events for astrological purposes, and many of their observations, such as the appearance of Halley's Comet in 12 BC, can be confirmed by modern calculations. According to Clark, Parkinson and Stephenson, there could be only one celestial event which would match the Chinese observation: a supernova, a colossal stellar explosion that, if occurring close enough to earth in our own galaxy, would appear suddenly, as if from nowhere, and remain for weeks as a brilliant point of light visible to the naked eye. In our galaxy, three such supernovae are known to have occurred in the last thousand years: in 1054, 1572 and 1604. The seventeenth-century astronomer Johannes Kepler described the one in 1604 as being visible even in broad daylight.

Shanghai, where the observation was made, is precisely on the same latitude as Judea, and consequently the supernova would indeed have been visible in Bethlehem around the time that Christ appears to have been born. By our modern dating, the Chinese event is recorded in the December of 5 BC, which means that it would have been visible until March the following year. If this was the star of Bethlehem, and there is no closer contender, then it means that we can narrow down Christ's birth to the winter months of 5–4 BC. (Jesus' birthday on 25 December is not based on any biblical account, or even early Christian tradition. It was celebrated on this date only after Constantine established the Catholic Church, as it was already an important Roman holiday.)

Is there anything in the Nativity story which fits with the historical events of late 5 or early 4 BC? According to the second chapter of Matthew's gospel, Herod learned from the wise men that Jesus was born to be King of the Jews. As the real king of the Jews, Herod evidently believed that the child would grow up to seize his throne. Learning that Jesus had been born somewhere in Bethlehem, in the hope of killing him Herod ordered that all the newborn children in the town should be murdered. Is there any historical record that Herod ever committed such an atrocity?

Indeed there is: at least, something very similar. According to Josephus, the emperor Augustus decreed that the eldest son of Herod's deceased son Antipater should be next in line to the Jewish throne. Just before he died in the spring of 4 BC, however, Herod decided that he wanted his son Philip to succeed him, and under suspicious circumstances Antipater's children vanished. It seems very likely that Herod had them murdered.

This was all happening at the very time that, according to Matthew, Herod ordered the massacre of the infants in Bethlehem in the hope of killing the baby Jesus. Is there some connection here? Perhaps so. If, at this time, some important travellers had arrived at Herod's court with rumours that a King of the Jews had been born in Bethlehem, the king might well have feared that the child in question was a surviving son of Antipater – the legitimate heir and a threat to his plans to make Philip his successor. This is actually the only scenario which makes historical sense of Matthew's account. Why else would Herod, with the full authority of Rome behind him, even bother himself with crazy tales of a royal baby?

So although there is nothing to confirm Luke's account of the manger, the shepherds and the angels, it does seem that Matthew's account is remarkably feasible. Jesus does appear to have been born during Herod's reign, there was a very unusual star visible from Bethlehem at the time, and Herod did have good reason to fear that a royal baby might undermine his plans. Indeed, the entire ambience of Matthew's narrative is far more feasible than Luke's account. Unlike in the Luke version, there are no angels flying around and Gabriel does not appear physically to Mary.

Just after midday, David and I lunched at the Astoria Restaurant on Casa Nova Street. It was a setting of strange contrasts. Although polite Arab waiters served traditional Middle Eastern dishes of *falafel* and *shwarma*, the decor was completely incongruous. One wall was covered by a huge photo mural of the Rhine Valley and another showed the Himalayas. As we ate we discussed the feasibility of the Matthew narrative.

'During the last year of Herod's reign Messianic expectancy ran high in Judea,' said David. 'Many Jews really thought the final days had come. Some of the Dead Sea Scrolls written at this time specifically refer to an imminent battle between the Sons of Light – the pious Jews – and the Sons of Darkness – the pagan Romans.' David explained how many Jews also found Herod's rule offensive. Although he was half-Jewish, the king was still thought of as an outsider, forced upon Judea by Rome. But in early 4 BC misgivings turned to hatred. While rebuilding the Jerusalem temple Herod committed an act considered so profane that it almost led to rebellion. The inner temple was an exact replica of Solomon's temple, and the scriptures taught that its precise design had been revealed by God. Every stone and piece of ornamentation had to match the description given in the Old Testament First Book of Kings (chapters 6–7). According to Josephus the building was considered so sacred that the masons were compelled to instruct ordained priests to carry out the actual construction work. Herod, however, added a touch of his own. He erected a huge golden sculpture of the imperial Roman eagle above the temple porch. This was not only a sacrilegious idol and a constant reminder of the presence of Rome, but a powerful symbol that the emperor was higher than God. Evidently, many Jews, such as the militant Zealots – the Judean resistance – began to spread the word that this was a sign that the final battle between light and darkness was at hand. It was time for the Messiah to come.

As I listened to David, I realized that yet another theme in Matthew's Nativity account made historical sense – the story of the wise men. In early 4 BC, against an atmosphere of Messianic expectation, an unprecedented celestial event occurs – a mysterious bright star appears from nowhere. The Bible story aside, there can be no doubt that many Jews took this to be a sign from God. A verse in the ancient Torah, and still contained in the biblical Book of Numbers, actually implied that a magnificent star would portend the birth of the Messiah:

And there shall come a Star out of Jacob [Bethlehem, where Jacob set up a pillar], and a Sceptre [a king] shall rise out

of Israel, and shall smite the corners of Moab, and destroy
all the children of Sheth. (Num. 24:17)

Anyone familiar with the scriptures would know that the
Messiah was expected to be born in Bethlehem. It would be
almost inevitable that at least some Jewish 'wise men' would
descend upon the town seeking a newly born male when the
star appeared. There would only have been a handful of
babies born in Bethlehem at the time, and few of them
would have had mothers who were of the house of David.
Jesus may indeed have been unique in this respect. If certain
rabbis, or holy men, really did visit the town in the early
weeks of 4 BC, they might well have decided that Mary's son
was the long-awaited Messiah.

As I looked across to the mural of the Himalayas, I
suddenly realized not only that such a scenario was feasible
but that a very similar thing had actually happened only a
few decades ago, in far-away Tibet. Until the Chinese
invaded the country, Tibet was ruled by the Dalai Lama –
in essence, a priest-king. In Buddhist belief, when a Dalai
Lama dies his soul is reincarnated into a newborn child and
certain select monks comb the countryside searching for
the infant. Various signs and omens, including astronomical
portents, are followed until an appropriate child is found.
This is precisely how the present Dalai Lama, now in exile
in India, was chosen in the 1930s. Buddhists believe that
the portents had led specifically to the true Dalai Lama.
Sceptics, however, would maintain that the child just happened to be in the right place at the right time. I could not
help but wonder what would have happened if the Buddhist
monks had not shown up at the home of the future Dalai

Lama in the 1930s. Would the boy have grown up to be just another Tibetan peasant? However, the Tibetan holy men *had* arrived and the boy became the spiritual leader of the nation. Had something similar happened in Bethlehem in the early weeks of 4 BC?

'Perhaps the entire course of world history was altered by a chance event,' I said as we left the restaurant and merged into a river of pilgrims. 'Mary gave birth to a son in the right place and at the right time to fulfil the expectations of a Jewish sect.'

Were the wise men – whoever they were – solely responsible for making Jesus what he became? If so, then, like the Dalai Lama, the boy would probably have been taken away for years of spiritual and religious training. The Dalai Lama's parents, devout Buddhists, were only too happy to have their son prepared for his chosen role. Perhaps Mary and Joseph, devout Jews, felt the same about their son Jesus.

Every aspect of Matthew's Nativity story really did fit into a genuine historical context. I had not fully appreciated it before, but David telling me of the eagle incident had woven the separate strands of evidence together. Herod's behaviour, the star and the wise men all fitted perfectly, as did the dating. I now had a fourth possible Mary: a peripheral character who had no active role whatsoever to play in the foundation of Christianity – a woman who, by chance alone, had given birth to a child under circumstances that others considered portentous.

I now knew my next move. In order to ascertain if Mary had any influence at all on her son's extraordinary religious career, I had to discover where Jesus spent his adolescence. From the Church perspective, he was not trained by anyone: he was divinely inspired. From a pragmatic perspective, though, he must have formulated his ideas somehow and it seems only reasonable to assume that someone, or some specific sect of Jews, helped prepare him for his ministry. Strangely, nowhere in the New Testament are we told what happened to Jesus in his formative years. Matthew does not tell us what became of him after Herod's death, merely that he dwelt in Nazareth. Even Luke only includes one brief episode in which Jesus teaches in the Jerusalem temple at the age of twelve. Jesus simply begins his ministry around the age of thirty with his religious knowledge, his powers of oratory and his healing abilities fully developed. Where had he spent these mysterious lost years?

According to the empress Helena, Jesus had spent his youth in Nazareth. She even found what she believed to be the site of his home on the heights overlooking the town. Here, in the Basilica of the Young Jesus, is a unique, but appropriate, marble statue of Jesus fashioned by the sculptor Bognio. It does not show the familiar bearded figure in his long desert robe but an adolescent Jesus, aged sixteen.

Early that afternoon I stood outside the Basilica looking down over Nazareth while David pointed out the sites. 'The Mensa Christi Church. It contains a stone slab said to be the table on which the resurrected Christ ate a last meal. Saint Gabriel's Church, which Greek Orthodox tradition associates with the Annunciation. Our Lady of Fright Chapel,' he said, pointing right across the town to a wooded hill shimmering in the heat haze. 'It's said to be the spot where Mary watched helplessly when the people of Nazareth attempted to throw Jesus off a cliff.'

The story suddenly had me thinking. According to Luke's gospel, at the beginning of his ministry Jesus preaches in Nazareth. The townsfolk, however, accuse him of blasphemy and try to throw him from a cliff. Somehow, he manages to escape and leaves the town. Before this episode, according to Luke (4:16), Jesus 'came to Nazareth, where he had been brought up'. This passage seems to imply that he had been absent from his home town for some time. Where had he been? After fleeing Nazareth Jesus heads directly for nearby Capernaum where all four gospels tell us he gathers his disciples. We are not told whether or not the disciples already knew Jesus but, judging by the fact that they immediately drop everything – wives, families and jobs – to follow him, we can hazard a guess that they did. Was it in the fishing village of Capernaum, on the shores of Lake Galilee, that Jesus spent his formative years? David was happy to take me to the site of ancient Capernaum, some thirty-five kilometres to the north-east.

At Kefar Nahum, in a remote bay in the north-western corner of Lake Galilee, is all that remains of biblical Capernaum – the ruins of an old synagogue and the foundation stones of an ancient fishing village, standing beside a small Franciscan monastery built in the nineteenth century. Here, just a few metres from the shore, Jesus' disciples had lived, worked and worshipped. I had by now become accustomed to the huge churches over the gospel sites, the myriad shops selling religious trinkets and the throngs of awe-struck pilgrims. Here, where Jesus apparently spent much of his ministry – where he preached to crowds, healed the sick, walked on water and fed a multitude with a few loaves and fishes – there was just one tiny priory, a kiosk selling tickets to the ruins and two families of Norwegian tourists.

'I can't believe it,' I said to David as we left the car in

the empty parking lot. 'Capernaum features in the life of Jesus far more than Jerusalem, Bethlehem or Nazareth. This should be the biggest resort of all.'

David smiled. 'Our old friend Helena never made it this far.'

It seems that the empress had returned home after visiting Nazareth and never got to found a basilica at Capernaum. A small octagonal chapel was built next to the synagogue around 450, but after the Arab invasion of the seventh century, when the village was renamed Tell Num, the location of Capernaum was forgotten altogether to Christians. In fact, it was not rediscovered until the 1800s.

Before exploring the ruins David led me down a narrow gully to the lakeside. Once more, I was completely surprised. I had expected a desolate rocky shoreline, with salt flats, arid rocks and sparse brown shrubs. Yet everywhere there were date palms, fig trees, lush subtropical vegetation and bubbling streams that trickled down into the waters gently lapping on to the sandy beach.

'In Hebrew Lake Galilee is called *Yam Kinneret* – "Sea of the Lute",' said David, 'because of the soothing harp-like sound of the waves.' I had often wondered why the Bible called it the *Sea* of Galilee: apparently the ancient Hebrews had only one word for a large expanse of water.

I looked south, down the twenty-kilometre length of the inland sea, its quiet waters broken only by the silent wake of a distant speedboat near the far-off resort of Teverya. I looked eastwards, towards the still grey hills of the Golan Heights, rising above the opposite shore some ten kilometres away. Unlike Nazareth, Capernaum really was as tranquil and mysterious as it must have been in biblical times. At last, I could not help but feel, I was in a land that Mary would recognize.

It was here, perhaps at this very spot, that Jesus called his first disciples. According to Matthew's gospel:

> And Jesus, walking by the sea of Galilee, saw two brethren, Simon called Peter, and Andrew his brother, casting a net into the sea: for they were fishers. And he saith unto them, Follow me, and I will make you fishers of men. And they straightway left their nets, and followed him. And going on from thence, he saw other two brethren, James the son of Zebedee, and John his brother, in a ship with Zebedee their father, mending their nets; and he called them. And they immediately left the ship and their father, and followed him. (Matt. 4:18–22)

After calling the four fishermen, Jesus went on to gather his other disciples from around Capernaum. John's gospel gives an account of Philip's call:

> The day following [the fishermen's call] Jesus would go forth into Galilee, and findeth Philip, and saith unto him, Follow me. (John 1:43)

According to John, Philip then fetches his friend Nathaniel, who also joins Jesus. The other gospels, however, call Nathaniel by the name Bartholomew, perhaps a new name that Jesus had given him. Jesus may have renamed all his disciples, as he did with Simon, whom he called the now familiar Peter (Matt. 16:18).

Another disciple included under two names is Matthew, the tax collector. The gospel writer Matthew describes his call:

> And as Jesus passed forth from thence, he saw a man, named
> Matthew, sitting at the receipt of custom: and he saith unto
> him, Follow me. And he arose, and followed him. (Matt. 9:9)

Mark also includes what must surely be the same man but calls him Levi:

> And as he passed by, he saw Levi the son of Alphaeus sitting
> at the receipt of custom, and said unto him, Follow me.
> And he arose and followed him. (Mark 2:14)

There are five other disciples referenced by all four gospels – Simon the Zealot, Judas Thaddaeus, Thomas, Judas Iscariot and James the son of Alphaeus – but none describe the circumstances in which they joined Jesus. From Luke, though, we can gather that the last five were chosen from amongst a large number of followers some time later, so as to make up the important Hebrew number of twelve (the number of Israelite tribes):

> And when it was day, he called unto him his disciples: and
> of them he chose twelve, whom also he named apostles;
> Simon, (whom he also named Peter) and Andrew his brother,
> James and John, Philip and Bartholomew, Matthew and
> Thomas, James the son of Alphaeus, and Simon called
> Zelotes, and Judas the brother of James, and Judas Iscariot,
> which also was the traitor. (Luke 6:13–16)

(The word 'apostle' must have been a transliteration of a now unknown Aramaic word, as it comes from the Greek *apostolos*, meaning 'messenger'.)

Seven of Jesus' apostles seem to have come from three families. Peter and Andrew are brothers, as are James and

John. James, son of Alphaeus (also called James the Less – the Younger – to distinguish him from the other James), and his brother Judas (also called Judas Thaddaeus – the large – to distinguish him from Judas Iscariot) must be brothers of Matthew, whom Mark also describes as son of Alphaeus. It is also apparent that the disciples already knew one another. Not only was Capernaum a small community, but the gospels make this clear. For instance, John (1:45) implies that Philip and Nathaniel (Bartholomew) were already friends, while Luke tells us that James and John were actually in business with Peter and Andrew: 'James and John, the sons of Zebedee, which were partners with Simon [Peter]' (Luke 5:10).

Despite the familiar scene from the movies and television depictions of Christ's life, which portrays Jesus as a mysterious stranger who suddenly arrives in the town, it is clear that he was already well known in the tight-knit community. It is not only the apostles who eagerly follow Jesus in Capernaum but, according to all four gospels, many of the local inhabitants too. According to Mark, for instance, right after Jesus calls Peter, Andrew, James and John he preaches in the synagogue:

> And they went into Capernaum; and straightway on the sabbath day he entered into the synagogue, and taught. And they [the people of Capernaum] were astonished at his doctrine: for he taught them as one that had authority, and not as the scribes. (Mark 1:21–22)

Again and again, Jesus preaches virtually unopposed in the Capernaum synagogue. For him to have done this without being arrested for blasphemy by the town elders he must already have had some religious standing in the area – an authority that had not been recognized in Nazareth.

'The remains of the synagogue stand on the very spot where Jesus seems to have preached,' said David, as he led me back up the path. A flight of weathered marble steps led up into the ancient open-air ruins: a paved courtyard flanked by two rows of stunted columns, some twenty metres wide, at the end of which, some forty metres away, was an almost intact wall, over ten metres high, set beyond four Corinthian pillars supporting a carved frieze. The crumbling structure looked more like a miniature Parthenon than a Hebrew temple.

'It looks like a *Greek* ruin,' I said.

'It is,' said David, 'as this clearly shows.' He pointed to an inscription on one of the four huge pillars. 'It's written in Greek.' He translated: ' "Herod, son of Monimus, and his son Justus, with his children, erected this column." It was a common practice for the Jews of the time to have their names inscribed on the parts of the building they had donated. These were Greek Jews who settled in the area around the late third or early fourth century.'

Evidently, excavations in the late 1960s showed that the site had been occupied from around the second century BC. However, although Capernaum survived the reprisals following the Jewish revolt in AD 70, it was sacked following a second Jewish revolt in 132, when the Romans killed over half a million people and destroyed 455 towns. About a century later the area was re-inhabited by Greek Jews, probably from Cilicia in modern Turkey, and it was they who erected the present building.

'I thought you said that Jesus would have preached here,' I said, confused.

'Look,' he said, bending down to remove some tufted grass from the foot of the wall. 'The walls are made from imported white limestone, but the foundations are made from local black basalt.' A narrow line of stones along the base of the wall was markedly darker than the structure above and made of more crudely cut bricks. 'This shows that there was a previous synagogue on the site, and it appears to date from the early first century – the time of Christ. The foundations of Peter's house – or what appears to have been Peter's house – have also been unearthed.'

Just outside the synagogue ruins, in the direction of the lake, was an area cordoned off by a low fence. Here, the substructures of an ancient village were clearly visible in the dusty soil. The 1960s excavations uncovered the foundations of several houses dating from Jesus' time. They were each laid out in the same style, with a series of rooms set around a central hall which contained a cooking hearth. In some of them, amongst broken pottery and tiles, fishing hooks were found, suggesting that they had been the dwellings of local fishermen. It seemed that the houses had a covered porch that opened on to the street which ran beside the synagogue.

Interpreting the gospels, it appears that Peter's house was right next to the synagogue. According to Mark, for instance, after Jesus has called the first four disciples and has preached in the synagogue he goes to Peter's house to heal his mother-in-law of fever:

And forthwith, when they were come out of the synagogue, they entered into the house of Simon [Peter] and Andrew. (Mark 1:29)

'The octagonal church built here in the fifth century was erected over one of these homes,' said David. 'When archaeologists dug down into the soil beneath the house they discovered shards of plaster that had once covered the walls of the original dwelling.'

He opened the guidebook that he had bought from the kiosk when we arrived and pointed to a photograph of a piece of stained plaster. On it was a Greek prayer which included the word *kephas*, the title that Jesus gave Peter when he told him that he would be the rock on which he would build his Church (John 1:42). (*Kephas*, or Cephas as it appears in today's Bible, means the same as the Latin *petra*, 'rock', from which the modern translation 'Peter' comes.) Many variations of Peter's name were found in graffiti scratched on to the plaster, David explained. Dating from the mid-second century, they appear to show that after the second Jewish revolt, Gentile Christians who moved into the area believed that the house had belonged to Peter – as, it would seem, did the fifth-century Christians who built the octagonal church over the site.

If this was Peter's house, then the family fishing business must have been lucrative. Archaeology has shown that the house was a large one with enough rooms to accommodate a considerable number of people. But however big Peter's house had been, it was not big enough to accommodate the multitude that descended upon Jesus to hear him preach. According to Mark:

And again he entered into Capernaum after some days; and it was noised that he was in the house. And straightway many were gathered together, insomuch that there was no room to receive them, no, not so much as about the door: and he preached the word unto them. (Mark 2:1–2)

'I don't suppose the archaeologists found anything with a disciple's name on it actually dating from his time,' I said, flicking through the guidebook.

'The next best thing,' said David.

Adjacent to the entrance to the site is a scenic garden, shaded by palm trees, where a number of architectural features discovered during the synagogue excavations are displayed. David took me past sections of a mosaic pavement, numerous carved stones and frieze blocks decorated with carvings of grapes and vines, then stopped at a section of an ornately sculptured column. It was a deep grey, very much darker than the buff-coloured 'white limestone' of the other exhibits.

'Black basalt,' he said. 'It comes from the original synagogue and has been dated to around the early first century – Jesus' time.' He indicated an inscription around the base. 'It's Aramaic: "Alphaeus, son of Zebedee, son of John, made this column." '

Remarkably, here were actual names from biblical Capernaum – names that appeared in the gospels: Alphaeus, the father of Matthew, James the Younger and Judas Thaddaeus; and Zebedee, the father of James and John.

'Alphaeus and Zebedee are rare names that appear nowhere else in the Bible,' said David. 'These may or may not have been the characters mentioned in the New Testament but the inscription does show that these particular names were used by a specific Capernaum family at the time Jesus lived. In all probability, the sons of Alphaeus and the sons of Zebedee were closely related, possibly cousins.'

'Perhaps being a disciple of Jesus was a family concern,' I quipped.

'Very likely,' he said seriously. 'Peter and Andrew were probably related, too. They were in business with Zebedee's sons. It would have been highly unusual in a small Jewish community of the time for someone to go into business with anyone outside their immediate family.'

It was getting late, and David had to be back in Jerusalem for a dinner date. During the three-hour drive back, I flicked through my copy of the Bible to see what the gospels said about Alphaeus and Zebedee. Alphaeus was mentioned only in passing by Matthew, Mark and Luke and in the Acts of the Apostles as the father of James the Younger, and by Mark as the father of Levi (Matthew). Zebedee was mentioned more often, not only by all four gospels as the father of James and John, but he actually appears in person in both Matthew's and Mark's accounts as being on the boat when his sons are called by Jesus. In Matthew's narrative Zebedee's wife is also referenced twice. Firstly, she is present with Jesus late in his ministry when he is preaching in Jericho (Matt. 20:20–9), and secondly, she is one of three important women present at Jesus' crucifixion:

> And many women were there beholding afar off, which followed Jesus from Galilee, ministering unto him [seeing to his needs]: Among which was Mary Magdalene, and Mary the mother of James and Joses, and the mother of Zebedee's children. (Matt. 27:55–6)

I was interested to find out who Zebedee's wife actually was, and consulting Mark's account of the Crucifixion I discovered that she was named:

> There were also women looking on afar off: among whom was Mary Magdalene, and Mary the mother of James the less and of Joses, and Salome. (Mark 15:40)

So the third woman with the two Marys – Zebedee's wife and the mother of James and John – was called Salome. Interestingly, the passage also told me that the second Mary was James the Younger's mother. As this James was the brother of Matthew and Judas Thaddaeus, she must have been Alphaeus' wife (see family tree, page 126). John's gospel also referred to this Mary as being present at the Crucifixion, but he called her 'Mary the wife of Cleophas' (John 19:25). Again it would seem we had another character who assumed two names, and under the name Cleophas, Alphaeus is a follower of Jesus who is present in Jerusalem after the Crucifixion (Luke 24:18). A family portrait was beginning to emerge. It was not only the apostles who followed Jesus throughout his ministry but their mothers and also, it seemed, at least one of their fathers.

It was while I was reading John's account of the women at the Crucifixion that I was suddenly transfixed. There, on the page before me, were three words that cast revelatory new light on my quest to discover the historical Virgin Mary. John's passage said the Virgin joined the other three women at the foot of the cross:

> Now there stood by the cross of Jesus his mother, and his mother's sister, Mary the wife of Cleophas, and Mary Magdalene. (John 19:25)

'His mother's sister'! There, as before, was Mary Magdalene and Mary, the mother of James the Younger, Judas Thaddaeus and Matthew, but this time the third woman – Salome, the mother of James and John – is described as Jesus' mother's sister. Salome was the Virgin Mary's sister! A completely new scenario had opened up. If Salome was Mary's sister this made her Jesus' aunt and so three of the disciples – her sons James, Judas and Matthew – were Christ's first cousins. Furthermore, if David was right then at least two of the other disciples were also closely related to him. It really was a family concern, Jesus' own family.

But there was more. Jesus' closest followers were apparently all related to him on his *mother's* side – as, also, was the man who actually prepared the way for his ministry: Mary's cousin's son, John the Baptist. It was beginning to look as if Mary might have been far more important in the scheme of things than I had thought – and it had something to do with her bloodline. She might not have been just one of many descendants of David, as I had assumed – perhaps she was the *direct* descendant of the ancient Israelite king.

I just had to find out more about Mary's family background and there was one vital lead – John the Baptist. According to all four gospels John had already amassed a considerable following before Jesus began to preach. With him, I might discover the true origins of Christianity. The search for John the Baptist would take me deep into the Judean Wilderness.

Summary

- The idea of the virgin birth appears to have arisen from a simple mistranslation. Around AD 130, when the Bible was translated into Greek and Latin, mistakes were inevitably made. One such mistake had been the word now rendered as 'virgin'. The original text did not employ the Hebrew word for 'virgin' – *betulah*; it used the word *almah* – 'a young woman'. Other aspects of the Nativity story, however, may be historically accurate.

- Because of a dating error made in the sixth century, Jesus was not born at the start of the year AD 1. In the New Testament account King Herod the Great is still alive. As Herod died in 4 BC, Jesus must have been born before this time. His most likely date of birth is during the winter of 4–5 BC, as what may have been the star of Bethlehem appeared at this time. In the contemporary records of Chinese astronomers there is reference to a brilliant star that appeared from nowhere and remained visible for three months. Astronomers now know this to have been a supernova, a colossal stellar explosion that appears suddenly, as if from nowhere, and remains for weeks as a brilliant point of light visible to the naked eye.

- According to Matthew's gospel, Herod learned from the wise men that Jesus was born to be King of the Jews. As the real king of the Jews, Herod evidently believed that the child would grow up to seize his throne. Learning that Jesus had been born somewhere in Bethlehem, Herod ordered that all the newborn children in the town should be murdered in the hope of killing Jesus.

- According to the first-century Jewish historian Josephus, the Roman emperor Augustus decreed that the eldest son of Herod's deceased son Antipater should be next in line to the Jewish throne. Just before he died in the spring of 4 BC, however, Herod decided that he wanted his son Philip to succeed him and under suspicious circumstances Antipater's children vanished. It seems very likely that Herod had them murdered.

- This was all happening at the very time that, according to Matthew, Herod ordered the massacre of the infants in Bethlehem in the hope of killing the baby Jesus. If, at this time, wise men from the east had arrived at Herod's court with rumours that a child called King of the Jews had been born in Bethlehem, the king may well have feared that the child in question was a surviving son of Antipater – the legitimate heir and a threat to his plans to make Philip his successor.

IV

THE MYSTERY YEARS

WHEN JESUS BEGAN his ministry, sometime around AD 30, his Judaic learning was highly proficient, his extraordinary oratory skills were completely developed and his remarkable philosophy was fully formulated. Unless, as fundamentalists believe, this was all directly inspired by God, then Jesus had to have been taught and trained by someone. I had reasoned that because of the portentous circumstances surrounding his birth – Herod's eagle, the appearance of the mysterious star and his mother's lineage – at least some contemporary Jews considered him to be the Messiah. I had also speculated, from Matthew's account of the 'wise men', that a particular Jewish faction had adopted Jesus for their cause. From infancy to the age of thirty, apart from the one brief teaching incident at the age of twelve, Jesus' life is a complete enigma. If I could discover where he had spent these lost years perhaps I could identify this mysterious sect. As the Bible reveals a little more about John the Baptist's early days than it does about Jesus', he was my best lead.

Thirty kilometres east of Jerusalem, where the River Jordan flows into the Dead Sea, Jesus' ministry began. According to the gospels, John the Baptist was preaching

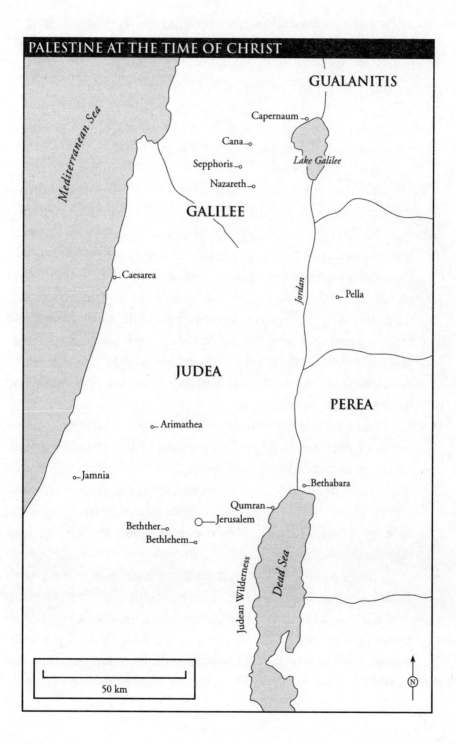

PALESTINE AT THE TIME OF CHRIST

GUALANITIS

Mediterranean Sea

Capernaum
Cana
Sepphoris
Nazareth

Lake Galilee

GALILEE

Caesarea

Jordan

Pella

JUDEA

PEREA

Arimathea

Jamnia

Bethabara

Qumran
Jerusalem

Bethther
Bethlehem

Judean Wilderness

Dead Sea

50 km

N

at Bethabara, modern Oasr el Yahud, when Christ came to him and asked to be baptized. Although John agrees and immerses Jesus in the river like all his converts, the Baptist tells his congregation that this is no ordinary man:

> This is he of whom I said, After me cometh a man which is preferred before me. (John 1:30)

John the Baptist is preaching an unusual form of Judaism – the teachings that would eventually be known as Christianity – even before Jesus begins his ministry. However, even though he has amassed many followers of his own, the moment Jesus appears on the scene John hands them over to his leadership. It seemed fairly safe to assume, therefore, that the same influences helped formulate both John's and Jesus' teachings. The two men may not only have been second cousins, they may also have belonged to the same unusual Jewish sect. So where did John the Baptist spend his formative years?

Today an Abyssinian monastery marks the spot on the banks of the Jordan where Jesus is said to have been baptized, and it was here that I met with Carole Snyder, a research student from the Hebrew University. David Deissmann had arranged the meeting as Carole was not only studying first-century Jewish history, she also had some interesting new ideas about John the Baptist.

I thought that I had got used to Israel's blistering temperatures, but I was wrong. The moment I left the comfort of the air-conditioned coach, the searing heat took my breath away. It was well over 30 degrees Celsius. 'It will get a lot worse where we're going,' said Carole after we got into her Jeep. 'The Judean Wilderness is one of the hottest places on earth.' According to the Bible, the Judean Wilderness was where John the Baptist spent much of his time.

Having concluded that Mary's immediate family came from Capernaum in northern Israel, I had reasoned that it was probably her own home town. But it was not, it seems, the town where Mary's cousin Elizabeth lived. Although she too may originally have hailed from Capernaum, she no longer lived there when her son John the Baptist was born. She apparently lived in her husband Zacharias' city, somewhere in Judea in southern Israel. Luke's gospel makes this clear when we are told of Mary's stay with Elizabeth when she learns that she has conceived Jesus:

> And Mary arose in those days and went into the hill country with haste, into a city of Juda [Judea]. And entered into the house of Zacharias, and saluted Elizabeth. (Luke 1:39–40)

John, though, does not remain in this unnamed city, or indeed in any town, when he becomes a man. Instead, according to Matthew, he spends his time in the Judean Wilderness:

> In those days came John the Baptist, preaching in the wilderness of Judea, And saying, Repent ye: for the kingdom of heaven is at hand. (Matt. 3:1–2)

The Judean Wilderness is a strip of inhospitable mountainous territory some twenty kilometres wide and seventy long to the immediate west of the Dead Sea. According to the first-century Roman historian Pliny the Elder, this sparsely populated area was the stronghold of the Essenes – a minority

Jewish sect to which many biblical scholars believe John the Baptist belonged.

In the 1950s a dry, rocky terrace was excavated at Qumran at the northern end of the Dead Sea and the remains of a huge Essene monastery were unearthed. As we drove south towards Qumran, along the western side of the seventy-six- by sixteen-kilometre inland sea, the landscape was in total contrast with the lush scenery around the Sea of Galilee, just over a hundred kilometres to the north. Burnt red mountains rose sharply from the cracked stone terraces which surrounded the green-tinged waters, the atmosphere heavy with the stench of salt. It was not the familiar, healthy smell of the seaside but a pungent chemical odour, like the fumes produced by an industrial blast-furnace. For the aptly named Dead Sea has a salt content over seven times that of the earth's oceans: so high that marine life just cannot survive. The enormous lake is an incredible four hundred metres below sea level – the lowest place on land anywhere in the world. Consequently, the waters from the Jordan that feed the Dead Sea have literally nowhere to go. They simply evaporate at a rate of 140 centimetres a year in searing temperatures that hover around 40 degrees for months on end. The salt washed down from rocks in the north just builds up in the water year after year.

I had never been anywhere so completely barren. It was like a vast acidic ocean in some lifeless, post-apocalyptic world. Yet it was here that the Qumran Essenes chose to make their home. As we turned into the dusty road that led to the ruins, Carole explained why.

Alexander the Great seized Palestine from the Persians in 331 BC and for two and a half centuries the area became a Greek province until it was annexed by the Romans. Alexander and his immediate successors were initially tolerant towards Judaism and allowed it to continue unhindered. In fact, many Greeks who moved into Palestine became Jewish converts, and the religion spread throughout much of the Greek empire around the eastern Mediterranean. By the second century BC, all this changed when the eastern empire broke away to form the Seleucid empire governed from Syria.

In 169 BC the Seleucid king Antiochus IV, fearing the spread of Judaism, decided to reverse the trend and attempted to Hellenize the Jews. Jewish practices were forbidden and scriptures were destroyed. Worst of all, Antiochus plundered the Jerusalem temple and erected a giant statue of the Greek god Zeus over the high altar. This so angered the Jews that in 167 BC Judas Maccabaeus, the son of the high priest, led a mass revolt against Seleucid rule. After a lengthy guerrilla campaign a new and tolerant administration was established in Palestine: the Hasmonean dynasty who, although Greek, put an end to the continual fighting by converting to Judaism. The two chief Jewish sects, the Sadducees and the Pharisees, both accepted Greek influence, but a third sect formed at this time to advocate a purer, fundamentalist form of Judaism – the Essenes.

The Essenes believed that the Messiah's coming was close at hand. In fact, the erection of the Zeus statue in the Jerusalem temple was seen as a direct portent of the event. To prepare themselves for the Messiah's birth, the Essenes withdrew into the seclusion of the Judean Wilderness where they founded various communities. Although the Messiah failed to arrive and deliver the people of Israel from foreign rule, the Essene movement survived and around 130 BC the Qumran monastery was built. By the time Jesus and John the Baptist were born, Qumran had become the chief centre of learning for the Essene sect.

On a rock-strewn terrace between the rugged cliffs beside the Dead Sea, a labyrinth of foundation stones, some hundred metres square, was all that remained of the once thriving community. Walking through the ruins of Qumran, I found it hard to believe that anyone could have lived here. The sun beat down mercilessly and the ground was so hot that the soles of my boots began to smell of smouldering rubber every time I stood on bare rock for more than a few seconds. Yet, Carole explained, despite the burning, arid conditions, despite the fact that less than five centimetres of rain falls in any year, the community that lived here at the time of Christ had all the fresh water they needed.

The site was excavated between 1953 and 1956 by the French archaeologist Roland de Vaux. His team discovered that an elaborate series of aqueducts, lined with an ingenious ceramic coating to prevent leakage, supplied the community with abundant water from springs in the surrounding hills. The water not only provided for the necessities of life, it was essential for the religious practices of the monastery. Large rectangular depressions were found at the dig: the remains of huge communal baths in which the inhabitants regularly immersed themselves for ritual cleansing.

The main feature of the site had been a three-storey tower which overlooked a central courtyard, surrounded on all sides by buildings of considerable size: workshops where day-to-day utensils were made, a long hall where the community gathered for meetings and meals, and a scriptorium where the Essenes' sacred manuscripts were written.

The Dead Sea Scrolls were just such manuscripts, and from them historians have pieced together the beliefs and religious practices of the Essenes. Since the chance discovery of the first scrolls by Arab shepherds in 1947, ten further caves have been excavated in the cliffs around Qumran to reveal an extensive collection of over eight hundred Essene manuscripts. It has taken half a century for the ancient library to be gradually reassembled from thousands of delicate fragments and, even though there is still much work to be done, an informative outline of Essene doctrine has been recovered. Although there were traditional Jewish scriptures found amongst the manuscripts, such as extracts from the Old Testament, there were also specific Essene scripts, such as *The Manual of Discipline* and *The Community Rule*, which detailed the convictions and daily rituals of the community at Qumran.

It seems that the people of Qumran were called the Sons of Light, a select group of Essenes who lived their lives in continual preparation for the Messiah's arrival. Like other Jews, they believed that the Messiah would drive out Gentile influence and re-establish the kingdom of Israel. However, they differed from most other Jewish sects in their belief that the Messiah would inaugurate a sort of communal Judaism in which each community lived as a co-operative, with collective ownership of property, collective organization of work and communal housing. Every member of the community would live for the general good of the others: something like a modern kibbutz. Religious matters, however, were subject to ridgid dogma.

The teachings had apparently originated with someone called the Teacher of Righteousness, the Essene leader who seems to have established the community around 130 BC. By living according to his strict regulations, the Essenes believed they could spiritually prepare themselves for the Messiah:

> They shall separate from the habitations of unjust men. And shall go into the wilderness to prepare the way of him. (*The Community Rule*)

The rules of Qumran religious devotion were austere. The devotees lived in humble tents or caves in the surrounding hillsides and came into the monastery each day to work and worship. Their clothes were plain, their food was modest and alcoholic drink was forbidden. Prayer to God was continuous:

> Before I move my hands and feet I will bless his name. I will praise him before I go out or enter or sit or rise. (*The Manual of Discipline*)

At the fifth hour of every day the members of the community had to spiritually purify themselves. This took the form of ritual bathing in which they put on a loincloth and immersed themselves in one of the communal baths.

'These particular Essenes have much in common with first-century Christians,' said Carole. 'Not only did the early Christians renounce material wealth but, from what we can tell, they lived in communes, sharing all they had. Specifically, the Qumran initiates have much in common with John the Baptist. Like the Essenes, John baptized his followers – spiritually cleansed them by immersing them in water.'

Carole went on to cite other similarities between the Qumran Essenes and John the Baptist. The dress code and eating habits of a Qumran devotee match John the Baptist as he is described in the Bible. According to *The Manual of Discipline*:

> I shall dress not as the rich man, but as one who has little. I shall eat not as the rich man, but as one who is poor. Neither shall wine pass my lips.

According to the Bible:

> And the same John had his raiment of camel's hair, and a leathern girdle about his loins; and his meat was locusts and wild honey. (Matt. 3:4)

> For he [John] shall be great in the sight of the Lord, and shall drink neither wine nor strong drink. (Luke 1:15)

'John is in the right place and does all the right things to have been an Essene,' concluded Carole. 'Enough to convince me, at least, that he spent time here.'

'Wasn't Qumran a separatist community?' I said. 'Would John have been permitted to leave?'

'Most of the community spent their whole lives here, but some did apparently leave to seek new converts. In fact, at the very time John was preaching around Judea, the Essenes seem to have been on something of a recruitment drive. Josephus explains that there were only around four thousand known Essenes living in Judea at the beginning of the first century, but after the Jewish revolt, just seventy years later, tens of thousands of them where butchered by the Romans.'

'So John might have been a part of this recruitment campaign?'

'It's possible.'

'Does anyone know why the Essenes suddenly began seeking new converts?' I asked.

'Anti-Roman feeling was running high. It may have been part of a general trend, as a number of new Judaic factions emerged at this time.'

'Like Christianity,' I said. 'Do you think Jesus himself spent time here?'

'That's the big question we would all like answered,' Carole said with a smile. 'The New Testament does not mention the Essenes and the Essene manuscripts don't mention the Christians, but when Christian teachings about Jesus and John the Baptist are taken together they do fall very much in line with Essene thought.'

Back in the Jeep, with the air-conditioning at full blast, Carole explained her fascinating theory. From what could be gathered from the Dead Sea Scrolls, the Essenes believed that there would actually be two Messiahs – the Messiah proper, the king who would be descended from David, and another who would precede him and prepare others for his coming. This first Messiah would be a preacher and a descendant of the prophet Aaron (the brother of Moses).

According to Carole, this was exactly how John the Baptist was depicted in the gospels. Even though many other New Testament characters had far more involvement with the establishment of Christianity, such as St Peter and St Paul, John is the only one apart from Christ whose birth was portrayed as divine. In fact, he is almost on a par with Jesus himself: his birth is foretold by the angel Gabriel, he is conceived under miraculous circumstances (as his mother had been considered barren), and, like Christ, he is filled with the Holy Ghost from the moment of his birth (Luke 1:5–36). Moreover, the authors of the gospels make it clear that the ancient prophets had specifically foretold that John would precede Christ. Matthew, for instance, says that John the Baptist had been predicted by the prophet Isaiah as one who would prepare the way for the Messiah's coming:

> For this is he that was spoken of by the prophet Esaias [Isaiah], saying, The voice of one crying in the wilderness, Prepare ye the way of the Lord, make his paths straight. (Matt. 3:3)

Matthew is paraphrasing a verse from the Old Testament Book of Isaiah:

> The voice of him that crieth in the wilderness, Prepare ye the way of the Lord, make straight in the desert a highway for our God. (Isa. 40:3)

This, Carole explained, was the very same verse that the Dead Sea Scrolls cite as evidence of a first Messiah, the voice in the wilderness. It was actually the reason the Essenes made their home in the Judean Wilderness to begin with: the prophecy implied that the first Messiah would arise here. The most indicative link of all, however, between John the Baptist and the first Messiah of the Essenes is that Luke's gospel says that John is descended from the prophet Aaron:

> ... and his [John's father's] wife was of the daughters of Aaron, and her name was Elizabeth. (Luke 1:5)

'There are just too many similarities between John the Baptist and the first Messiah of the Essenes to be mere coincidence,' Carole concluded. 'In my opinion there are only two possibilities: either the early Christians were influenced by the Essenes or John and Jesus had been Essenes themselves.'

That evening, back in my Jerusalem hotel room, I reflected on my informative meeting with Carole Snyder. Was the mysterious sect I was seeking the Essenes? Were the 'wise men' in Matthew's account actually Essene priests?

Although the familiar Nativity play invariably portrays the 'wise men' as three oriental kings from a far-off land, this is purely down to the imagination of Victorian times when the pageant became popular. Matthew's gospel simply says, 'there came wise men from the east to Jerusalem' (Matt. 2:1). Not a word about kings, the orient, how many there were or how far they came. (Although Matthew says that when the 'wise men' left Bethlehem 'they departed into their own country' [Matt. 2:12], the word 'country' is often used in the Bible to refer to a district.) If there was some connection between the Essenes and early Christianity, then the gospel writers might well have referred to Essene priests as 'wise men', and if they came from Qumran, they would indeed have come from the east of Jerusalem.

This was pure speculation, but there was a far more tangible link between the Essenes and Matthew's account of Jesus' birth. Of all the Jews, the Essenes are the ones most likely to have sent a delegation to Bethlehem to seek a newborn Messiah when the star appeared. Other Jews believed that a Messiah would come, but the Essenes spent their entire lives preparing for the event. They would have been constantly on the lookout for just such an omen and would have known full well when it came that the place to search was Bethlehem. Moreover, when Herod erected the imperial eagle over the gateway of the Jerusalem temple, the Essenes, more than any other Jews, would have taken it as a portent of the Messiah's imminent arrival. It had been just such an act of sacrilege by the Seleucid king Antiochus IV, when he erected the statue of Zeus over the temple altar, that instigated the Essene movement in the first place.

According to Matthew, before reaching Bethlehem the 'wise men' visited King Herod.

Had a delegation of Essene priests visited Herod's court at the time Jesus was born? The most complete historical source covering the period was the works of Josephus, written at the end of the first century. It was time to re-examine Josephus. I decided that the next day I would visit the vast library at the Hebrew University.

The National Library on the campus of the Hebrew University, close to the Shrine of the Book in modern West Jerusalem, is said to be the largest in the Middle East. Students and researchers from all over the world study here, and most of its Hebrew manuscripts have an English translation. In an alcove in an empty corner of the huge reading room, I settled down with an English version of the complete works of Josephus. I was initially disappointed, as they contained no more about the Essenes than Carole had already mentioned. But Josephus was most enlightening regarding the political backdrop at the time of Christ's birth. At the very time Jesus was born in Bethlehem, Herod's court was entangled in a web of conspiracy, murder and political intrigue that would change the country for ever.

A Greek Jew like the Hasmoneans before him, Herod had been installed as king of all Jewish Palestine by the Romans in 37 BC. Although he was answerable to the Romans he had almost complete autonomy in domestic affairs, and his reign was a relatively peaceful one until the few months before he died in the spring of 4 BC.

Herod had nine wives and numerous sons, but his favourite son and heir, from his first wife Doris, was Antipater. Antipater spent much of his time in Rome where he became a close friend of the emperor Augustus. Augustus not only endorsed Antipater as heir to the Jewish throne, he also decreed that kingship would thereafter pass to Antipater's descendants. According to Josephus:

> Antipater was appointed to be his [Herod's] successor: and that if Antipater should die first, his son by the High Priest's daughter should succeed.

Like his father, Antipater also had a number of wives, something which Roman law did not recognize. Accordingly, the daughter in question was his first wife Mariamne, whose father was Matthias, the high priest of the Jerusalem temple. Other sons from other wives would only succeed if Mariamne had no surviving children.

Back in Jerusalem, Herod's sister Salome was furious at the emperor's decision. She had long contrived to secure the Jewish throne for her favourite nephew Philip. Philip was a pliable young man, completely under his aunt's influence and, through him, Salome hoped to seize effective control of Palestine for herself. Now, however, Philip was excluded completely from the line of succession. Immediately Salome began to plot the death and disgrace of Antipater and his family. Her chance came when Pheroras, her half-brother, tried to poison Herod and failed by accidentally poisoning himself. With Pheroras dead and unable to contradict her, Salome got one of her scribes to fake a letter which would incriminate Antipater in the plot. It purported to have been sent to Antipater by his close friend Antiphilus, a high-ranking official in Egypt, and in it the entire conspiracy was supposedly detailed. Evidently, Herod spent his last few months in a state of progressive paranoia, seemingly due to an illness that Josephus describes as distemper. Accordingly, the resourceful Salome had little difficulty persuading Herod that the letter was genuine.

Back in Rome, blissfully unaware of any of this, Antipater received word from his father requesting his presence in Jerusalem. Having no idea of the fate that awaited him, Antipater returned home only to find himself arrested and thrown into jail. Although the prince vehemently protested his innocence, he eventually confessed under brutal torture. Herod would have executed his son there and then, but Salome reminded her brother that, since he was a friend of the emperor, more evidence was required to convict Antipater. In reality, given that the emperor had decreed that if Antipater died Mariamne's son should succeed Herod, Salome knew that simply killing Antipater would not secure the throne for Philip. She needed to implicate Mariamne. On Salome's advice, Herod arrested Antipater's mother Doris, who was tortured into confessing not only to her own involvement in the scheme but also to Mariamne's guilt.

Before Mariamne could be arrested, the situation came to the attention of the emperor's envoy, Quintilius Vara, the Roman governor of Syria who was visiting Jerusalem. Although Herod was king in Palestine, Quintilius had military jurisdiction of the Roman empire throughout the eastern Mediterranean. Suspicious of the entire affair, Quintilius demanded to further question the suspects himself. Herod, however, was now so convinced of Antipater's guilt that he flew into a rage, had Doris spirited out of the palace and ordered the guards to kill his son in his cell.

Although the outraged Quintilius wrote to Augustus requesting permission to remove Herod from office, the emperor had more pressing concerns of his own and left the matter in abeyance for some weeks. It was at this time that Herod erected the eagle effigy in the Jerusalem temple, evidently in the hope of pleasing the emperor if he should decide to hold him to account for Antipater's death. A furious mob, led by the priests, soon tore down the blasphemous idol and Herod had the culprits rounded up and burnt alive. The high priest himself, Mariamne's father Matthias, was arrested, stripped of his office and was never heard from again.

Before Herod died, a few weeks later, Salome persuaded him to make Philip his heir. But the emperor, fearing that Jewish Palestine might degenerate into civil strife, decided to resolve the matter by dividing the country between Herod's three surviving sons who would act as tetrarchs, or provincial rulers. Salome's favourite Philip got the northern district of Gaulanitis, Herod Antipas inherited Jesus' province of Galilee in central Palestine and also Perea along the east bank of the Jordan, while the important province of Judea, which included Jerusalem, fell to Archelaus. Ten years later, however, in AD 6, when Archelaus proved incompetent, Augustus removed him from office and appointed a Roman governor to rule Judea.

Josephus was annoyingly silent about the very person at the heart of the affair – Antipater's son. He did not even give the child a name. He also failed to say what happened to the boy or his mother, Mariamne. As I read through various commentaries on Josephus by modern historians, I discovered that the general consensus was that they were murdered in the bloody purge that followed the supposed attempt on Herod's life. It was reasoned that, had the son survived, Augustus would have made him king. In fact, as Antipater had more than one wife and other sons, Herod may well have killed a number of innocent children to prevent them from succeeding him.

All this had been happening in the early weeks of 4 BC, around the very time that Jesus was born in nearby Bethlehem. There was now no doubt in my mind that Matthew's account was based on historical events. If Jesus was believed by some to be the King of the Jews, albeit from the ancient lineage of David, he would indeed have been in mortal danger from Herod's soldiers as they combed the countryside looking for any son of Antipater who might still survive.

Unfortunately, there was nothing in Josephus concerning Jesus' birth, his mother or the 'wise men'. Or so I thought. It was then that I discovered a reference to a controversial theory propounded by a Jewish scholar in 1956. In his book, *The Laws of the Jews*, Israeli historian Joseph Schreiber claimed to throw startling new light on the entire story of Jesus' birth.

Luckily, the library had an English copy of Schreiber's book and, fascinated, I settled back to read. Schreiber began by following Rudolf Bultmann in dismissing the notion that Mary was a virgin. Like Bultmann, he concluded that Jesus had an earthly father. However, Schreiber did not accept that the father was Joseph. He pointed out that both the Matthew and Luke narratives were confusing concerning Mary and Joseph's marriage. After stating that Joseph was Mary's husband when Jesus was conceived, Matthew and

Luke apparently contradicted themselves by saying that the couple did not even know each other at the time. According to Luke, when the angel appeared to Mary to tell her that she would bear Jesus, she answered, 'How shall this be, seeing I know not a man?' (Luke 1:34). Matthew went even further by saying that Joseph and Mary were strangers until Christ's birth: 'And [he] knew her not till she had brought forth her firstborn son' (Matt. 1:25). To Schreiber, it was clear that Joseph and Mary were unacquainted when Jesus was conceived.

According to Schreiber, his hypothesis made sense of an otherwise mysterious episode in Luke's account: namely, Mary's stay with Elizabeth. Why, he argued, should Mary mysteriously go and stay with her cousin if she had a husband at home? The Jewish critics of Christianity, writing in the second-century Talmud, questioned the story of Jesus' divinity by claiming that he had been the illegitimate son of a Roman officer. Schreiber believed that Matthew's and Luke's earlier, contradictory verses concerning Mary's marriage to Joseph were later insertions to counter such accusations.

As I continued to read, Schreiber dropped his bombshell: he claimed to know the true identity of Jesus' father. It had been hidden away for centuries, he proposed, in the biblical story of Jesus' trial.

According to the gospel accounts, when Jesus challenged the authority of the temple priesthood the Jewish elders conspired to have him killed. He was arrested and tried by the Sanhedrin on the charge of blasphemy for claiming to be the Messiah; he then appeared before the Roman governor Pontius Pilate who reluctantly sentenced him to death. Even though some aspects of the gospel narratives are suspect as later interpolations, this part of the story was most likely based on historical events. Not only are Pilate and Caiaphas (the high priest at Jesus' trial) known historical figures, but the Roman historian Tacitus actually makes reference to 'Christus' having been executed by Pontius Pilate.

However, Schreiber argued, claiming to be the Messiah was not in itself blasphemy – one day someone would have to be the Messiah. The claim would only be blasphemous if it could be shown to be false. The onus was therefore on the priesthood to prove Jesus wrong. This was easier said than done: Jesus had been doing everything that was expected of the Messiah.

According to the Old Testament prophets, the Messiah would be born in obscurity in David's home town of Bethlehem, and would travel throughout Israel spreading God's unifying message. Ultimately, he would enter the holy city of Jerusalem riding on an ass as prophesied by Zechariah (Zech. 9:9). Here, he would challenge the corruption of the temple and would be proclaimed King of the Jews as foretold by Isaiah (Isa. 66:5–6, 9:6–7). This is precisely the Jesus the gospels portray. He is born in obscurity in Bethlehem; he preaches unity and proclaims that the Kingdom of Heaven is at hand; he rides into Jerusalem on an ass, where he ransacks the temple; and he is hailed by his followers as King of the Jews. Moreover, the prophet Daniel referred to the Messiah as 'the Son of man' (Dan. 7:13–14), which is exactly how Jesus repeatedly refers to himself in all four gospels.

One option open to the elders which would permit them to condemn Jesus as a fraudulent Messiah would be to demonstrate that he was not descended from David on his mother's side, as the prophecy required. But Jesus must have been able to prove that he was – otherwise, the Sanhedrin would have ordered him stoned to death on the spot, which they did not.

The Sanhedrin failed to condemn Jesus. Instead, they sent him to the Roman governor of Judea, Pontius Pilate. This was a clever manoeuvre from the priesthood's perspective. The province of Judea had been subject to direct Roman rule since AD 6, and under the terms of the occupation the Sanhedrin only retained power over Jewish religious matters. Jesus may have been innocent of any religious infringement, but the elders considered that, by claiming to be King of the Jews, he was guilty of sedition under Roman law.

According to Joseph Schreiber, when Jesus rode into Jerusalem somewhere around AD 33, there was only one person that Roman law would have recognized as king of the Jews – a surviving son of Antipater. It was a law that still remained on the statute books and it was a law that could not be repealed. It had been decreed by the emperor Augustus who, now dead, had been ordained a god by the new emperor Tiberius and by the Roman senate. A decree by the god Augustus could not be undone. Jesus, however, in claiming to be the Messiah was, by definition, claiming descent from David, a dynastic lineage that was not recognized under Roman law. Such a declaration would be pure sedition, the penalty for which was death.

In John's gospel, Pilate asks Jesus straight out, 'Art thou the King of the Jews?' Jesus' eventual answer is 'To this end was I born.' If this referred to his claim to be a descendant of David, then Pilate would have ordered him crucified immediately. On the contrary, Pilate's deliberation to the Jewish elders is 'I find in him no fault at all.' For the episode to fit into any kind of historical context, Pilate finding no fault in Jesus' claim to be King of the Jews means that Jesus must have been claiming to be the only person Rome would have recognized to hold the title – the son of Antipater.

Although in the end Jesus did perish on the cross, according to the Bible it was a reluctant Pilate who condemned him to die. The governor, in the hope of preventing a riot instigated by the Jewish priesthood, washed his hands of the matter and let the mob decide. The mob, egged on by the priesthood, called for Jesus' blood and Pilate finally agreed to send him to his death. In all probability, Schreiber argued, Pilate ultimately decided that it was best to rid himself of a case that, if proved before the Roman senate, would effectively remove him from office.

If Schreiber was right and Jesus was Antipater's son, then Mary had been one of Antipater's wives. Although Schreiber was virtually ignored by other Jewish academics, Christian scholars took exception on this point. They maintained that Mary, a devout Jewish woman, would never have married a man who had other wives. This criticism, however, Schreiber easily countered. Although modern Judaism prohibits polygamy, he explained, this was not so in the first century. Different sects had different ideas about marriage and those who advocated polygamy cited Jacob, whom the Book of Genesis portrays as having numerous wives. Mary, said Schreiber, could indeed have been married to a man with other wives and still have been considered a good Jewish woman.

Despite a number of minor peripheral aspects of Schreiber's argument addressed by his Christian critics, as far as I could tell no one seemed to have refuted his main contention. If Jesus did claim before Pilate that he was King of the Jews, then the governor would certainly have 'found fault' in him if the claim had been made by anyone other than Antipater's son.

Later that afternoon I sat on a bench in the shade of an ancient olive grove, studying the photocopied pages from Schreiber's book. I was in the most appropriate place to consider the implications of his startling theory – the Garden of Gethsemane, the very place where Jesus was arrested and led off for trial. It was incredible to think that these gnarled olive trees, at the centre of the little garden at the foot of the Mount of Olives, just to the east of Old Jerusalem, were some of the oldest trees on earth. They had been dated to over two thousand years old. Not only were they here when Mary and her family had lived, but Jesus himself may actually have stood beneath them on his last night of freedom. A light breeze rustled through the ancient branches as I made notes.

Although Schreiber's theory had been virtually ignored by his peers, for me it answered many questions concerning Mary's mysterious background. I had already concluded that she was a far more influential character at the advent of Christianity than the New Testament writers let on. Why else would so many members of her immediate family have been at the heart of the movement? Moreover, for her lineage to have been so widely accepted as the true bloodline of the Messiah, she must have been from a more aristocratic household than Church tradition maintains.

Schreiber had placed Mary in precisely the historical context I had suspected. Not only would she have needed high-ranking connections to have married the prince, but the same line of reasoning that implied that Jesus was Antipater's son also said much about Mary's lineage. The Sanhedrin, the Jewish elders, would have stoned Jesus to death if he had not been able to prove that his mother was of David's bloodline. Mary must have been from an extremely important family to have even possessed such a convincing family tree.

Mary's true parents may have been very different people from the humble Joachim and Anna of Church tradition. But who were they? The story of Joachim and Anna cannot be traced back earlier than the second-century *Protevangelium* of James of Ephesus. No one before James even mentions Mary's parents. There is no Joachim anywhere in the Bible, but there is an Anna, whom the third-century Christian writers Origen and Clement of Alexandria believed to have been Mary's mother. She is the only Anna in the Bible and appears just once, in Luke's account when Mary takes the infant Jesus to the Jerusalem temple:

And there was one Anna, a prophetess, the daughter of Phanuel, of the tribe of Aser: she was of a great age . . . And she was a widow of about fourscore and four years, which departed not from the temple, but served God with fastings and prayers night and day. And she coming in that instant gave thanks likewise unto the Lord, and spake of him to all them that looked for redemption in Jerusalem. (Luke 2:36–8)

Here, the prophetess Anna is recognizing Jesus as the Messiah. If the account is in any way true, then the woman would seem to have been too old to be Mary's mother. Nevertheless, the Church eventually accepted her as Mary's mother and she was canonized as St Anna (or St Anne in the English Church). Interestingly, here was yet another tradition associating Mary with the Jerusalem temple.

According to James of Ephesus, Joachim and Anna had placed Mary in the custody of the high priest, while Origen and Clement say that Mary's mother was the prophetess in the temple. Could these traditions have any historical validity?

Although Mary could not, as James of Ephesus maintained, have been an altar girl in the inner temple, she might have had some other role in the massive temple complex. Women were allowed into the Royal Portico and the outer courtyard, and there were a number of holy women who, like Anna the prophetess, were allowed to attend to certain religious tasks. The Jewish priesthood were permitted to marry and some of their wives played active roles in temple life. Did the traditions that Mary's guardian was the high priest and that her mother was the prophetess, in some way reflect that her true parents were officials in the Jerusalem temple? If Mary really was of David's line, if she really was Antipater's wife, then it would have been quite possible for her parents to have been highly placed in religious circles. The most exalted religious leaders in the Jewish world were the temple priesthood, and a number of Jewish princes had married their daughters.

Just below the Garden of Gethsemane, a narrow, shrub-lined path led down into the Valley of Jehosaphat. Here, below the Church of the Assumption, was the rock-cut tomb where Joachim and Anna were believed to have been buried. It seemed a fitting place to end the afternoon.

Halfway down the long flight of worn marble steps that led deep underground, two craggy recesses were cut into the rock, one to either side. It was in one of these that Severus, the bishop of Antioch, apparently discovered the bodies of Mary's parents in AD 517. The other, he believed, contained the bones of Joseph. Severus' most controversial claim. however, was that the long stone chamber at the bottom of the steps, twelve metres below ground level, had contained the bones of Mary herself.

Inside the rock-hewn cavern, a service was in progress and a Greek Orthodox monk politely told me that I had to wait at the foot of the stairs. In fact, there were two services going on. The long, candle-lit chamber was flanked on either side by very different altars: one for the Armenian Church, the other for the Greek Orthodox Church. Before them, a priest from each denomination was silently at prayer. A number of monks in attendance were swinging incense burners, filling the place so full of smoke that I could hardly see the niche at the other end of the chamber where Mary's body was said to have been laid. The Armenian and Orthodox Churches share the shrine between them but the Catholic Church has no involvement. The reason for this unusual lack of a Catholic presence lies in the controversial history of the Virgin's tomb.

Even when Severus found the tomb in the early sixth century, the Church was divided on the issue of the Assumption. Had Mary been buried like anyone else, or had she, like her son, ascended bodily into heaven? The idea of Mary's Assumption can be traced back only to around AD 380, when Gregory, the influential bishop of Nyssa, reasoned that Mary must have ascended bodily into heaven simply because she was so exalted. Other churchmen vehemently disagreed. As far as they were concerned, only Jesus, as the son of God, could have done that. Besides which, they argued, there was not one word of Mary's death or ascension into heaven anywhere in the Bible. Gregory countered by using the sort of inverted logic that characterized the Church of his time, saying that if Mary had *not* ascended bodily into heaven the Bible would have said so. The arguments raged on until AD 430, when a Greek manuscript appeared in Rome which was claimed to be an eyewitness account of the Assumption. Known as *The Testament of John*, and attributed to the disciple John, it purported to be the complete story of Mary's death.

According to the manuscript, after Christ's crucifixion Mary spent her last years in Jerusalem, often praying at her son's empty tomb. Eventually, the angel Gabriel appeared to her and told her she was to be reunited with Jesus in heaven. As a final request, Mary asked to see the apostles one last time and her wish was granted. Wherever they were in the world, the Holy Spirit took them up in cloud and brought them to her house. When Mary died the apostles took her away for burial. Here, Christ himself appeared, raised her from the dead and took her, body and soul, into heaven.

The manuscript said that Mary had been buried somewhere in the Valley of Jehosaphat and it was for this reason that Severus was searching the area when he came across the tomb. Severus reopened the entire debate when he claimed that the bones he found in the cavern were Mary's earthly remains. The Church remained divided on the issue. Those who advocated the doctrine of the Assumption said that Severus only learned that the bones were Mary's in a spurious dream, while those who opposed the doctrine claimed that the John manuscript was a fake.

Either way, the so-called Tomb of the Virgin in the Valley of Jehosaphat posed a problem for Catholic unity. In the Middle Ages when the Crusaders seized Jerusalem from the Moslems, pilgrims began flocking to the tomb, and the Vatican was forced to act. As a compromise, the Church of the Assumption was built over the tomb. Pilgrims of either persuasion could worship as they saw fit: either in the church if they believed in the Assumption or at the shrine if they believed that it had contained Mary's body. However, when the Assumption was declared dogma by Pope Pius XII in 1950, the Catholic Church decided to distance itself from the site altogether, leaving it to the Armenian and Greek Orthodox Churches to tend.

Many Catholics, however, still visit the shrine, as I discovered when I was eventually allowed inside. The party of Italian students who joined me in the smoky, candle-lit cavern immediately crossed themselves and began reciting the rosary. After a while the man in charge, evidently their tutor, began to give a lecture, presumably about the Virgin Mary, as he kept repeating the only word I could understand – Maria.

Feeling that both *The Testament of John* and Severus' dream were somewhat suspect and that the shrine had little to do with the historical Mary or her parents, I decided to leave. It was then that I heard the tutor mention another familiar name – Mariamne.

I stopped in my tracks. Mariamne! That was the name of Antipater's wife. I could not leave without asking the man what he was talking about. Mariamne, he explained, was the Greek version of the name Mary. Just as Jesus came from Greek *Iesos*, which in turn came from the Hebrew Yeshua, Mary or Maria came from the Greek Mariamne, which came from the Hebrew Miriam – thought to mean 'Beloved of Heaven'.

Schreiber had assumed that Mary may have been one of Antipater's lesser wives. Perhaps she was actually the Mariamne in Josephus' account – Antipater's first wife and the chosen mother of the Jewish heir. Could Josephus' Mariamne have really been Mary, the mother of Christ? Mary or Miriam was, it seems, a fairly common name at the time, so Antipater could have had two wives of that name. But there was something that did link the two women: both were associated with the Jerusalem temple. In fact, Mariamne's father had been the high priest, as was, according to tradition, Mary's guardian. Had I found the Mary of history?

Consulting my notes back in my hotel room, I began to reconstruct the lives of Mary and her son as they might have been before Jesus' ministry began.

Mary comes from an aristocratic family in Capernaum. Her father Matthias, perhaps originally the priest of the Capernaum synagogue, is ultimately ordained the most important religious leader in the country, the high priest of the Jerusalem temple. Mary marries Prince Antipater, and her cousin Elizabeth marries another priest. According to Luke's gospel, Elizabeth's husband Zacharias is also a priest of the Jerusalem temple:

> There was in the days of Herod, the king of Judea, a certain priest named Zacharias . . . According to the custom of the priest's office, his lot was to burn incense when he went into the temple of the Lord. (Luke 1:5–9)

When Mary conceives Jesus, Elizabeth is already pregnant with John. According to Luke, when Jesus is conceived the angel Gabriel tells Mary:

> And, behold, thy cousin Elizabeth, she hath also conceived a son . . . and this is the sixth month with her . . . (Luke 1:36)

Six months before Mary gives birth to Jesus, Elizabeth gives birth to John the Baptist, presumably in Jerusalem. Just before Jesus is born, Antipater is framed by his aunt Salome for the attempted assassination of Herod. When Antipater and his mother Doris are arrested by the mentally unstable king, Mary somehow manages to escape.

The Church tradition concerning Mary's youth has the high priest placing her into the care of the elderly Joseph, who first acts as her guardian and ultimately marries her. This might reflect that the historical Matthias manages to find his daughter a safe hiding place in the home of Joseph, perhaps a sympathizer, when she is sought by Herod. If so, that safe hiding place would appear to be in Bethlehem.

In Matthew's gospel, Joseph seems to live in Bethlehem and initially to have no connection with Nazareth. His account begins with Mary and Joseph already in Bethlehem: they only move to Nazareth when they return to Israel after their flight to Egypt.

> When Herod was dead, behold, an angel of the Lord appeareth in a dream to Joseph in Egypt, Saying, Arise and take the young child and his mother, and go into the land of Israel . . . But when he heard that Archelaus did reign in Judea in the room of his father Herod, he was afraid to go thither . . . he turned aside into the parts of Galilee: And he came and dwelt in a city called Nazareth. (Matt 2:19–23)

Luke's conflicting account of Mary and Joseph's journey from Nazareth to Bethlehem at the time of Jesus' birth is questionable because of the inaccurate dating. The author places the event during the census of AD 6, ten years after Herod's death. The date, however, is interesting. This is precisely the year that Archelaus, the ruler of Judea, was removed from office by Augustus and banished from Judea. Matthew tells us that Joseph is afraid to set foot there while Archelaus is still in charge. Perhaps Luke's source confused Jesus' birth in Bethlehem with a later visit by Joseph and his family when Archelaus is dismissed and they feel it is safe to return.

If Jesus was born in Bethlehem in the winter of 5–4 BC, then he cannot have been the specific son of Antipater mentioned by Josephus when he refers to Augustus' decree concerning the Herodian line of succession. However, if that particular child was already deceased or had fallen into Herod's murderous hands, then, with Antipater dead, the child that Mary was carrying – Jesus – may have been the legitimate heir.

When the mysterious star appears, the Essenes of Qumran take it as a portent of the Messiah's birth and send a delegation to Bethlehem to seek out an appropriate child. Here they discover the newborn Jesus and decide that he is the one they seek. Perhaps they also consider Jesus' cousin John to be the first Messiah. Not only is he a descendant of Aaron, as the prophecy required, but he had been born just a few months earlier.

In Matthew's account, after Jesus is born in Bethlehem Herod learns of the child's existence from the 'wise men'. Fearing that Jesus will usurp him, Herod summons his chief priests who tell him of the prophecies concerning the Messiah's birth in Bethlehem (Matt. 2:4–6).

Here, again, there might have been a mix-up between two different accounts: one account of Essenes finding Jesus in Bethlehem, and the other of Jewish priests telling Herod where the baby is. Essenes or not, the 'wise men' had to have been Jewish, or they would not have been seeking the Messiah in the first place. Any Jewish 'wise man' would have known that Bethlehem was where the Messiah was supposed to be born. There is therefore no reason for them to go to Herod's court and ask for his help. Herod, however, did summon his chief priests at this very time. According to Josephus they are Mariamne's father Matthias and his assistant Judas:

> There was one Judas, the son of Saripheus, and Matthias, the son of Margalothus, two of the most eloquent men among the Jews, and the most celebrated interpreters of the Jewish laws . . .

Josephus says that Herod flew into a rage and dismissed Matthias because his followers had torn down the eagle. Perhaps he also interrogated the high priest concerning his daughter and her newborn son. If so, then he probably tortured Matthias into revealing their whereabouts. In Matthew's account Herod sends his men to find the child and bring him to him:

> And he sent them to Bethlehem, and said, Go and search diligently for the young child . . . (Matt. 2:8)

Luke's account of the baby Jesus being laid in a manger, so presumably in a stable, may reflect the fact that Mary had to hide her baby from Herod's men. Matthew tells us that the holy family manage to escape Herod because Joseph has been warned in a prophetic dream:

> Behold, the angel of the Lord appeareth to Joseph in a dream, saying, Arise, and take the young child and his

mother, and flee into Egypt, and be thou there until I bring thee word: for Herod will seek the young child to destroy him. When he arose, he took the young child and his mother by night, and departed into Egypt. (Matt. 2:13–14)

The most likely place for Antipater's wife to have fled was indeed the land of Egypt. Antipater's close friend Antiphilus, whom Salome had also falsely implicated in the plot, was a high-ranking official in that country.

According to Matthew, Herod is so furious that Jesus has escaped him that he: 'sent forth, and slew all the children that were in Bethlehem, and in all the coasts thereof' (Matt. 2:16). However, the psychotic king fails to kill Jesus, who is already safely away.

With Antipater dead, Joseph marries Mary and the couple ultimately live a low-profile existence in Nazareth, where Jesus spends his early years as a carpenter. When they are old enough Jesus and John join the Qumran community, where they spend many years preparing for their chosen roles.

Around AD 30 John the Baptist emerges from Qumran and begins to recruit new Essene followers. Unlike many other characters who feature in Jesus' life, John's historical existence is attested to by Josephus:

[John] was a good man and commanded the Jews to exercise virtue, both as righteousness towards one another, and piety towards God, and so to come to baptism; for that the washing would be acceptable to him.

His influence over the people seems to have been considerable because Josephus tells us that Herod Antipas (Herod's

The tomb of the Virgin in Jerusalem's Valley of Jehosaphat. Its very existence divided the established Church for centuries. (All pictures Graham Phillips unless otherwise credited)

The High Altar at the ruins of the Church of the Most Holy Virgin at Ephesus.
It was built directly over the tomb said to contain Mary's mortal remains.
(Lorraine Evans)

Nazareth, showing the Church of the Annunciation.

The Chapel of the Annunciation, where Mary is believed to have
divinely conceived the son of God.

Herod watches the killing of the First Born in a relief from Chartres Cathedral. Was this murderous tyrant really Jesus' grandfather? (Ancient Art & Architecture Collection Ltd)

Old Jerusalem and the Church of the Holy Sepulchre.

The Grotto of the Nativity in Bethlehem, said to be the site of Christ's birth.

The Judean wilderness where John the Baptist prepared the way for the Messiah.

The cave dwellings at Qumran where Jesus may have spent his formative years.

The Garden Tomb in East Jerusalem, believed by many to be the true sepulchre of the Resurrection.

Above: A fourth-century gold coin bearing the effigy of the Roman empress Helena. She was responsible for establishing the many shrines associated with Mary's earthly life. (Hebrew University)

Right: One of the trees in the Garden of Gethsemane which actually dates from the time of Christ.

Above: The Roman city of Ephesus. It was here that the Mary of history became the Mary of faith. (Lorraine Evans)

Left: One of the many ancient statues depicting Mary as the goddess Artemis in the Church of the Most Holy Virgin at Ephesus. (Lorraine Evans)

The Vatican in the 1850s, when Pope Pius IX proclaimed the Immaculate Conception church dogma. (Grigori Grigo'evich Chernetsov 1801–65, The Bridgeman Art Library)

Vatican grotto chapel celebrating the Assumption of the Virgin Mary, a church tradition not endorsed by the papacy until 1950. (The Bridgeman Art Library)

Seventeenth-century painting of the Assumption, from the Lombardy School. Even in the Renaissance, Mary was still being depicted as the moon-goddess Artemis. (The Bridgeman Art Library)

son) actually feared he might incite a revolt in his province of Perea, along the River Jordan:

> [Herod Antipas] feared lest the great influence that John had over the people might put it into his power and inclination to raise a rebellion, for they seemed ready to do anything he should advise.

After some time, Jesus himself leaves the Qumran community and joins John in Bethabara, where the Baptist proclaims him the Messiah. John's own days of preaching are soon over for, according to both the gospels and Josephus, Herod Antipas has him arrested and executed. Jesus' remarkable ministry then begins.

As I stood on the balcony watching the first evening star twinkling over the Judean hills, I had the strangest feeling. If my speculation about Jesus' birth was in any way correct, then it was almost as extraordinary as the gospel writers believed.

The ancient Hebrew prophecies required that the Messiah quite literally become King of the Jews. According to the Old Testament prophet Isaiah, even though the Messiah may bring peace and even though he has the power of God himself, he must sit upon the throne of David and be king of Israel (Isa. 9:6–7). In early first-century Palestine there could be only one way that anyone could hope to become King of the Jews, accepted by both Romans and Jews alike. He not only had to satisfy Roman law by being the son of Antipater, he also had to satisfy Judaic requirements and be descended from David. Jesus' father Antipater, heir to the Herodian throne; his mother Mary, heir to the throne of ancient Israel! – This could have been arranged: a kind of Messianic scheme. However, for the star – the supernova – to have appeared at precisely the time that a legitimate King of the Jews was born in Bethlehem cannot, by any stretch of the imagination, have been arranged. It was a truly astonishing coincidence. Only three such celestial events have occurred in the last thousand years (see page 67).

Was it a remarkable series of coincidences that started Christianity? Or was there, as Christians maintain, more to it?

It was time to investigate Jesus' teachings. It was his teachings regarding salvation for the whole of humanity that really established Christianity as the most influential movement the West has known. His teachings quite literally changed the world. This was not, though, what his followers had been expecting.

The Hebrew Messiah was only relevant to the Jews: the Kingdom of God that it was foretold he would bring about was a united kingdom of Israel, an earthly Jewish state, free from foreign occupation and Gentile influence. The Hebrew Messiah was certainly not expected to die on the cross. When Jesus died his new religion would probably have died with him if it had not been for his unique beliefs. The Christ portrayed in the gospels claims to have come to earth to redeem all mankind, Jews and Gentiles alike. He prepares the way for souls to enter a very different Kingdom of Heaven – Resurrection in God's afterlife. When Jesus began his ministry, and deviated from traditional Jewish thought, he appears to have fallen out with his immediate family. He also, it seems, rejected his mother.

Summary

- According to the gospels, when Jesus challenged the authority of the temple priesthood the Jewish elders conspired to have him killed. He was arrested and tried by the Sanhedrin on the charge of blasphemy for claiming to be the Messiah – the King of the Jews.

- The Sanhedrin failed to condemn Jesus. Instead, they sent him to the Roman governor of Judea, Pontius Pilate. This was a clever manoeuvre from the priesthood's perspective. The province of Judea had been subject to direct Roman rule since AD 6, and under the terms of the occupation the Sanhedrin retained power only over Jewish religious matters. Jesus may have been innocent of any religious infringement, but the elders considered that, by claiming to be King of the Jews, he was guilty of sedition under Roman law.

- When Jesus was tried around AD 33, there was only one person that Roman law would have recognized as king of the Jews – a surviving son of Antipater. This had been decreed by the emperor Augustus who, now dead, had been ordained a god by the new emperor Tiberius and by the Roman senate. A decree by the god Augustus could not be undone. Jesus, however, in claiming to be the Messiah was, by definition, claiming descent from David, a dynastic lineage that was not recognized under Roman law. Such a declaration would be pure sedition, the penalty for which was death.

- In John's gospel Pilate asks Jesus, 'Art thou the King of the Jews?' Jesus' eventual answer is 'To this end was I born.' If this referred to his claim to be a descendant of David, then Pilate would have ordered him crucified immediately. On the contrary, Pilate's deliberation to the Jewish elders is 'I find in him no fault at all.' For the episode to fit into any kind of historical context, Pilate finding no fault in Jesus' claim to be King of the Jews means that Jesus must have been claiming to be the only person Rome would have recognized to hold the title – the son of Antipater.

- According to the Jewish historian Josephus, Antipater's first wife was called Mariamne, which is the Greek version of the name Mary. Although this was a common name at the time, Mariamne does have something in common with Jesus' mother. According to early Church tradition Mary was raised by the high priest of the Jerusalem temple. Mariamne was the high priest's daughter. Interestingly, shortly after Antipater's death Mariamne mysteriously disappeared.

V

THE FAMILY OF CHRIST

IN 1970 ISRAELI archaeologists uncovered the foundations
of a first-century dwelling near the Wailing Wall in
Jerusalem. It had been destroyed by the Romans in the
blood-bath that followed the Jewish revolt in AD 70. As there
was some evidence that it might have been the home of an
early Christian family, I decided to visit the site the next
morning.

Rebellion against the despotic rule of the emperor Nero
finally broke out in Palestine in AD 66 and, because of trouble
elsewhere in the empire, the rebels held the city of Jerusalem
for almost four years. However, after Vespasian became
emperor and Rome had solved its internal troubles, the
general Titus was sent to retake the city. This he did with
ruthless efficiency and thousands of innocent men, women
and children were butchered in the streets.

The so-called Burnt House is actually the basement of a
wealthy Jewish home which had been filled with rubble ever
since it was torched by the Romans during the massacre.
Amongst the ruined walls, some ten metres square, archaeologists found the broken remains of storage pots, wine
bottles and perfume jars, just as they had fallen when the

MARY'S FAMILY TREE

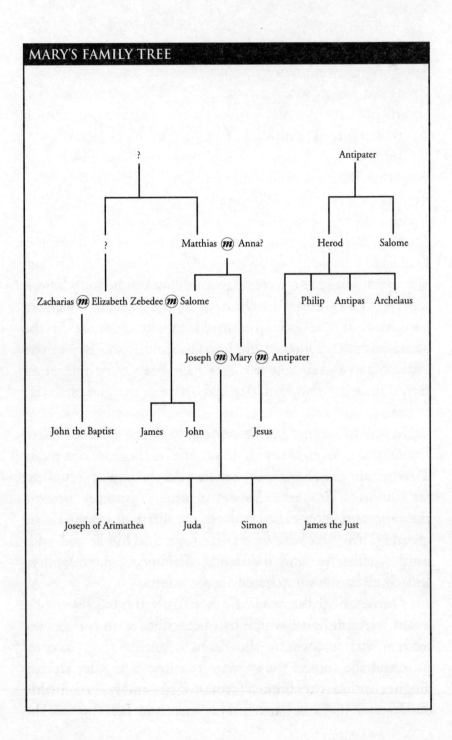

upper storeys collapsed in the fire almost two thousand years ago. The only human remains were the skeletal arm of a young woman in her early twenties. She must have been just one member of the unfortunate family to have been mercilessly slaughtered in the atrocity.

Items found amongst the debris were inscribed with the householder's name: Bar Kathros, a well-to-do priest. Remarkably, he was a known historical figure. Contemporary Jewish records, preserved in the second-century Talmud, list him amongst dissident priests of the Jerusalem temple. Evidently, disillusioned by mainstream Judaism, he had openly criticized the temple and joined a breakaway Jewish sect. He may even have been a Christian. The Romans only permitted one Jewish faction to survive after AD 70: the Pharisees, who had been relatively tolerant of Roman rule. Like many other Jewish sects, the Jerusalem Christians were completely wiped out in the massacre.

These followers of Jesus who had preached around Jerusalem for four decades since the Crucifixion were not called Christians at the time: this was a much later Roman term. The earliest Jewish writings concerning them, such as the texts of the Talmud, refer to them as the Nazarenes – the followers of 'Yeshua of Nazareth'. From the New Testament, in the Acts of the Apostles, we can gather that they were strict Jews who worshipped daily at the Jerusalem temple, although they differed from traditional Jews by living a communal life, sharing everything they had. Their first leader was the disciple Peter, but within a few years the movement was taken over by Jesus' brothers.

Although, since the fourth century, the Church has taught that Mary remained 'forever virgin' and had no further children after Jesus, this is not what the Bible says. The

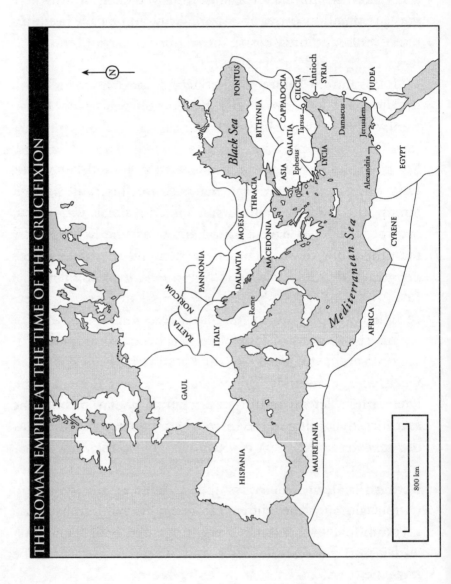

THE ROMAN EMPIRE AT THE TIME OF THE CRUCIFIXION

gospels tell us that Mary had other children besides Jesus. Jesus' siblings appear, for instance, in Mark's account, where they are mentioned by the townsfolk of Nazareth when they reject Jesus' authority to preach:

> Is not this the carpenter, the son of Mary, the brother of James, and Joses, and of Juda, and Simon? And are not his sisters here with us? (Mark 6:3)

To avoid confusion with disciples of the same name, the early Christians called James, James the Just and Simon, Simon the Blessed. The two of them, along with Juda, became successive leaders of the Jerusalem Church up until the time of the revolt. James is the first and is initially Peter's deputy. Paul refers to him in his letter to the Galatians:

> Then after three years I went up to Jerusalem to see Peter, and abode with him fifteen days. But other of the apostles saw I none, save James the Lord's brother. (Gal. 1:18–19)

Even before Peter's death, James appears to have taken over as leader. According to the third-century writings of Clement of Alexandria:

> Peter, James and John, after the Ascension of our Saviour, though they had been prepared by our Lord, did not contend for the honour, but chose James the Just as Bishop of Jerusalem.

There was actually no such thing as a bishop in the first century. However, Clement's source clearly implied that James was chosen as leader of the Christians, even over the three chief apostles. James is also mentioned by Josephus, who tells us of his death in AD 62:

> So he [the high priest] assembled the Sanhedrin of the judges, and brought before them the brother of Yeshua, who was called the Christ, whose name was James, and some others [his followers], and when he had formed an accusation against them as breakers of the law, he delivered them to be stoned.

According to the second-century Jewish writer Hegesippus, James was succeeded by his brother Juda. Juda is thought to have been the St Jude who wrote the last but one book in the New Testament – The General Epistle of Jude. It begins with the writer referring to himself as 'Jude, the servant of Jesus Christ, and brother of James [the Just]'. According to Hegesippus, Juda was ultimately succeeded by Jesus' surviving brother Simon, the last head of the Jerusalem Church before its extermination by the Romans following the revolt.

Strangely, these brothers who led the Christians for the first four decades after Christ's death played no role whatever in the movement during Jesus' ministry. Not only did Jesus apparently exclude his brothers almost completely from his life, he also seems to have shunned his mother.

By the time Jesus begins to preach, Joseph is completely absent from the gospel accounts so he is presumably dead. Mary, however, is very much alive. Nevertheless, she hardly features at all in the gospel narratives at any time during Jesus' ministry. Even when she *is* included she is far removed from the Queen of Heaven that she later became in the eyes of the Church. In John's account Jesus seems almost rude to his mother. The episode in question occurs at the very beginning of his ministry when, after he has gathered his first disciples in Capernaum, he travels to nearby Cana to attend a wedding. His mother Mary is there, seemingly in charge of the festivities.

> And the third day there was a marriage in Cana of Galilee; and the mother of Jesus was there: And both Jesus was called, and his disciples, to the marriage. And when they wanted wine, the mother of Jesus saith unto him, They have no wine. Jesus saith unto her, Woman what have I to do with thee? (John 2:1–4)

Jesus seems most offhand towards his mother, whom he admonishes for badly organizing the wedding feast. After the wedding, Mary and his brothers return with him to Capernaum:

> After this he went down to Capernaum, he, and his mother, and his brethren, and his disciples: and they continued there not many days. (John 2:12)

In John's narrative, none of them appear again until the Crucifixion. Matthew, Mark and Luke, however, do make reference to one further episode in which Jesus makes it quite clear he has no time for his family. He is preaching, perhaps in Peter's house in Capernaum, when his mother and brothers arrive outside and ask to see him.

> While he yet talked to the people, behold, his mother and his brethren stood without, desiring to speak with him. Then one said unto him, Behold, thy mother and thy brethren stand without, desiring to speak with thee. But he answered

and said unto him that told him, Who is my mother? and who are my brethren? And he stretched forth his hand toward his disciples, and said, Behold my mother and my brethren! For whosoever shall do the will of my Father which is in heaven, the same is my brother, and sister, and mother. (Matt. 12:46–50)

After this, the brothers do not show up again until the Crucifixion and Mary only appears briefly, standing at the foot of the cross. Strangely, as soon as Jesus is executed they are all back on the scene. The Acts of the Apostles include them amongst the Christian leaders who meet secretly in a house in Jerusalem shortly after Jesus has died.

[The disciples] continued with one accord in prayer and supplication, with the women, and Mary the mother of Jesus, and with his brethren. (Acts 1:14)

There was undoubtedly discord between Jesus and his family, and the reason appears to have been his radical teachings. The link between Jesus and the Essenes seemed fairly certain, as far as I was concerned. However, there were glaring discrepancies between Jesus' philosophy and Essene thought. If his family had become involved in the Essene sect, then perhaps it was Jesus' departure from their uncompromising doctrine that created the rift.

The Dead Sea Scrolls speak of a final war between the Sons of Light and the Sons of Darkness: the Essenes and the occupying forces. Eventually, we are told, there would be a last battle, a cataclysmic struggle between the two. The second Messiah of the Essenes would not only be a holy man and a king, he would also lead them as a warrior like David before him. According to *The Manual of Discipline*:

> He shall cleanse you not with water but with fire, so that you may stand boldly behind him on the field of battle.

This seems to be the Messiah that John the Baptist was expecting:

> I indeed baptize you with water; but one mightier than I cometh, the latchet of whose shoes I am not worthy to unloose: he shall baptize you with the Holy Ghost and with fire. (Luke 3:16)

For the Essenes, the Messiah would transform the present order and return Israel to a former golden age of statehood and independence. As other Jews believed, this Kingdom of Heaven was not in the life to come but here on earth, and the Essenes were expected to fight for the Messiah. *The Manual of Discipline* actually included an entire section devoted to military training. One verse even instructed their elite warriors how to wage the holy war:

> One thousand men shall be ranked seven lines deep and they shall each hold a shield of bronze, burnished with mirrors. And on the points of their javelins they shall write, 'shining javelin of the power of God, bloody spikes to bring down the slaying of the wrath of God, flaming blade to devour the wicked, struck down by the judgement of God'.

This was no analogy – the Essenes really intended to slay the Romans. The Dead Sea Scrolls taught them to hate their enemies. According to *The Community Rule*:

Everyone who wishes to join the congregation of the elect, must pledge himself to live according to the rule of the community. To love all the children of light and to hate all the children of darkness.

The Essenes also believed that the Sons of Light had to be 'bodily whole', and they refused admission to anyone who was physically disabled. *The Community Rule* specifically excluded the blind, the deaf and the lame from Qumran. It excluded the deaf because they could not hear the scriptures, the blind because they could not read them, and the lame because they would scare away the angels. Women were also excluded from Qumran.

Jesus' teachings depart from Essene doctrine in all these respects: his Kingdom of Heaven was the Resurrection in the afterlife; he taught his followers to love all others, even their enemies; he advocated they renounce violence and turn the other cheek; he preached compassion for the sick and gladly welcomed women into his fold. If Jesus had originally been an Essene, which the John the Baptist link seemed very much to imply, then at some point he was inspired by a new philosophy and broke away from the sect. This might have been the reason for the split with his mother and brothers.

Perhaps the major cause of the friction between Jesus and his family was his insistence on preaching to the Gentiles. Although he deliberately fulfilled the prophecies expected of the Hebrew Messiah, Christ sees his messianic role as an emissary of a new covenant between God and *all* mankind. He believes that the word of God is intended for everyone and not just the Jews. Even the disciples abandoned his teachings in this respect.

We know this from the letters of St Paul. When he was imprisoned at Caesarea around AD 57, Paul wrote many letters to his fellow Christians. Some are still preserved in the New Testament, and in them he complains that the disciples had rejected Jesus' instructions to preach to the Gentiles. The disciples, it seems, had come round to seeing things a little more in line with Jesus' brothers, which would explain why Christ's family joined the movement after his death. Paul, however, broke away from them all and began to convert the Greeks. As I left the Burnt House, that last morning of my visit to Israel, I could not help but wonder whether Christianity would have perished completely in the flames of the Jewish revolt had it not been for St Paul.

David Deissmann had offered to drive me to the airport, but as my flight did not leave until the evening, he took me to see the Roman ruins of Caesarea where Paul had been imprisoned, just over forty kilometres up the coast from Tel Aviv.

Set between an eighteen-hole golf course, an affluent country club and a luxury hotel are the ruins of ancient Caesarea. Overgrown with thick vegetation there is a huge hippodrome: a chariot-racing stadium which would once have seated over twenty thousand spectators. Partially submerged in wind-swept sand are the great rounded arches of an aqueduct which once supplied the town with water from the north. Most impressive of all, there is a classical theatre, where an audience of five thousand would once have enjoyed the entertainment of the day. The open-air theatre, which has been fully restored to its former glory, was excavated by a team of Italian archaeologists in the 1960s. Here, they unearthed one of the most publicized biblical finds of recent years – the only known inscription bearing the name of Pontius Pilate.

At the entrance to the site there is a reproduction of the find. (The original is in the Israel Museum in West Jerusalem.) The limestone block, 82 centimetres high, 20 centimetres thick and 68 wide, bears the Latin words: *Tiberieum Pontius Pilatus praefectus Judaeae* – 'Temple of Tiberius [built by] Pontius Pilate, governor of Judea'. The stone apparently commemorated Pilate's building of a nearby temple which had been dedicated to the emperor Tiberius.

Herod the Great had originally built the town in a completely Roman style as the chief harbour and seaport of his kingdom. He named it after his benefactor Augustus Caesar. It later served as the headquarters of the governor of Judea when the province came under direct Roman rule in AD 6. The remains of the governor's palace were unearthed near the theatre in 1997, and it was here that Paul is believed to have been imprisoned by one of Pilate's successors, Claudius Felix.

Other than Jesus, Paul is arguably the most important figure in Christian history, for it was via him that Christ's teachings found their way into the Gentile world. There is no real evidence that any of Jesus' disciples preached to anyone other than the Jews or, at least, those who converted to Judaism. This is demonstrated in Paul's biblical letter to the Galatians, for instance, where he refers to the disciples' insistence on circumcision (Gal. 2:8). From the New Testament we learn that the early apostles did travel outside Palestine, but only, so far as can be gathered, to preach to other Jewish communities. The notion that they intended to convert the entire world comes from a Christian tradition established many years later. (For example, the popular belief that, as first head of the Church, St Peter preached in Rome does not originate with the Bible but with the writings of the Christian scribe Irenaeus in AD 170.) Regardless of what Jesus may have believed concerning the Gentiles, soon after his death Peter and the other disciples evidently decided that his message was only intended for the Jews. Paul makes this clear on many occasions in his letters. He also makes it blatantly apparent that he disagrees: he, like Jesus, intends to preach the word to all mankind. For example in Galatians 2:8:

> For he that wrought effectually in Peter to the apostleship of the circumcision, the same was mighty in me toward the Gentiles.

According to the biblical account, Paul never knew Jesus personally but was converted to his teachings by a vision on the road to Damascus around a decade after the Crucifixion. One of Paul's first acts was to visit the disciples in Jerusalem and ask to join them. Although he was initially welcomed, bitter divisions soon emerged. In his letter to the Galatians, we are told of a stormy meeting in Antioch, in present-day Turkey, during which Paul and Peter quarrelled. The main point of contention was Peter's insistence that Gentiles had to convert to Judaism if they wanted to join the Nazarenes:

> But when I saw that they walked not uprightly according to the truth of the gospel, I said unto Peter before them all . . . why compellest thou the Gentiles to live as do the Jews? (Gal. 2:14)

A further reason for the dispute seems to have been the disciples' refusal to sanction Paul's authority. In his first letter to the Corinthians, Paul complains that he has been rejected by the disciples who saw him as no true apostle – they had known Jesus personally, he had not. Paul, however, believes he has as much authority as any of them as he knew Christ in his heart:

> Am I not an apostle? am I not free? have I not seen Jesus Christ our Lord? are not ye my work in the Lord? If I be not an apostle unto others, yet doubtless I am to you: for the seal of mine apostleship are ye in the Lord. Mine answer to them that do examine me is this, Have we not power to eat and to drink? Have we not power to lead about a sister, a wife, as well as other apostles, and as the brethren of the Lord, and Cephas [Peter]? (I Cor. 9:1–5)

Judging by the fact that Paul also rebukes Jesus' brothers ('the brethren of the Lord'), it seems to have been Peter's decision that Jesus' message was intended only for the Jews that finally won them over.

After the meeting at Antioch the two parties seem to have split permanently, as the Bible gives no indication that they ever met again. It was one of the most significant turning points in Christian history. Two rival Churches had formed – the Church of the Nazarenes, with its message for the Jews, and the Pauline Church, intent on converting the Gentiles.

Unlike the Jerusalem Christians, Paul travelled widely, converting many Greek communities throughout the Near East. Only three centuries earlier, the Greeks had ruled much of what became the Roman empire and many Greeks still lived around the eastern Mediterranean. It was to these pagan Greeks, particularly in what is now Turkey, that Paul successfully preached Christ's message. Perhaps the main reason why Paul's teachings were so readily accepted by the Greeks is that Paul was Greek himself. According to the Acts of the Apostles, he came from Tarsus in what is now Turkey but at the time it was a major Greek city. Although Paul claims to have been a Hebrew from the tribe of Benjamin, this would appear to have been an adopted heritage, seemingly through marriage.

Evidence of his Gentile background comes from both historical sources and literary research. According to Epiphanius, a fourth-century bishop of Salamis, Paul was the son of Greek parents and adopted Judaism only after spending time in Jerusalem and marrying a Jewish woman. Paul's Greek origins are also confirmed by linguistic studies of his biblical letters, which reveal that all his Old Testament quotations are from the Greek translation, the Septuagint, even where its text wrongly diverges from the Hebrew original. Paul, therefore, must have consulted the Greek Old Testament rather than the Hebrew version, which would not have been the case if he was born a Jew and had understood the Hebrew language.

Paul's home city of Tarsus was a centre of Stoicism, a Greek philosophy which taught self-control in adversity and the acceptance of a universal law; it emphasized the equality of men and women, denounced slavery and advocated a worldwide human brotherhood, devoid of national frontiers. Paul clearly saw Jesus' teaching in terms of Stoicism, which would have had little difficulty assimilating the concept of a single, universal God, and it was the Stoic philosophy of internationalism which probably persuaded Paul to preach to the Gentiles.

Around AD 57, shortly before Jesus' brother James was stoned to death, Paul also came into conflict with the Jewish elders in Jerusalem who accused him of preaching against Judaic law. According to the Acts of the Apostles, to save Paul from a lynching, Roman soldiers took him away under heavy guard to Caesarea. In reality, the Jewish elders probably handed him over to the Romans. Paul was from Tarsus and hence a Roman citizen, and the Sanhedrin had no jurisdiction over him. Perhaps the elders hoped that the Roman governor Felix would execute him for sedition as Pilate had ultimately executed Jesus. But although like Pilate's original deliberation concerning Christ, Felix could find no fault in Paul, to avoid antagonizing the Sanhedrin the governor kept Paul locked up in prison and waited for things to calm down.

In the summer of 1997 Israeli archaeologist Yosef Porat excavated the foundations of a large complex of buildings near the theatre at Caesarea, thought to be the seat of Roman administration in first-century Judea. The site included the palace of the governor, a luxurious bath-house and large ornamental courtyards. In one building was a mosaic floor bearing the Latin inscription: *Adiviorib[us] Offici Custodiar* – 'I came to this office – I shall be secure.' Yosef Porat believed that the inscription implied that the building had been a part of the administrative complex that dealt with internal security. As such, it may well have contained Paul's cell.

For two years Paul remained imprisoned at Caesarea while Felix dithered. When a new governor, Portius Festus, was appointed in AD 59, Paul demanded his right as a Roman citizen to appeal directly to the emperor. The Acts of the Apostles include his appeal to Festus:

I stand at Caesar's judgement seat, where I ought to be
judged: to the Jews have I done no wrong, as thou very well
knowest. For if I be an offender, or have committed any
thing worthy of death, I refuse not to die: but if there be
none of these things whereof these accuse me, no man may
deliver me unto them. I appeal unto Caesar. (Acts 25:10–11)

After an eventful voyage to Rome, Paul appears before
the emperor Nero – or more likely one of the emperor's
officials – and he is set free. Five years later Paul is again in
the capital, seeking converts, when the great fire of Rome
destroyed much of the city. It is a mystery how the fire
actually started, but rumours circulated that the psychotic
Nero had started it himself. The emperor, though, countered
the rumours by blaming the defenceless Christians, and along
with hundreds of others Paul was rounded up and killed.

These earliest Christians in Rome were undoubtedly the
Greek followers of Paul and not the Jewish followers of Peter.
After the persecutions by Nero, the Christians of the capital
were forced to meet in secret in the city's catacombs: burial
sites consisting of hundreds of subterranean galleries connected by miles of passageways. The Christians illustrated
these galleries with devotional paintings, many of which still
survive today. In them we find clear evidence that the first
Christians were the Greeks and not the Jews, as the paintings
are accompanied by Greek inscriptions and not by any in
Hebrew or Aramaic. Moreover, we find the ambience of
these early depictions of Jesus completely detached from
Judaism. Taken alone, there is nothing to connect them with
the Hebrew world: Christ is not shown in a Judaic setting
but in a context of Greek mythology.

The problem that confronted early Christianity was that

the Greeks outside Palestine had no concept of Judaism. Jesus' role as the Messiah, the heavenly king who had come to amend ancient Judaic law, meant absolutely nothing to the Greeks. Consequently, they began to interpret Jesus in their own familiar contexts. The Roman catacomb paintings show that the first Christians made frequent use of Greek mythology for devotional purposes. For instance, Ulysses and the Sirens symbolized the Christian rejection of pagan lust, while Orpheus' lute symbolized Jesus' message of love, and the rebirth of the god Adonis symbolized the Resurrection of Christ.

The Christians in Rome had been driven into hiding by Nero and, soon after, the Christians in Jerusalem were wiped out in the persecutions that followed the Jewish revolt. In AD 70, the Romans destroyed the Jerusalem temple, uprooted the Jewish ruling class and greatly reinforced their military presence. They reorganized the Sanhedrin and moved it to Jamnia, about forty-five kilometres north-west of Jerusalem, and eliminated any sect they considered subversive. The Jerusalem Christians, indeed Christians throughout all Palestine, seem to have vanished completely. Although an early Church tradition holds that some of them managed to escape the Jerusalem massacre and settle in Pella, about forty kilometres south of Lake Galilee, no archaeological evidence of their presence at the site has been found. There were certainly Christians in nearby Capernaum in the mid-second century, as demonstrated by the graffiti in 'Peter's house', but, as the inscriptions were in Greek, these would appear to have been Gentile Christians who had moved into the area from Cilicia in the north.

The new religion might simply have faded away had it not been for Paul's most successful community of Christians

– in the seaport city of Ephesus. It was here, on the Aegean coast of what is now Turkey, that Christianity really evolved. It was also in the city of Ephesus that the Mary of history became the Mary of faith.

As the plane climbed above the clouds and the coast of Israel disappeared from view, I once again flicked through my copy of *The Living Faith*, this time wondering what Father Rinsonelli would have made of what I had learned. I was sure that he would have dismissed out of hand any notion that Mary was a daughter of the high priest, the wife of the crown prince and the mother of the heir to the Jewish throne. To Father Rinsonelli, Mary was unquestionably co-redeemer of the universe and the Queen of Heaven. As far as the Bible is concerned, however, Mary has no active role in the establishment of Christianity.

Following the Crucifixion Jesus' brothers lead the Jerusalem Christians, yet Mary is strangely absent. She is not even present at three of the most important events in the New Testament. In no gospel account is she there when the empty tomb is discovered; she is not present at Christ's Ascension; and she is not there at Pentecost when the disciples are divinely inspired by the Holy Ghost. She is not even visited by the risen Christ, although he appears to all his disciples and to his friend Mary Magdalene. After the Acts of the Apostles refer to her presence at the secret meeting in Jerusalem Mary simply disappears. We are not told where she lived, how she died or where she was buried. If the New Testament is to be believed, she not only played no part in Jesus' ministry, she had no active role at all in establishing Christianity. How, then, did she become for the Church the most important woman who ever lived? Why was she so exalted in the eyes of later Christians?

It all began with the second Jewish revolt of AD 131. Across the Mediterranean, a thousand kilometres from Jerusalem, the Christians of Ephesus were thriving. Paul had established one of his first Christian communities in the city, as can be gathered from his biblical letter, The Epistle to the Ephesians. Irenaeus the bishop of Lyons, writing around AD 177, tells us that when the Jerusalem Christians were decimated by the Romans there were already thousands of Gentile Christians in Ephesus. This may be an exaggeration, but a contemporary historical source certainly confirms that by the early second century Ephesian Christianity was thriving. In AD 112 the emperor Trajan wrote to the governor of Bithynia asking him to report on the growing Christian movement in the city. The governor, Pliny the Younger, wrote back saying that, although they were numerous, the emperor had nothing to fear from the Christians. Evidently, they were a peaceful and law-abiding group who met together at daybreak and 'sang a hymn to *Christus* as to a god'. Although these Christians were Gentiles, Pliny regarded them as a Jewish sect. They were, it seems, still open about their Judaic religious heritage. All this was to change two decades later when the Ephesian Christians chose to distance themselves from Judaism altogether.

In AD 131 the second and final Jewish revolt broke out in Palestine. It was led by a mysterious figure called Simeon Bar Kokhba. Little is known about his background but the Talmud says that he claimed descent from the Davidic line and set himself up as the divine King of the Jews. Unlike Jesus, Bar Kokhba saw himself as the warrior-Messiah, come to rid Israel of foreign rule. It seems that he started off as a minor resistance leader, waging a feckless guerrilla campaign from a base-camp somewhere in the Judean Wilderness. In 131, when the emperor Hadrian decided to build a pagan shrine on the site of the demolished Jerusalem temple, rioting broke out in the streets. Seizing the opportunity, Bar Kokhba rallied the mob and took control of Jerusalem. So outnumbered were the Roman forces that the governor, Tinus Rufus, had no alternative but to order an evacuation of the city and the Roman forces retreated to Caesarea. The Jews once again had control of their ancient capital and in the euphoria thousands hailed Bar Kokhba as the true Messiah. Even the previously pro-Roman Sanhedrin got caught up in the excitement and officially sanctioned his claim.

The emperor immediately sent a new legion to Palestine, but Bar Kokhba's frenzied rebels managed to wipe them out before they got anywhere near Jerusalem. After this, the emperor played safe and assembled a full-scale invasion force, drawing men and equipment from units stationed as far afield as Syria, Arabia, Mysia and Egypt. Led by the veteran general Julius Severus, this new army progressively reconquered Palestine, destroying whole towns and massacring entire populations as they went. In AD 135 Bar Kokhba was finally surrounded at the fortress of Bethther, some twelve kilometres south-west of Jerusalem, and after a lengthy siege the Romans breached the walls and slaughtered the surviving defenders, including Bar Kokhba himself.

After Bar Kokhba's defeat, the recriminations were dreadful; far worse than anything that followed the first revolt. The emperor decided to make an example of the Jews, and an estimated half-million lost their lives. It did not stop there, and for years a succession of emperors persecuted and oppressed the Jews. The Christians of

Ephesus accordingly decided to distance themselves from Judaism. They made certain that the Romans realized that Christ had been born to amend Jewish law – he had come to show the Jewish elders the error of their ways. It was around this time that the gospels began to assume their present form and some biblical scholars believe that they were altered to make them more pro-Roman than they had originally been. For instance, to place the blame for Christ's death on the Jews in general, the episode where the Jewish mob demanded that Pilate execute Jesus was inserted:

> Pilate therefore, willing to release Jesus, spake again to them. But they cried, saying, Crucify him, crucify him (Luke 23:20–1)

In all probability, although he could find no fault in Jesus, Pilate decided that it was best to rid himself of a troublesome claimant to the Jewish throne.

If the original gospel sources had mentioned anything about Jesus as Antipater's son or Mary as Antipater's wife, this is when it would have been removed. Any claim by the Christians that their founder had been a real king of the Jews, rather than an allegorical one, would have been highly dangerous. In no way would the Ephesian Christians have wanted Jesus tarred with the same brush as Simeon Bar Kokhba. Isolated completely from Judaic tradition, they began to adopt an ever more Hellenistic manner of worship. Unlike the Jews, for centuries the Greeks had worshipped the images of pagan gods. Ephesus had been the chief cultic centre of the goddess Artemis, and it was not long before the Virgin Mary took her place.

*

After a brief stay in England, I decided to travel to Turkey and visit Ephesus. I knew that the ruins of the Roman city had been unearthed, and I knew the excavation covered a large area, but I had never expected anything quite so huge.

On a broad, flat plain, set between rolling green hills, the ruins seemed to go on and on for ever. Before me, a wide Roman road stretched off into the distance, its white marble paving glaring in the bright morning sun. Either side, stone pillars, colonnades and broken statues lined the avenue which would long ago have been the central thoroughfare of the ancient city. Just like the plan of a modern city, other streets led off at regular intervals into the administrative and commercial districts of the town. Now, however, all that remained of the once multistorey buildings, with their ornate columns, covered walkways and classical façades, were the foundation stones. Acre upon acre of white limestone walls spread out like a vast labyrinth as far as the eye could see.

Ephesus is said to be the largest archaeological excavation in the world: an entire Roman city some fifteen kilometres square, where the remains of arenas, bath-houses, libraries and mansions are still being excavated today. Here and there an area would be cordoned off where archaeologists were hard at work uncovering the colourful tiles of yet another mosaic, once the lavish floor of some important public building.

About two kilometres to the north-east of the ancient thoroughfare, with ruins stretching all the way between, was the remains of the once gigantic Temple of Artemis: now just a pile of dusty bricks rising above a sea of tiny yellow flowers. Artemis was the Greek goddess of the moon and the deity of chastity and virginity. The Romans also venerated Artemis under the name Diana and built the massive temple in her honour. The temple became a chief centre of pagan worship for people from all over the Roman world, and it enjoyed the services of an army of temple maids, virgin prophetesses and eunuch-priests. It seems that as Christianity grew in the city, the converts found it difficult to embrace the new and intrinsically alien religion without a similar divinity to replace the ancient goddess. Mary, the mother of God's son, now portrayed as a divine virgin, quickly became the new Artemis. Many Christian devotional artefacts depicting the Virgin Mary have been uncovered at Ephesus, dating from as early as the mid-second century AD. From them, it is clear that there was originally a fine dividing line between the goddess Artemis and Mary the mother of Christ.

The oldest surviving depictions of the Virgin Mary made by the minority Christian movement in Rome are paintings found in the catacombs of Priscilla. The earliest, dating from around AD 150, show her as a robust, serious-faced woman, holding a child in her arms. She is bare-headed and wears a plain white robe. In none of these early Roman depictions is Mary in any way ethereal, nor is she the object of worship. She is simply one of many characters depicted in scenes from the gospels. In Ephesus, however, Mary is depicted very differently. In statues, her arms are outspread, inviting prayer, and in her fresco portraits she is young and beautiful and surrounded by a halo of heavenly light. She also wears a distinctive blue robe and is often depicted wearing a crown and sitting on a crescent moon – exactly as the moon goddess Artemis is depicted in pagan art.

The oldest surviving writings concerning the worship of Mary at Ephesus can be found in the works of the early Christian missionary Justin Martyr. Justin was a pagan, born in Nablus in Palestine, but was converted to Christianity when he visited Ephesus around AD 140. He wrote three works that still survive and became one of the most influential Christians of the era. In his writings Justin exalts Mary almost to the level of Christ himself. He portrays her as the Queen of Heaven and the absolver of original sin. Christians believed, and still do, in the doctrine of original sin. By disobeying God and tempting Adam with the forbidden fruit of the Tree of Life, Eve brought sins upon humanity. Thereafter, all human beings were born sinners and only through Jesus Christ could their sins be forgiven. Justin, however, taught that it was also through the intercession of the Virgin Mary that sins could be absolved. He praises her as the new Eve whose very existence cancelled out the sins of the first.

When Ephesus was eventually sacked by the barbarian Goths in AD 262, much of its three-hundred-thousand population moved to Rome. Here, the Ephesian Christians greatly outnumbered other Christians, and by the time of Constantine and the Council of Nicaea in AD 325 they had become the dominant faction in the Christian religion. It was through the influence of Ephesian Christianity that Mary finally became such an important figure to the established Church. To begin with, however, there was considerable friction between the Roman and Ephesian factions.

Although the two were now joined in one unified Church, for some decades after the Council of Nicaea many leading figures in the newly formed Catholic Church were uncomfortable with Mary's role as Queen of Heaven. They were only too aware that she played no such part in the gospels, but were most troubled by Paul's biblical letters which made no reference to her at all. How could she be a central theme of Christian devotion, they protested, when St Paul himself seemed completely unaware of the fact?

One of the leading exponents of Marian devotion (as this devotion to the Virgin Mary became known) in the fourth century was Athanasius, the bishop of Alexandria. In 357 he wrote of a series of mystical visions he claimed to have experienced concerning Mary's coronation as Queen of Heaven. His work became extremely influential and many Christians mistakenly cited it as an historical eyewitness account. But the emperor Julian remained uneasy with Athanasius and the Ephesian-inspired view of Mary's exalted status. He saw no biblical evidence for her role as Queen of Heaven and was especially disturbed by the link between Mary and the pagan moon goddess Artemis.

Eventually, a solution to the dilemma was provided by one of the leading churchmen of the time: Epiphanius, the bishop of Salamis in Cyprus. In his book the *Panarion* ('The Refutation of All Heresies'), written around 375, he claimed to have found an oblique reference to both Mary's lunar associations and her role as Queen of Heaven in the last book of the Bible, the Book of Revelation. Accredited to a mysterious Christian visionary, St John the Divine, the Book of Revelation concerns the author's visions of the Apocalypse, the final days of the world. In chapter 12 there is a reference to a crowned woman who appears in heaven giving birth to a child:

And there appeared a great wonder in heaven; a woman clothed with the sun, and the moon under her feet, and upon her head a crown of twelve stars: And she being with child cried, travailing in birth, and pained to be delivered. (Rev. 12:1–2)

As the child was 'to rule all nations' and 'was caught up unto God, and to his throne' (Rev. 12:5), Epiphanius equated him with Christ. By association, therefore, the crowned woman seated over the moon must have been his mother, the Virgin Mary. As far as Epiphanius was concerned, this proved that Mary was biblically represented as a queen of heaven and was associated with the moon, regardless of any similar pagan depictions of Artemis. Even though the Book of Revelation was full of symbolic imagery which was nigh on impossible to interpret – although there was no way to date its authorship to before or after the Ephesians had portrayed Mary in this way – Epiphanius' theory satisfied the Church's need for a unifying solution to the Marian debate. Mary could be accepted as the lunar Queen of Heaven, free from pagan associations.

The Ephesian notion of Mary being 'forever virgin' could also be severed from the pagan veneration of Artemis as a perpetual virgin. In fact, it was considered a self-evident aspect of Christian doctrine. Around AD 380 the emperor Theodosius I's religious adviser, Ambrose the bishop of Milan, wrote:

> Would the Lord Jesus have chosen for his mother a woman who would defile the heavenly chamber with the seed of a man?

Some two kilometres to the north of the Temple of Artemis are the remains of the Church of the Most Holy Virgin, once a massive basilica built after the Romans had retaken Ephesus from the Goths. Like so many of the holy sites in Israel, it was erected in the early fourth century on the orders of the empress Helena. In stark contrast with the white limestone buildings of the earlier Roman town, the ruins are of deep-red brick. The original church has been partially reconstructed: Corinthian pillars, friezes and archways of the 260- by 30-metre edifice have been painstakingly re-erected from the rubble. It was here, in AD 431, that Mary's status was finally debated by the Supreme Council of the Church.

Celestine, the bishop of Rome, had been satisfied by the works of Athanasius, Epiphanius and Ambrose and was happy to formally accept Mary's divinity. Nestorius, the equally powerful bishop of Constantinople, was not. His main objection was to Mary being given the title 'Mother of God'. Since Constantine's Council of Nicaea, Jesus had been considered not only God's son but God himself: he was 'of the same substance as the Father' – a doctrine known as the 'essential union'. To the fifth-century Church, Christ had literally been God incarnate. Although he accepted that Jesus' teachings were divine, Nestorius disagreed on this point. He believed that God had manifested only his will through Jesus – not his entire being. Christ had been a man like anyone else and so his mother could not be literally the 'Mother of God'. 'Divine nature cannot be born,' he wrote. 'It can have no mother.' Mary, he advocated, may have been a good and pious woman, but she should not be deified as 'Queen of Heaven'. Nestorius had a considerable following and, once again, Church unity was threatened. Something had to be done.

In the early fifth century the emperor was still the highest authority in the Church and, as such, Theodosius II convened an ecumenical council to resolve the matter. In 431 almost two hundred bishops and other religious authorities met at Ephesus and for three months they hotly debated the issue. Finally, on the emperor's insistence, they sanctioned the divine motherhood of Mary. She was officially given the titles 'Queen of Heaven' and 'Mother of God' and was accepted as co-redeemer of mankind. Nestorius, however, was excommunicated and exiled to Antioch.

Following the Council of Ephesus, Mary's holy days became mandatory and the 'Hail Mary' was composed as an essential prayer for all Christians. In Luke's account of the Annunciation, when Gabriel appears to Mary and tells her she has conceived Jesus, the angel says: 'Hail, thou that art highly favoured, the Lord is with thee: blessed art thou among women' (Luke 1:28). Also in Luke's account, when Elizabeth learns that her cousin Mary has conceived Christ, she proclaims: 'Blessed art thou among women, and blessed is the fruit of thy womb' (Luke 1:42). The verses were combined to form the salutation that became as customary as the Lord's Prayer:

> Hail Mary, full of grace, the Lord is with thee: blessed art thou among women, and blessed is the fruit of thy womb, Jesus.

And a petition was added:

> Holy Mary, Mother of God, pray for us sinners now and at the hour of our death.

Mary had become what she would remain to all Roman Catholics to this day: 'the most superior and wholly unique member of the Church . . . the co-redeemer of the universe'.

Ephesus was not only the city where the Mary of history became the Mary of faith, it was also, according to the

Ephesian Christians, where Jesus' mother died and was buried.

Shortly after the Council of Ephesus *The Testament of John* appeared, purporting to be an eyewitness account of Mary's bodily ascension into heaven. Although it would be over fifteen hundred years before the Assumption was made Church dogma, many Christians readily accepted it as fact. Surely, they argued, if Mary was, with her son, co-redeemer of humanity, she too must have ascended bodily into heaven. But this was not the prevailing Christian view when the empress Helena visited Ephesus in the 320s. The Ephesian Christians actually believed that Mary had spent her last days in their city and was eventually buried there. In fact, Helena built the first Church of the Most Holy Virgin over a tomb that she was told contained Mary's body.

Excavations on the site have failed to discover the original tomb and it is feared to have been destroyed when the Byzantine emperor Justinian rebuilt the church around AD 530. The house where Mary is said to have lived can still be seen, however, so I decided to take a look.

About three kilometres from the archaeological zone, in a remote clearing on the wooded hillside of Panaya Kapula, is the House of Mary: a simple hut built from roughly hewn stones. Here, it is said, Mary spent her last days. Surprisingly, there was no one to be seen in the quiet little glade: no tourists, no nuns or monks; not even an attendant to charge for admission. The only people anywhere around were two women kneeling silently at prayer before the simple wooden altar which stood at one end of the single windowless chamber inside.

The building, I soon discovered, has only been regarded

as Mary's house since 1891 when a German woman, Catherine Emmeric, experienced a vision in which the Virgin Mary appeared to her to tell her that this is where she had died. In reality the little building was a reconstructed Byzantine chapel, originally built sometime around AD 600. Most people in the area were somewhat sceptical of Frau Emmeric's vision, as she had experienced the mystical revelation at home and never actually visited Ephesus. From what I had been reading about Church history, I seriously doubted whether Mary had visited Ephesus either.

Although by the empress Helena's time it was generally accepted in Ephesus that Mary had lived and died there, there is not one surviving manuscript which actually documents the story. All that remains is the works of Helena's contemporaries, such as Bishop Eusebius, merely making reference to the fact that Mary died there. The only reason, so far as I could gather, to link Mary with Ephesus was by association with the disciple John, the son of Zebedee. The tradition held that when John came to Ephesus to preach, Mary came with him. However, the story that John came to the city is itself suspect.

It is first referenced by Irenaeus of Lyons around AD 170, but the full account does not appear until about half a century later, in the works of Clement of Alexandria. In the narrative, John arrives in Ephesus some years before St Paul. At first he has little success converting the citizens, so decides to prove God's existence by calling upon his power to destroy the Temple of Artemis:

> The altar of Artemis split into many pieces, and all the offerings laid up in the temple suddenly fell to the floor and its goddess was broken, and so were more than seven images.

Half the temple fell, so that the priest was killed at one stroke as the roof came down.

Judging by its clearly legendary content – not least the fact that the Temple of Artemis was still standing three centuries later – the story seems unlikely to have originated with a reliable historical source. Even if John did visit the city, there is nothing in the account to explain why Mary was believed to have come with him. She makes no appearance in the story whatsoever. Why, then, was she thought to have come to Ephesus at all?

According to the gospel of John, after the Crucifixion Mary spends her remaining days with an unnamed disciple. When Jesus is on the cross, we are told, he asks the disciple to look after Mary and to treat her as his own mother. This he apparently does, as she stays with him for the rest of her life:

> Now there stood by the cross of Jesus his mother, and his mother's sister, Mary the wife of Cleophas, and Mary Magdalene. When Jesus therefore saw his mother, and the disciple standing by, whom he loved, he saith unto his mother, Woman, behold thy son! Then saith he to the disciple, Behold thy mother! And from that hour that disciple took her unto his own home. (John 19:25–7)

Nowhere in the account is the disciple named, but he appears on three other occasions in John's gospel, each time the author referring to him only as the 'disciple whom Jesus loved'. The mysterious disciple seems to be someone especially close to Jesus, for the first time he is mentioned, during the Last Supper on Jesus' last day of freedom, he is sitting at Christ's side with his head resting on his chest:

> Now there was leaning on Jesus' bosom one of his disciples, whom Jesus loved. (John 13:23)

The second occasion is when he is at the foot of the cross, and the third is early on Easter morning when Mary Magdalene has discovered the empty tomb and runs and tells two of the disciples:

> Then she runneth, and cometh to Simon Peter, and to the other disciple, whom Jesus loved . . . (John 20:2)

The last time he is mentioned is at the end of the gospel account when the risen Christ appears to the disciples on the shores of Lake Galilee:

> Then Peter, turning about, seeth the disciple whom Jesus loved following; which also leaned on his breast at supper . . . Peter seeing him saith to Jesus, Lord, and what shall this man do? Jesus saith unto him . . . He shall not die; but, if I will that he tarry till I come, what is that to thee? This is the disciple which testifieth of these things, and wrote these things: and we know that his testimony is true. (John 21:20–4)

Here we are told that the 'disciple whom Jesus loved' is the person who originally wrote down the events. By Helena's time it was unquestioned that the gospel writer was the disciple John. Accordingly, it was reasoned that as John was the 'disciple whom Jesus loved' and Mary spent the rest of her days with him, then she must have accompanied him to Ephesus.

Most biblical scholars now doubt that the author of the gospel was the apostle John. Yet even if he was, the author makes it very clear that the mysterious disciple is someone else. He tells us: '*we* know that *his* testimony is true'. The author, whoever he is, is saying that the 'disciple whom Jesus loved' had provided him with the story of Jesus' life; not that he himself is that man. Consulting the Bible, I seriously doubted that the disciple was John at all.

At the beginning of the passage concerning Christ's final appearance to the disciples on the shore of Lake Galilee we are told that there are seven disciples present:

> There were together Simon Peter, and Thomas called Didymus, and Nathaniel of Cana in Galilee, and the sons of Zebedee [James and John], and two other of his disciples. (John 21:2)

This would seem to rule out John as being the mysterious disciple, since he is described here, as he usually is, as one of the sons of Zebedee. If, in this verse, John openly calls himself the son of Zebedee, why, immediately after, obliquely refer to himself as 'the disciple whom Jesus loved'? The disciple in question seems more likely to have been one of the two unnamed ones.

Strangely, the mysterious disciple is present at the foot of the cross when all the apostles have apparently gone into hiding. After Jesus' arrest, even Peter is afraid to admit knowing his master, let alone be anywhere near the cross (John 18:15–27). Perhaps the mysterious disciple was not actually one of the twelve apostles at all. Indeed, nowhere else in the New Testament are any of them singled out as 'the disciple whom Jesus loved'. The twelve are not the only people the New Testament describes as disciples. For example:

There was a certain disciple at Damascus, named Ananais. (Acts 9:10)

Now there was at Joppa a certain disciple named Tabitha. (Acts 9:36)

A certain disciple was there, named Timotheus. (Acts 16:1)

Although the gospels tell us that the twelve are all present at the Last Supper, we are not told whether or not anyone else is there. In fact, John's account seems to imply that the mysterious disciple is someone other than one of the twelve. Jesus tells his disciples that one of them will betray him, and they all look at one another in confusion. The unnamed one, in his privileged position next to Christ, is asked by Peter to query Jesus about his suspicions:

When Jesus had thus said, he was troubled in spirit, and testified, and said, Verily, verily, I say unto you, that one of you shall betray me. Then the disciples looked one on another, doubting of whom he spake. Now there was leaning on Jesus' bosom one of his disciples, whom Jesus loved. Simon Peter therefore beckoned to him, that he should ask who it should be of whom he spake. He then lying on Jesus' breast saith unto him, Lord, who is it? (John 13:21–5)

Why would Peter need to ask this other disciple to question Christ about his suspicions, unless the man was on more intimate terms with Jesus than he? As Peter is Jesus' chosen successor and the leader of the twelve, the mysterious disciple cannot presumably be one of them.

The mysterious disciple is present at the foot of the cross. There are, in fact, only two of Jesus' male followers present at the Crucifixion in any gospel account, and neither of them is one of the twelve. They are Nicodemus and Joseph of Arimathea (a small village about fifty kilometres north-west of Jerusalem). John refers to them being there to take away Jesus' body when he dies.

> And after this Joseph of Arimathea, being a disciple of Jesus, but secretly for fear of the Jews, besought Pilate that he might take away the body of Jesus: and Pilate gave him leave. He came therefore, and took the body of Jesus. And there came also Nicodemus, which at the first came to Jesus by night . . . Then took they the body of Jesus, and wound it in linen clothes with the spices, as the manner of the Jews is to bury. (John 19:38–40)

Interestingly, Joseph of Arimathea is actually described as 'a disciple' of Jesus. He is, however, a secret disciple, as also, it seems, is Nicodemus. Nicodemus appears three times in John's account as a high-ranking Pharisee priest who is sympathetic to Jesus' cause: 'There was a man of the Pharisees, named Nicodemus, a ruler of the Jews' (John 3:1). He regards Christ as 'a teacher come from God' (John 3:2), but he has to keep his association with Jesus secret: 'Nicodemus . . . came to Jesus by night, being one of them' (John 7:50).

So both Joseph of Arimathea and Nicodemus are secret disciples of Christ. If one of them is the mysterious disciple this may account for his name being omitted from important sections of the narrative. Indeed, they may both have been the unnamed disciples in the final passage. But the one most likely to have been the 'disciple whom Jesus loved' is Joseph of Arimathea. This Joseph, it seems, was Jesus' own brother.

The person Jesus chose as Mary's guardian cannot have been just any disciple: it had to have been his oldest surviving brother. It was the Jewish custom for the eldest son to look after his widowed mother. We know from both Matthew's and Mark's gospels that Mary had other sons besides Jesus. We also know from the Acts of the Apostles and the letters of Paul that they were still alive at the time of the Crucifixion. When Jesus says to his mother, 'Woman, behold thy son!' and to the disciple, 'Behold thy mother!', he must be speaking literally. He is handing his mother over to the care of his eldest brother. (The special love and peculiar intimacy the disciple apparently shares with Jesus are understandable if the man is his brother.)

According to Jewish tradition it would also have been Jesus' closest male relative who would have been responsible for his burial. In all four gospels it is Joseph of Arimathea who organizes the funerary rites and places the body in the tomb. According to Matthew, he actually places Jesus in his own tomb:

> When the even was come, there came a rich man of Arimathea, named Joseph, who also himself was Jesus' disciple: He went to Pilate, and begged the body of Jesus . . . And when Joseph had taken the body, he wrapped it in a clean linen cloth. And laid it in his own new tomb . . . (Matt. 27:57–60)

The only person other than Jesus' eldest brother who would have had the right to arrange the burial would have been Jesus' father (or adopted father), Joseph. Joseph of Arimathea is clearly not this Joseph, as he is not a carpenter but a political figure. Mark's and Luke's gospels both tell us that he was a 'counsellor' – a lay member of the Sanhedrin. If Joseph the carpenter was dead, then Joseph of Arimathea must be Jesus' eldest surviving brother. According to the New Testament, Jesus did indeed have a brother called Joseph. He is named in the reference to his siblings:

> Is not this the carpenter . . . the brother of James, and Joses, and of Juda, and Simon? (Mark 6:3)

The name Joses is actually the same as Joseph. Just as Jesus was the Latin rendering of *Iesos* (which, as we have noted, was the Greek rendering of the Hebrew *Yeshua*), Joses was the Latin rendering of *Iesoph*, which in turn was the Greek rendering of the Hebrew *Yoseph*. When the English translation of the New Testament was made in the early seventeenth century, others called Joses – and there were fourteen of them – had their names transliterated as Joseph, but somehow two of them, including Jesus' brother, missed out.

I already suspected that Joseph of Arimathea had been entrusted with Mary's care. But it was not until I was left alone in the tiny chapel that afternoon that the implications suddenly struck me.

Before the cross on the simple little altar that the two women had been praying before when I entered Mary's house was a small brass communion chalice. I was reminded of the Grail chapel in the Pre-Raphaelite painting by Edward Burne-Jones – the chapel, which according to legend, had been built by Joseph of Arimathea. Romantic literature of the Middle Ages portrayed Joseph as the Grail guardian. Although many different artefacts were depicted as Grails in medieval times, in the Joseph story the 'Holy Grail' was the cup used by Jesus at the Last Supper. It was said to have contained a few drops of Christ's blood and Joseph had been charged by Jesus himself to look after it after his death. The Holy Grail not only had divine power, it was said to hold a great secret.

Was Joseph's Holy Grail actually the Virgin Mary? Is this what Giovanni Benedetti had meant: 'The Holy Mother was the Holy Grail'? From what I could gather from Father Rinsonelli's Holy Office report, Benedetti claimed to have found Mary's tomb. In the legend, Joseph of Arimathea is charged by Jesus with the safety of the Grail. In the Bible he is charged by Jesus with the safety of his mother. In the legend, Joseph flees Palestine with the Holy Grail – the vessel that bore Christ's blood. If I was right he had actually fled Palestine with the Virgin Mary – the vessel that brought Christ into the world. Was the secret of the Holy Grail really the secret of Mary's tomb?

If Mary spent her last days with Joseph, then she may have died where he is said to have died – in the British Isles. Was this where Benedetti had found her tomb?

Summary

- According to Church tradition Mary spent the years after the Crucifixion with the apostle John in the Greek city of Ephesus. Although the Bible does not say where Mary lived out her life or where she died, John's gospel asserts that she spent her final days with an unnamed disciple.

- When Jesus is on the cross he asks the disciple to look after his mother. This he apparently does, as we are told she stays with him for the rest of her life. Although the disciple is not named, Church tradition holds that he was the apostle John. However, this seems highly unlikely. The gospels tell us that the apostles all went into hiding after Christ was arrested. (There were disciples of Jesus – close followers – who were not chosen as apostles, the twelve.)

- There are, in fact, only two of Jesus' male followers present at the Crucifixion in any gospel account, and neither of them is an apostle. They are Nicodemus and Joseph of Arimathea. John's gospel refers to them being there to take away Jesus' body when he dies. Joseph of Arimathea is actually responsible for Jesus' burial.

- The disciple in question is far more likely to be Joseph of Arimathea. Not only is he actually described as 'a disciple' of Jesus, he is the only candidate who places the account into an historical context. In Jewish tradition Mary's closest male relative would have been responsible for her welfare, and her son's closest male relative would have been responsible for his burial. Joseph buried Jesus, so he must have been his closest male relative and, therefore, Mary's too. So Joseph of Arimathea would have been responsible for taking care of the widowed Mary.

- As his father was dead, the burial arrangements should have fallen to Jesus' eldest surviving brother. According to the New Testament, Jesus did have brothers. Mark's gospel names one of them as Joses. The name Joses is actually the same as Joseph. Joses was the Latin rendering of *Iesoph*, which in turn was the Greek rendering of the Hebrew *Yoseph*. Joseph of Arimathea may well have been this particular brother.

VI

THE NEW JERUSALEM

JOSEPH OF ARIMATHEA does not appear in the New Testament after the account of the Crucifixion. (Neither does Jesus' brother Joses.) Like Mary, he simply disappears. According to early Christian tradition, however, he came to Britain. The story of Joseph's journey to the British Isles was popularized in the Middle Ages by the Burgundian author Robert de Boron in his *Joseph d'Arimathie*, written around the year 1200. According to the story, once the Sanhedrin discovered that Joseph was a disciple of Christ he was dismissed from office and thrown into prison. He eventually escaped and, along with Nicodemus, fled Judea and travelled north. Ultimately, after a series of adventures, he crossed the Channel to settle in Britain where he built a special chapel to contain the Grail. Robert fails to name his source, except to say that it was a book written by a group of Christian clerics.

Although this was the first detailed account of Joseph's journey to Britain, there survive two much earlier references to the tradition, dating from almost a thousand years before Robert de Boron's time. The fourth-century *Evangelium Nicodemi* and its contemporary *Vindicta Salvatoris*, purported to

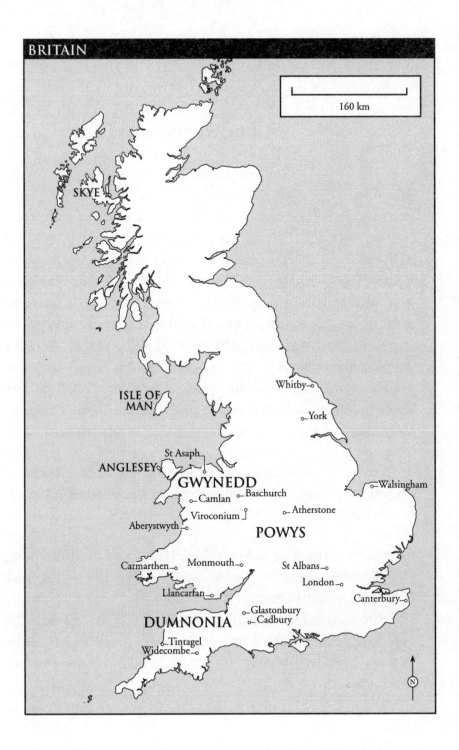

BRITAIN

160 km

SKYE

ISLE OF
MAN

Whitby

York

St Asaph
ANGLESEY
GWYNEDD
Camlan Baschurch
Viroconium Walsingham
Aberystwyth Atherstone
POWYS
Carmarthen Monmouth St Albans
London
Llancarfan Canterbury
Glastonbury
DUMNONIA Cadbury
Tintagel
Widecombe

N

have been written by Nicodemus, both refer to Joseph's journey; but, like Robert, they fail to say where his chapel is located.

Robert does not include Mary as one of Joseph's followers during the flight from Judea. Might she, as Giovanni Benedetti evidently believed, have been secretly represented by the Grail? Robert's Grail is said to be the cup of the Last Supper, but the word itself apparently held deeper, symbolic meaning. The origin of the word 'Grail' is something of a mystery. Robert is not the first author known to have used it; that was the French poet Chrétien de Troyes, around 1190, who portrays the Grail as a communion plate. Another author, the German poet Wolfram von Eschenbach, writing around the same time as Robert, refers to a magic stone as a Grail. It seems, therefore, that the word was applied to anything that was especially sacred. As I reread Robert's *Joseph d'Arimathie*, it became evident that his Grail was being used to symbolize something other than Jesus' chalice. He refers to 'the great secrets which one calls the Grail'. Immediately after, he appears to allude to these secrets when he says:

Now hear how Joseph came to England, but at the time it was called Britain, then fifteen years with Our Lady, as I understand, Joseph waited upon her.

Our Lady is the Virgin Mary. Unless this was itself intended as a symbolic reference, then Robert is actually saying that Mary came to Britain. Furthermore, he seems to imply that the secrets of the Grail are in some way associated with her. Joseph serves the Grail and he waits upon Our Lady. Perhaps Benedetti was right: the Grail and Mary are one and the same.

When I first read the account of Joseph's journey to

Britain, I wondered if such a thing was feasible in the early first century. It turned out that there was nothing unreasonable about it at all. Britain was in no way the primitive backwater one might imagine. There may not have been a city-building civilization here until the Romans arrived, but the country's rich mineral deposits had been attracting Mediterranean traders for at least five hundred years. Tin, copper and lead had been exported from Cornwall, Somerset and Wales from the fifth century BC, and in 460 BC the Greek historian Herodotus describes the trade. It was to secure such valuable resources that Julius Caesar tried in vain to conquer Britain in 55 BC.

From Caesar's time there were Roman roads all the way to the north coast of France and trading ships frequently crossed to Britain. Indeed, a few years before the emperor Claudius successfully invaded the country in AD 43, there was a Roman trading settlement near modern St Albans in Hertfordshire. The Roman Museum in the town has numerous artefacts which have been dated to the reign of Tiberius, an emperor who died eighteen years before the invasion. Not only was Britain accessible to anyone from anywhere in the Roman empire, there were already Roman citizens living and working here.

Rome had a massive empire stretching from the Persian Gulf to the north of France, and Britain was just about the only place where any political or religious dissidents could safely settle beyond its frontiers. There is actually an early historical reference to some of Jesus' disciples doing just that. According to the British monk Gildas, writing in the mid-sixth century, some of Jesus' original disciples came to Britain in the last year of Tiberius' reign – AD 37. This is only a few years after the Crucifixion and some years before St Paul began his teachings. If Gildas is right – and modern scholars consider him to have been an accurate historian who consulted reliable historical texts – then Joseph of Arimathea and his followers are the best candidates. Most of the other leading disciples are accounted for in Palestine until well after this time.

The problem was that none of these references to Joseph of Arimathea or to disciples in Britain actually said where they settled. Where was Joseph's chapel thought to be? Any church built in the early first century would have been a simple structure which might long ago have crumbled. Luckily, from their earliest years the Christians repaired and rebuilt original churches, often making them grander with each passing century. In Britain, most medieval ecclesiastical buildings are on the sites of churches dating back to Saxon and even Roman times. It was possible, therefore, that a church, abbey or cathedral still stood on the site of Joseph's original chapel.

Nevertheless, there were thousands of churches in Britain; where should I start? My only lead was Benedetti. If I was right, he had found what he believed to be Mary's tomb. There were no official records, at least that I could obtain, as to where Benedetti had gone in search of Mary's tomb. Consequently, I had to reconstruct his thinking. If he believed that Mary was the Grail then, like I do, he must have associated her with Joseph of Arimathea. Accordingly, he would have come to Britain. But where would he have started his search? As far as I knew, there was only one place in the country ever said to have been associated with Mary's earthly life. That, I decided, is where Benedetti would have begun.

*

There must have been fifty people crammed into the tiny, one-roomed chapel. In one harmonious voice they were singing the 'Ave Maria', as hundreds of prayer candles flickered and smoked on shelves around the walls. This was the so-called Holy House, a replica of the Virgin Mary's home built on the very spot she is said to have lived. I was not in Nazareth, Jerusalem or even Ephesus. I was in Walsingham, near the Norfolk coast of eastern England.

One day in 1061 Richeldis de Faverches, the lady of Walsingham manor, claimed she was at prayer when the Virgin Mary appeared to her. Apparently, Mary told her that she had once lived on that spot and that in her memory Richeldis should rebuild her house. This she did, and for the next five hundred years the little stone hut became one of England's most popular centres of pilgrimage. During Henry VIII's dissolution of the monasteries in the 1530s the shrine was closed, and during the Civil War it was destroyed by Puritans. In the 1930s, however, the Holy House was rebuilt by the local priest, Father Alfred Patten, and a huge church was erected around it.

Although no record survives of the precise details of her vision, Richeldis de Faverches apparently believed that Mary had spent her last days in England and had died in Walsingham. Whether or not the vision told her why Mary came here or whom she came with is unknown. We do know, though, that Richeldis's claim created a dilemma for the English Church. They were happy to have a shrine to Mary on their home soil, but the official Church position was that Mary died at Ephesus. Stigand, the archbishop of Canterbury, came up with a compromise and interpreted Richeldis's vision to mean that the Virgin had wanted a replica of her house in Nazareth to be erected on the site. From then on the shrine was known as England's Nazareth, and to this day that is the version of the story that pilgrims are told.

I very much doubted that Benedetti would have taken Lady Richeldis's vision as proof that Mary had lived in Walsingham, but he may have searched for historical evidence of an earlier tradition which associated the Virgin with the village. After all, if Mary had no traditional link with the area, why would Richeldis have been taken so seriously? I was sure Benedetti would at least have visited the shrine. I was right. Remarkably, I managed to trace an elderly lady who actually remembered Benedetti staying in the village. Edna Bowen had been one of the shrine's voluntary attendants for over fifty years and remembered the excitement when the Vatican official had stayed at the local Catholic hospice in 1950.

As I waited to meet with Mrs Bowen at the shrine that lunchtime, I watched the throng of pilgrims who filled every corner of the church. Around the Holy House there were no less than fifteen separate little chapels, one for each of the 'mysteries' – important episodes from the lives of Jesus and Mary. Roman Catholics are required to contemplate the 'mysteries' as they recite the rosary after confession, starting with the Annunciation and ending with Mary's coronation as Queen of Heaven. The rosary is the culmination of Marian devotion. Dating from the twelfth century, it is a series of 180 prayers, usually recited while holding a bead-string to keep count. Demonstrating just how important Mary had become to the established church, it includes one hundred and fifty repetitions of the 'Hail Mary'.

The altar in the Annunciation chapel said it all. Here Mary was represented in a white marble relief as seated before the angel Gabriel. The angel is not only announcing

Christ's conception, he is kneeling before Mary and actually praying to her. So, also, were the pilgrims, who seemed transfixed by the Virgin's image.

When Mrs Bowen arrived we sat in the vestibule, and she told me of Benedetti's visit. She remembered clearly that Benedetti believed that Mary had come to England and, more importantly, that he was here because he *was* searching for her tomb.

'Did Benedetti believe Mary's tomb was in Walsingham?' I asked.

'He did at first, I think, but he eventually decided that she had lived in another part of the country.' Mrs Bowen tried to remember the details. 'It was to do with someone – in the eighteen hundreds, I think – who thought Our Lady came to England. Somebody famous who had written a book or something while he was staying at an old manor house on Dartmoor. Mr Benedetti went there himself after he left us.' Mrs Bowen could not recall the name of the writer or the manor house. All she could remember was that the manor was supposedly the scene of a series of appearances or visions of the Virgin Mary.

'Did Benedetti believe in these visions?' I asked.

'I think he had one himself. When he wrote to thank us for our hospitality, he said that he had seen something in the manor that told him where Our Lady had lived.'

Although I was naturally sceptical about any historical lead Benedetti might have got from a vision, I thought it worth pursuing. After all, it seemed that the Holy Office had taken him seriously enough to silence him. But where was the manor house? Dartmoor was an awfully large place.

It took some weeks, but eventually I managed to track it down. I reasoned that there could not be many reported appearances of the Virgin Mary, particularly in a manor house. As Benedetti had actually learned of it, it must presumably have received coverage. After trying the Catholic archbishop's office, the Press Association and numerous cuttings services, I finally found references to what must surely have been the case in question in the archives of the Society for Psychical Research. Apparently, the apparition of a woman in shining white had been seen by various occupants of Elton Manor near the Dartmoor village of Widecombe. They had firmly believed she was the Virgin Mary. The sightings began in 1805 when Emily Reddington, the lady of the manor, had apparently been cured of tuberculosis by the vision. There was also a famous writer associated with the house. In 1899 the celebrated novelist Sir Arthur Conan Doyle had stayed there.

As well as being the creator of Sherlock Holmes, Conan Doyle was fascinated by the paranormal. He regularly attended spiritualist meetings and seances and stayed in houses that were said to be haunted. He was also a member of the Theosophical Society, a mystical group who believed in the physical manifestations of angels. When he heard about the Virgin Mary's supposed appearances at Elton Manor, Conan Doyle decided that it was really an angel and stayed at the house for a period of two weeks. He did not witness the apparition himself, but he did find the manor so eerie that it inspired the setting for his most famous Sherlock Holmes mystery, *The Hound of the Baskervilles*.

Elton Manor had to be the place I was looking for and Sir Arthur Conan Doyle was presumably the famous writer whose name Mrs Bowen could not recall. She had said that the man had written something while staying in the manor which had persuaded Benedetti to visit the house. Conan

Doyle had supposedly started work on *The Hound of the Baskervilles* there. However, I could find nothing in the book which, by any stretch of the imagination, related to the Virgin Mary. The only thing remotely connected with the supernatural was the hound itself: a legend of a phantom dog that the villain of the story manipulates to frighten the Baskerville heirs to death. Evidently, there was a real legend of such a creature on Hound Tor, overlooking Elton Manor.

When I phoned Margaret Timmings, the current owner of the manor, she was very helpful but knew nothing of Giovanni Benedetti. The owners of the property in 1950 had been an elderly couple who died in the 1960s. She knew all about the apparition, though. In fact, it had apparently been seen as recently as two years ago. The owners at the time, Christine and Robert Morton, both claimed to see what they called the 'Lady of Light' appear once in the dining-room and once at the head of the stairs. They were not religious, however, so did not believe it was the Virgin Mary. They had no idea who she was. The Mortons had moved out and Mrs Timmings had never seen the apparition personally. Nevertheless, she told me that she could arrange for me to speak to someone who had seen the Lady of Light: Steve Jowett, a local paranormal researcher whom the Mortons had invited to their house. He had agreed to come over to the manor that morning.

Descending into the Widecombe valley, the lane wound steeply downwards, through thick hedgerows and into a dense wood at the heart of which stood Elton Manor. As my car crunched to a halt on the gravel forecourt I understood why Conan Doyle would have been so inspired by the building. With its castellated façade and decorated chimney-stacks, the black and white half-timbered building was the ideal setting for any Gothic chiller. I almost expected to see a hunchbacked butler appear on the porch to inform me that his master awaited. Instead, a smiling lady in a heavy tweed suit emerged to greet me.

'No trouble finding your way?' She beamed, striding forward and seizing me firmly by the hand. 'Margaret Timmings.'

After the customary discussion about the weather, I followed her into the house. The musty hallway was panelled in dark wainscoting, framing heavy oak doors which led to the many ground-floor rooms. Facing the entrance, a broad staircase wound upwards to a balustraded balcony, its newel posts carved with heraldic beasts and family crests. Mrs Timmings's voice echoed through the building as she told me of the manor's strange history.

'Besides the Lady of Light, other odd things go on in the house,' she said. 'Electrical appliances are always going wrong, light-bulbs keep blowing, static on the TV and radio – you name it.' Mrs Timmings led me into what I discovered was the dining-room. 'This is where it all began,' she continued. 'The first appearance of the lady in 1805.' It was like stepping into the past. Buff-papered walls, leaded windows, and a great fireplace with a panel above bearing the opening verse from William Blake's famous hymn, 'Jerusalem'. 'The lady has given the manor quite a history,' Mrs Timmings said. 'Blake actually stayed here in 1810 in the hope of seeing her for himself. They say he wrote "Jerusalem" while he was here. And, of course, there's Sir Arthur Conan Doyle. This was where he started to write *The Hound of the Baskervilles*.'

It was easy to imagine the room redolent of tobacco smoke, with Sherlock Holmes standing before the roaring fire, drawing thoughtfully on his pipe as he revealed his discoveries to Dr Watson.

When Steve Jowett arrived about half an hour later I was quite surprised. I had expected him to be somewhat eccentric but he turned out to be very down-to-earth. He was a psychology student at Exeter University who said he had been sceptical of the apparition until the night he had stayed at Elton Manor. Apparently he and the previous owner, Robert Morton, had together seen what Steve described as a shimmering, crackling column of luminous mist hovering above the landing. Steve seemed sincere, but I was more than a little sceptical. 'It doesn't sound much like the Virgin Mary,' I said.

'I think it was some form of natural phenomenon. Ball lightning, plasma, something like that.'

'But Robert had seen it before, hadn't he? He described it as a lady.'

'They said it took the form of a woman before, yes.'

'If they're right, then it can't be ball lightning,' I said.

'I think that when people are confronted with something so strange their imaginations take over – their religious beliefs, if they see it as the Virgin Mary.'

'So what do you think causes it?'

'I don't know. Something about this valley. The granite, perhaps. Over a hundred people witnessed something very similar in the church over there.' He pointed through the window to the spire of the parish church poking above the trees.

Steve explained that on the evening of 21 October 1638, during a packed service in Widecombe's St Pancras Church, a ball of fire mysteriously appeared, hovering above the altar. Crackling and whining, it floated right down the central aisle before the eyes of the stunned congregation. Finally, it shot up into the air and exploded, bringing down half the roof and killing four people. At the time it was taken to be the work of the devil. An old memorial in the church still commemorates those who died, together with a more recent plaque attributing the tragedy to ball lightning.

'What exactly *is* ball lightning?' I asked.

'A rare phenomenon in which an ionized gas of highly charged particles ignites like a massive electric spark.'

I didn't know what to make of the story. Steve seemed convinced. All the same, what possible connection could the apparition of Elton Manor, real or imagined, have with Benedetti's search for Mary's tomb?

After Steve had left, I thanked Mrs Timmings for her help and got into my car. 'Drive carefully,' she said as I buckled the seat-belt. 'They've forecast a heavy fog this afternoon.' I looked up to where the lane wound steeply on to the moors. A thick bank of mist was already descending into the valley.

As I drove off, I tried to imagine what had persuaded Benedetti to visit Elton Manor. Although he may have caught vision fever once he was staying at the house, something more substantial must have made him go there in the first place. But what? As far as I could gather, even those who thought they saw the Virgin Mary at the manor never said anything about her tomb. If Mrs Bowen was right, it had something to do with whatever it was that Arthur Conan Doyle wrote while in the house. But what could have made the Vatican archaeologist take the story of Elton Manor seriously? I could see Conan Doyle, a spiritualist, lapping it up, and I could understand William Blake, a self-confessed visionary, visiting the manor, but . . .

I slammed on the brakes and almost skidded into the hedge. It had suddenly struck me: Benedetti had not seen the apparition at all. He never said he had. Like Mrs Bowen, I had got it all wrong. His visit to the manor had nothing to do with the apparition. Quickly, I drove back to Elton Manor and asked a surprised Mrs Timmings if I could take another look at the dining-room.

'What is it?' she said, as I stood before the fireplace.

'That,' I said, pointing to the verse from Blake's hymn. 'How long has it been here?'

'Since the early eighteen hundreds. The Reddingtons put it up because Blake had composed "Jerusalem" while he was staying with them.'

I asked Mrs Timmings if I could use her phone and called Mrs Bowen to ask her if the famous nineteenth century person who had written something while he was staying at the manor was William Blake.

'I'm sorry, I just can't recall,' was the response.

'Blake wrote a hymn,' I said. 'I think that . . .'

'A hymn!' said Mrs Bowen excitedly. 'Yes, that sounds right!'

That confirmed it. I had assumed that Benedetti had gone to Elton Manor because of something Conan Doyle had written there. But it had been William Blake that had drawn him to the place. There, above the fireplace, was the verse that said it all:

> *And did those feet in ancient time*
> *Walk upon England's mountains green?*
> *And was the Holy Lamb of God*
> *On England's pleasant pastures seen?*

I had sung those words so many times as a schoolboy: it had never struck me what they meant. Not until now. The Holy Lamb of God is Jesus. Blake is implying that Jesus Christ came to England.

I flicked through the pages of Mrs Timmings's copy of a Blake biography. Blake was a writer, a painter and something of a mystic. Most of his works were said to have been inspired by visions. Evidently, he did believe that Jesus had come to Britain before he began his ministry in Palestine. Blake even claimed to have seen documentary evidence of it. Unfortunately, he never produced it as proof or, so far as the biographer knew, told anyone where it was. The biographer didn't take the claim very seriously, but maybe Benedetti did. That must have been the reason he visited Elton Manor. He was trying to discover Blake's evidence. If Jesus had come to England, then perhaps Joseph of Arimathea had built his chapel where Christ had founded a church. Benedetti must also have hoped to discover the location Blake had in mind when he wrote the hymn. The hymn is all about building a new Jerusalem in England: evidently, in the same place that the 'Holy Lamb of God' had walked. Unfortunately, Blake never publicly revealed where he had in mind. But here was the answer. Below the verse was a faded little painting of a solitary hill with a stone tower on top. At the base of its gilded frame was a panel bearing the title, the artist and the date: ' "Jerusalem" – Emily Reddington 1810'.

'Emily, she was the first person to see the lady,' said Mrs Timmings. 'The painting has hung over the fireplace for almost two hundred years. I think it's quite valuable.'

It was valuable all right. And not just because it was old. Blake had been a guest of the Reddingtons when he composed 'Jerusalem'. Emily Reddington would no doubt have known the location he had in mind. Benedetti said in his letter that he saw something in the dining-room that told him where to look. We had assumed that he was referring to an apparition speaking to him. It was the *painting* that he must have seen. *It* had told him where to look. And the scene it depicted was the unmistakable profile of Glastonbury Tor.

I already knew that the Grail legend was associated with the Somerset town of Glastonbury, but had long dismissed it as a medieval invention. Perhaps it was time to rethink. One way or the other, Glastonbury must have been Benedetti's next stop.

Beside the main roads entering the market town of Glaston-bury, signboards welcome the tourist to 'The Ancient Avalon' – the island of Arthurian fame. Nestling amidst a small cluster of hills at the heart of the Somerset marshes, Glaston-bury was almost an island in early Christian times. It is certainly an imposing location, for its highest hill, Glaston-bury Tor, with its solitary stone tower at the summit, can be seen for miles around on the fertile Somerset plain.

In his account, Robert de Boron tells us that Joseph of Arimathea founded his first Christian community in Britain in 'the Vale of Avalon'. Here he built a chapel in which the Holy Grail was kept. Unfortunately, Robert gives absolutely no hint as to where Avalon actually is. The oldest surviving reference to it by name is of little more help. In his *History of the Kings of Britain*, written around 1135, the Welsh bishop Geoffrey of Monmouth says that it is an island somewhere in the west of Britain. He does not mention Joseph of Arimathea or the Holy Grail but he does link the island with King Arthur. According to him, after a last battle, the wounded Arthur was taken to the island, to a healing sanctuary to be tended by nine holy maidens.

Glastonbury's link with Avalon arose as the result of a discovery said to have been made in the local abbey in the late 1100s. The impressive ruins of Glastonbury Abbey that survive today date from the late twelfth century, replacing much older buildings destroyed by fire in 1184. In 1190, during reconstruction after the fire, the monks claimed to have discovered a grave containing the bones of a tall man. Along with the remains a lead cross was said to have been found, bearing the Latin inscription: *Hic iacet sepultus inclitus Rex Arturius in Insula Avalonia* – 'Here lies the renowned King Arthur in the Isle of Avalon.' Since that time, Glastonbury has been widely accepted as the ancient isle of Avalon, and Glastonbury Abbey is said to be where Joseph of Arimathea built his church. So was it here that the Virgin Mary spent her last days? Was she too buried somewhere nearby?

The town's claim to be the mystical isle of Avalon is virtually unquestioned by its thousands of annual visitors. However, I was far from convinced that Glastonbury was really the location of Avalon that Geoffrey of Monmouth had in mind. The cross inscription had identified both the body as Arthur's and the site as Avalon, yet in Geoffrey's account Arthur is not actually buried on Avalon. He was merely taken to the island for his wounds to be nursed. Geoffrey does not actually say where Arthur died or where he was finally laid to rest.

At midday I met up with James Whitmore, an archaeologist from Bristol University who had helped me to research my Grail book. As we stood in the scenic abbey ruins we discussed my suspicions. Before us, a signboard identified where the monks had found the grave.

'In 1962 the area was excavated by archaeologists and they did find evidence of an old grave,' said James.

'But you doubt it was Arthur's?' I said.

'The discovery was a bit fortuitous, if you ask me. The abbey desperately needed funds for rebuilding. Arthurian stories were immensely popular and relics were big business.'

Holy relics were the earthly remains of saints: their bones or, in some cases, a mummified appendage. They were believed to hold divine power: they could heal sickness, protect against evil and secure spiritual well-being. In the Middle Ages relics were priceless and highly sought-after, and their acquisition became an international obsession. For many monks it was a sacred duty to seek them out and return them to their abbots. In abbeys throughout Europe relics were displayed in public shrines, to be visited by thousands of pilgrims in the hope that they might be helped, cured or enlightened by their close proximity to the remains. Pilgrims were prepared to pay to view or touch the relics and vast wealth was donated to the churches, abbeys and cathedrals which contained the bones of the most famous saints. Often a religious centre would grow rich and powerful solely from the proceeds of its relics. Although Arthur was not a saint, he was said to have been a great king and the bones of powerful rulers were believed to hold their own miraculous properties which bought success, wealth and influence.

'I don't doubt that the brothers found an old grave,' said James. 'It's the cross that worries me. Along with the bones, it was kept in the abbey until it disappeared during the Reformation. So it can't be examined. All the same, the purported inscription itself suggests a hoax. It's just too convenient. It told the world not only that the bones were

Arthur's, but that Glastonbury was the mysterious island of Avalon.' James pointed to an ancient gravestone set against the ruined abbey wall. 'Would it have made any sense for anyone to have inscribed that with the words: "Here lies the renowned Abbot Thomas in the town of Glastonbury"? At the time he was buried everyone would know the name of the town.'

'But these people were monks: men of God,' I said. 'Would they really have resorted to fraud?'

'Well, they deliberately tampered with an historical manuscript in order to associate Joseph of Arimathea with their abbey.'

James explained how the official history of the abbey, which was written sixty years before the grave was uncovered, was amended to associate the town with Avalon. In 1130, the respected historian William of Malmesbury wrote *The Ecclesiastical History of Glastonbury.* An original copy still survives in Trinity College, Cambridge, and in it William makes no reference to King Arthur, the Grail, Avalon or Joseph of Arimathea. In 1247, after the supposed discovery of Arthur's remains, the monks produced a revised edition of the work. It too survives in the British Library and in it a new passage has been inserted, telling how the first church on the abbey site had been built by Joseph of Arimathea.

That evening I sat in the George and Pilgrim bar, flicking through a copy of William of Malmesbury's original work. James was right: William did not associate Glastonbury with Joseph of Arimathea. In fact, he did not even consider Glastonbury to be the site of the first British church. That was apparently on another island. It was when I read the passage concerning this original church that I almost choked on my beer. William said that when the Pope's envoy Augustine visited Britain in AD 597, he was shown a church that was said to date from the time of Christ. William quoted from a letter that Augustine sent to the Pope:

> In the western confines of Britain there is a certain royal island of large extent, surrounded by water, abounding in all the beauties of nature and necessaries of life. In it the first Neophytes of Catholic Law, God beforehand acquainting them, found a church constructed by the hands of Christ himself . . . He continues to watch over it as sacred to Mary, the Mother of God.

Incredibly, the letter implied that Augustine had actually found a church built by Christ himself. By 'the first Neophytes of Catholic Law' Augustine was referring to Christ's original followers. Apparently, after Jesus' death, some of them had returned to Britain to establish a Christian community around the church. But there was more: he said it was sacred to Mary. Until the eighth century churches were only dedicated to saints whose tombs they were believed to contain. That is why Empress Helena dedicated the church in Ephesus to the Virgin Mary. If Augustine was right, then this church had also been dedicated to the Virgin Mary. Here, apparently, was a fourteen-hundred-year-old reference to Mary's tomb actually being somewhere in the British Isles.

Was this the evidence of Christ's visit to Britain that Blake claimed to have found? William of Malmesbury is considered by modern scholars to have been an extremely reliable historian, so there was no reason to doubt that the letter was genuine. But what about Augustine himself? Was he to be trusted? Excitedly, I telephoned James and told him what I had discovered.

James remembered reading the passage in William of Malmesbury's book but had merely read over it. 'I just thought Augustine was referring to a local folktale,' he said.

'Do you think Augustine himself would have made up the story?' I asked.

The line was quiet for a moment. 'No I don't,' he said eventually. 'Now that I think about it, Augustine must have had some pretty convincing evidence that the church really was associated with Jesus and Mary.' James's reasoning lay in the political backdrop to Augustine's visit to Britain.

By the mid-fourth century Christianity was the state religion of the Roman empire. The emperor Constantine had hoped that the Catholic religion would unify the Roman world, but in 364, only three decades after the Council of Nicaea, the Roman empire split in two. The western empire was governed from Rome, while the eastern empire was centred on the city of Constantinople in what is now Turkey. The eastern empire became known as the Byzantine empire (after Byzantium, the Greek name for Constantinople), and it survived until it was finally extinguished by the Ottoman Turks in the fifteenth century. The western empire, however, soon fell to a succession of barbarian invaders.

'Barbarian' was the name the Romans gave to peoples outside the empire, and the first barbarians to break through the Roman frontiers were the Germanic tribes. The Goths, the German tribes east of the Rhine, had never been conquered by the Romans. They had been no real threat to Rome until, in the early fifth century, they were themselves attacked by the Huns of central Asia. Driven at first by a series of disastrous crop failures, the fierce and warlike Huns surged westwards towards the Ostrogoths (the eastern Goths), who were uprooted from their homelands. The vanquished Ostrogoths in turn were compelled westward and forced the Visigoths (the western Goths) across the Rhine. With the western empire no longer strong enough to defend its borders the Visigoths moved south, and by 408 their king, Alaric, was laying siege to Rome itself.

To meet this challenge, Honorius, the western emperor, was compelled to withdraw troops from Britain. With the Roman forces severely diminished, it was not long before problems arose on British soil. In the north, the Picts of Scotland began a series of increasingly daring raids across Hadrian's Wall, and in 410 the British administration appealed to the emperor for help. Honorius, however, had troubles of his own, for in the same year Rome was sacked by Alaric's Visigoths. So not only did the British receive no reinforcements, they also lost the soldiers they still possessed. With the empire in tatters, the Roman army totally withdrew from Britain.

Britain had been part of the empire for three and a half centuries, the fabric of government long reliant on its military muscle. This had provided stability for longer than anyone could remember. Now, suddenly, it was gone and anarchy threatened the land. Every freeborn Briton had long been a Roman citizen, and few would have danced in jubilation on the white cliffs of Dover as the last boatload of soldiers disappeared over the horizon.

Precise records during this period of British history are few and far between, but an overall picture can be gleaned from St Germanus, the bishop of Auxerre, who visited Britain in 429. According to his biographer Constantius, although there were serious troubles in the north, a Roman way of life persisted in most British towns. Before long, matters grew progressively worse and over the following two decades central administration seems to have collapsed. In many parts of the country the Britons reverted to tribal allegiances and regional warlords soon established themselves. With continual territorial squabbles, the island slid inexorably into anarchy and the Dark Ages. It was into this divided and troubled country that the Anglo-Saxons came.

As a result of the attack by the Huns on the Goths there were mass migrations right across the European continent, an unprecedented domino effect which continued until the Huns were ultimately defeated by a joint Roman–Visigoth army in 453. As a result, coastal dwellers from what is now part of Denmark and north Germany began to cross the English Channel to invade eastern Britain. These people were of mixed tribal groupings, Jutes, Angles and Saxons – later collectively called the Anglo-Saxons, or just Saxons. Fragmented and disorganized, the native Britons, the Celts, were easily defeated. The Anglo-Saxons' homeland had not been part of the Roman empire and, like the Huns, they had never been Christianized. Once Britain was invaded by these newcomers, much of the country reverted to paganism.

Remarkably, the Church in Rome managed to survive. On the night of 24 August AD 410, Alaric stormed the walls of Rome and his men pillaged the city for three days. For the first time in eight hundred years Rome had been sacked. It seemed to be the end, not only for the western empire but for the Roman Catholic Church. In far-away Bethlehem, where Christianity had begun, Jerome, a leading churchman of his time, wept as he wrote: 'The city which has taken the whole world is itself taken.'

In the first of a series of almost miraculous escapes, Rome was saved: Alaric died suddenly and his army retreated north

of the Alps. Safe in the city of Ravenna, the emperor Honorius made peace with the new Visigoth chieftain and forged
an alliance against the Huns. As part of the alliance the
Visigoths converted to Christianity. The emperors continued
to rule from the more easily defensible Ravenna and when
Attila, the mightiest of the barbarian warriors, reached Rome
with his Hun army in 452, the city was helpless. In an
incredible gamble, Leo, the bishop of Rome, met with Attila
and persuaded him to spare the city with a considerable
ransom in gold. In 455, after the Roman–Visigoth army was
weakened from their war with the Huns, another barbarian
tribe, the Vandals of northern Germany, surrounded Rome
and ransacked the city for fourteen days. Leo again got the
barbarians to retreat – this time, by converting their leader
Gaiseric and persuading him to return home. In 493 the last
western emperor, Odoacer (actually a German warlord who
had served as a general in the Roman army), was defeated
by Theodoric, chief of the Ostrogoths. Luckily, Theodoric
had already converted to Christianity while in the eastern
empire and he too spared the city of Rome. After Theodoric's
death in 526 the Byzantine emperor Justinian reconquered
much of Italy, and Rome came under the protection of
Constantinople. The eastern emperor had no interest in
moving his court back to the old, crumbling capital. Instead
he allowed Felix, the bishop of Rome, to rule the city in his
place. In political terms, this was the birth of the papacy.

Today's Church holds that the bishop of Rome – the
Pope – holds an office that has direct continuity from
the time of St Peter. According to Catholic doctrine, Jesus
had appointed the disciple Peter as his successor and
according to Church tradition Peter had gone to Rome. In

the capital, Peter appointed a successor, who in turn appointed a successor, and so on down to the present day: 261 of them in all, from Peter to John Paul II. They had all been the 'father' of the Church, in Latin *papa*, from which we get the name 'Pope'. This is known as the apostolic succession and the bishopric of Rome is the apostolic see – the seat of St Peter himself.

The real history of the bishops of Rome is nowhere near so certain. The first twelve such bishops are almost certainly an invention. The list originates with Irenaeus of Lyons in the late second century. Around AD 180 he wrote his *Proof of the Apostolic Preaching*, the oldest known writing to include the doctrine of the apostolic succession. Irenaeus' work is also the earliest surviving reference to the tradition that Peter came to Rome. Where Irenaeus obtained his information is unknown, but he claimed that these first bishops were descended by direct line of appointment from St Peter. Apart from one, nothing is known about any of them, and even the one we do know something about, St Clement (*circa* AD 100), seems unlikely to have been an actual *bishop* of Rome.

The word 'bishop' comes from the Greek *episkopos*, meaning 'overseer', and applied to the Christian leader of a particular city. Until Constantine's time, however, there was no unified Church and each congregation worshipped as they saw fit. Neither was there an organized constitution or ecclesiastical hierarchy. Although the word 'Church' is often used by historians to refer to early Christianity, the term is misleading as there was no such thing as an overall Church until the Council of Nicaea in AD 325. When Irenaeus compiled his work, the person whom he referred to as his contemporary bishop of Rome, Eleutherius, would by no means have spoken for all the Christians in the city – probably only the faction supported by Irenaeus himself.

The first real bishop of Rome, in the modern sense of the word, was Sylvester, when he was recognized as such by Constantine in 325. Sylvester, however, was far from head of the newly formed Church. Not only was that the emperor's status, but Eusebius, the bishop of Caesarea, and Athanasius, the bishop of Alexandria, were the leading bishops of their time. In fact, Bishop Sylvester did not even attend the Council of Nicaea, where the Catholic Church was formed.

It was not until 380 that the bishops of Rome first claimed to speak for the entire Church. In that year Bishop Damasus used Irenaeus' work to bolster his assertions of papal infallibility. Much to the anger of the emperor, Damasus declared that he, and he alone, spoke with the authority of Christ. He greatly annoyed other bishops, in particular the bishops of the east, by referring to them not as the usual 'brother', but as 'son'. Damasus insisted that they all called him 'father' – *papa* – or Pope.

Although the Pope's authority was growing in the west, in 364, when the empire split in two, the eastern Church refused to recognize him as anything but another bishop. This eventually led to a split in the Church itself: the Roman Catholic Church in the west, led by the Pope, and the Orthodox Church in the east, led by the bishop – or patriarch – of Constantinople.

When the eastern emperor allowed Felix to rule Rome in 526, the Pope became the political leader of what remained of the western empire. Outside Italy, though, this was little more than a loose alliance of Celtic and Germanic tribes, many of which were only nominally Christian. When

Gregory the Great became Pope in 590, all this was to change.

In the second half of the sixth century the Germanic Lombards pushed the Byzantines out of Italy and by 593 they were besieging Rome. Pope Gregory had been a soldier before he entered the Church, and he drew upon his military expertise to fortify the city and successfully saw off the attack. So impressed were the Lombards with this warrior-Pope that many converted to Christianity and offered their services as protectors of Rome. With the Lombards in Italy and the Visigoths in France now converted, Gregory decided to establish a new empire in the west – a Christian empire in which he was head of state. He set about organizing an army of monks to travel western Europe, establishing papal authority over the wavering Christian lands. The old empire had included Britain, and it was here that Gregory met with his greatest challenge. The island had been virtually cut off from Roman influence for over one and a half centuries and, under Anglo-Saxon control, much of the country had reverted to paganism.

Accordingly, in 597 Gregory sent Augustine and his team of priests to Britain to convert the pagan kings. By this time Anglo-Saxon England was divided into twelve separate kingdoms, and, remarkably, Augustine had immediate success converting the three largest. In recognition, he was appointed the country's first archbishop, and from his see in Canterbury he set about converting the rest of the island. It was then that he met with a completely unforeseen problem.

Like the Pope, Augustine imagined that Christianity had long ago died out in Britain. He was wrong. The Anglo-Saxons had failed to conquer much of the west, and here Christianity survived. Although the Celtic Church had once been a part of Constantine's Universal Catholic Church, it had been developing in isolation for almost two hundred years. It differed from Roman Catholicism in many ways. Most significantly, it was a monastic form of religion which recognized no central authority. Each community was virtually a law unto itself. This was completely unacceptable to Pope Gregory's new world view. Although the Celtic Church eventually did join with the Catholic Church in 664, Augustine's initial attempts to return them to the Roman fold failed miserably. He responded by preaching against them; Gregory went further and denounced them as heretics.

When we met next day in the George and Pilgrim bar, James told me why he was so sure that Augustine would not have lied. 'In his letter Augustine says the church was on an island in the west. This would have been Celtic Britain. The chapel would have been a shrine of the Celtic Church. Augustine had nothing to gain and much to lose by making such a claim. If he was going to invent the story of a church built by Christ himself – one which contained Mary's tomb – then he would have said it was in the east – in lands under his own jurisdiction.'

'What about the people who told Augustine?' I said. 'Perhaps *they* made it up.'

'According to William of Malmesbury, Augustine claimed to have seen the church himself,' he said, looking through the account. 'In fact, his assistant Paulinus actually helped repair it.'

'There might have been a church,' I agreed. 'But perhaps its association with Jesus, Mary and the first disciples was nothing but legend.'

'I'm not so sure,' said James. 'Augustine must have had a pretty good reason for believing the story, otherwise he would never have written to the Pope. By claiming that Jesus founded his first Church in Britain, the Britons were claiming an alternative apostolic succession.'

James was right. According to the Bible, Peter was the rock on which Jesus would build his Church and Catholic doctrine taught that Peter's Church was the Church of Rome. If Jesus really had come to Britain as Augustine seems to have believed, then it would presumably have been during the mystery years preceding his ministry in Palestine. Consequently, he would have founded a Christian movement in Britain *before* he appointed Peter.

'The ramifications for Church doctrine would be immense,' said James. 'Augustine would never have written to the Pope about it unless he had some pretty convincing evidence.'

Was it Augustine's letter that convinced Blake that Jesus came to Britain? If I was right, Blake had accepted the local tradition that Glastonbury was Avalon. If he saw the letter, then he must have assumed that Augustine's island *was* Glastonbury. But it can't have been. By no stretch of the imagination did the town match Augustine's description. Glastonbury during his time was simply a cluster of hills surrounded by marshland, hardly a 'royal island of large extent, surrounded by water, abounding in all the beauties of nature and necessaries of life'.

What about Giovanni Benedetti? Had he accepted Glastonbury's claim? At the time he wrote to Mrs Bowen and her friends, it seems that Emily Reddington's painting had led him to believe that Glastonbury was where Mary was buried. Perhaps after visiting Glastonbury he had arrived at the same conclusion as I had and decided that it could not have been the isle of Avalon. Whether or not he had moved on, I had no way of knowing, but at least I now had historical evidence from which I could decide upon my own next move. The problem was, where was Augustine's mysterious island? There are literally dozens of islands off the west coast of Britain and some of them are indeed 'of large extent', such as the Isle of Man or the Isle of Skye.

Neither Augustine nor Pope Gregory was of any further help. As far as I could discover no record has survived of what, if anything, the Pope did about the church. There was probably little he could do except try to hush it up. Celtic Britain would be outside papal influence for the next half-century. As Augustine never mentioned it again, Gregory presumably told him to forget it and keep quiet.

What leads did I have? If Mary came to Britain with Joseph and she was buried in Augustine's church then it may have been the historical building behind the legendary Grail chapel. Perhaps, therefore, the 'certain royal island' was the same place that Robert and Geoffrey called Avalon.

There is now no longer a place in Britain called Avalon. If ever there was, its whereabouts were long forgotten by the twelfth century. Neither Geoffrey of Monmouth nor Robert de Boron – indeed, none of the medieval authors of the Grail stories – says where the island actually is. My only lead was King Arthur. According to Geoffrey, he was taken to Avalon for his wounds to be tended, after a final battle. All the medieval Arthurian stories link Arthur with the Grail and the Grail is said to be on Avalon. If I could find the historical King Arthur, perhaps I could find the mysterious isle. I had already done much research into the Arthurian legend for my book *King Arthur: The True Story*, co-authored with my colleague Martin Keatman. So I had somewhere to start.

Summary

- Joseph of Arimathea seems to have come to Britain. Now in the Vatican Library, the fourth-century *Evangelium Nicodemi* and its contemporary *Vindicta Salvatoris* both record that Joseph fled Palestine and settled outside the Roman empire, somewhere in the far north. The twelfth-century Grail romances all portray the land as Britain. If Joseph really did come to this country, then presumably so did Mary. Unfortunately, although these sources say that Joseph built a church here they fail to say where he settled.

- There may not have been a city-building civilization in Britain until the Romans arrived, but the country's rich mineral deposits had been attracting Mediterranean traders for at least five hundred years. Tin, copper and lead had been exported from Cornwall, Somerset and Wales from the fifth century BC, and in 460 BC the Greek historian Herodotus describes the trade. In Joseph's time there were Roman roads all the way to the north coast of France and trading ships frequently crossed to Britain.

- Rome had a massive empire stretching from the Persian Gulf to the north of France, and Britain was just about the only place where any political or religious dissidents could safely settle beyond its frontiers. There is actually an early historical reference to some of Jesus' disciples doing just that. According to the British monk Gildas, writing in the mid-sixth century, some of Jesus' original disciples came to Britain in the last year of Tiberius' reign – AD 37.

- Any church built in the early first century would have been a simple structure which would long ago have crumbled. Luckily, from their earliest years the Christians repaired and rebuilt original churches, often making them grander with each passing century. In Britain, many medieval ecclesiastical buildings are on the sites of churches dating back to Saxon and even Roman times. It is possible, therefore, that a church, abbey or cathedral still stands on the site of Joseph's original chapel.

- In 597 St Augustine came to Britain as an envoy of the Roman Catholic Church. After travelling widely, he wrote to the Pope telling him that on an island in the west of the country there was a church where some of Jesus' original disciples had worshipped. It was, he said, 'sacred to Mary, the Mother of God'.
- If Augustine was right, then this church had been dedicated to the Virgin Mary. Until the eighth century churches were only dedicated to saints whose tombs they were believed to house. Here, apparently, is a fourteen-hundred-year-old reference to Mary's tomb actually being somewhere in the British Isles.

VII

KING OF KINGS

In Robert de Boron's account Joseph of Arimathea came to Britain and here spent fifteen years 'with Our Lady' – the Virgin Mary. If this is to be taken literally it means that Mary lived in this country for the last one and a half decades of her life. According to Gildas, the disciples – presumably Joseph and his companions – arrived in Britain in AD 37. Mary, it would seem, died in AD 52, perhaps around the age of seventy-five.

By this time the Romans had invaded eastern Britain, but the west was still in native hands. It was indeed in the west of Britain that Augustine was shown the mysterious church which seemingly housed Mary's mortal remains. In Robert's account Joseph's church was to be found on the isle of Avalon.

Find Avalon, and I might well be closer to finding Mary's tomb.

According to the oldest surviving reference to Avalon, in Geoffrey of Monmouth's work, King Arthur is taken to the island for his wounds to be seen to after he is mortally wounded at the battle of Camlan. (He is not, however, buried there, as he is in later accounts.) The Avalon that

Geoffrey depicts is an important holy isle, to be found somewhere in Arthur's kingdom. Arthur apparently lived during the late fifth and early sixth centuries, about a century before Augustine's visit, a time when Britain was divided into numerous small kingdoms. Where exactly was Arthur's kingdom?

The casual reader would be forgiven for thinking that Arthur was a medieval invention. True, the king in shining armour who fought dragons and rescued damsel in distress certainly was a work of fiction, but the character himself appears to have been based on an authentic British hero. Following Geoffrey of Monmouth's work around 1135, numerous tales were written about King Arthur and his famous knights. Although many themes within these so-called Arthurian romances are clearly invention, a much earlier manuscript – written centuries before these tales were composed – records that Arthur was the last British leader to make a successful stand against the invading Anglo-Saxons.

This oldest surviving reference to Arthur by an historian is found in the work of Nennius, a monk from the monastery of Bangor in North Wales. (There are two earlier passing references to Arthur in Dark Age war-poems.) In his *Historia Britonum* ('History of Britain'), written around AD 830, Nennius writes:

> In that time the Saxons strengthened in multitude and grew in Britain... Then Arthur fought against them in those days with the kings of the Britons, but he himself was leader of battles.

Nennius does not say where or precisely when Arthur lived but he does list twelve of his battles, and the last of them, the battle of Badon, is datable from a separate historical source. The British monk Gildas actually wrote within living memory of the battle. In his *De Excidio Conquestu Britanniae* ('On the Ruin and Conquest of Britain'), dating from the mid-sixth century, he makes reference to the event. Gildas verifies the victory of the Britons at Badon, but unfortunately neglects to name their leader. He does tell us that the battle occurred forty-four years after the Saxons first arrived in the country, which would mean that it took place somewhere around AD 500.

The years of anarchy and tribal feuding in Europe which followed the collapse of the western empire are called the Dark Ages because so little is known concerning their history. In Britain, from the time when the Roman legions left in AD 410 to the arrival of Augustine almost two hundred years later, hardly any contemporary records have survived. Unfortunately, it is right in the middle of this period that Arthur is said to have lived.

This is not the historical period of the Arthur now depicted in popular fiction – the High Middle Ages. There were no knights in shining armour or huge Gothic castles in the Dark Ages. The historical Arthur that Nennius records would not have worn a steel helmet with a plume and visor, but a skull-cap made of iron plates, leather strapping and bronze panels to protect the face. His body armour would have been little more than a short-sleeved mail shirt. Living conditions would also have been far removed from the huge castles of the later Middle Ages. Most chieftains would have lived in little more than a single-roomed hall with wattle-and-daub walls and a thatched roof; defences would not have been stone walls, battlements and drawbridged moats, but timber stockades, earthen banks and water-filled ditches.

The reason that Arthur and his warriors found themselves placed in the wrong historical setting is that the authors of the Middle Ages would often depict ancient tales, such as the myths of Greek and Rome, in a contemporary, medieval context.

Having established Arthur's true historical era, we now turn to location. Where, precisely, did he come from? Nennius fails to tell us, and the battle sites he names can no longer be identified. Many centuries after Nennius' time, however, writers began to speculate on Arthur's origins and the location of his court. After Geoffrey of Monmouth's work the medieval romancers came to portray Arthur's birthplace as Tintagel Castle on the north coast of Cornwall. Arthur is said to have been the son of Igraine, the duchess of Cornwall. Historically, though, the story is not feasible. There was no such thing as a duchess of Cornwall around the year 500: Cornwall was merely part of the much larger kingdom of Dumnonia, which also covered Devon and part of Somerset. Neither could the castle have been the birthplace of a warrior who had lived in the late fifth or early sixth century: it was built for Reginald, the duke of Cornwall, only in the early 1100s.

The only real archaeological excavation undertaken in a search for King Arthur took place in the 1960s at Cadbury Castle, an Iron Age hill-fort in Somerset. Cadbury had long been proposed as the site of Arthur's city of Camelot. But unfortunately, although the dig showed that the fort, like many other similar sites, had been used during the late fifth and early sixth centuries, no evidence was unearthed to specifically associate it with the historical King Arthur. Although this does not in itself rule out Cadbury as the seat of the historical Arthur, the reason why it was thought to have been Camelot in the first place makes it an unlikely candidate. Cadbury had first been proposed as the site of Camelot by Henry VIII's royal historian John Leland in 1542. Leland arrived at his conclusion on the strength of the word 'Camel' being found in the names of two nearby villages: Queen Camel and West Camel. However, the very name Camelot is misleading in the search for Arthur. It is unlikely that a place with that name ever existed. Although in the earliest stories of Arthur, the king is depicted as ruling from an impressive fortified city, it is not actually named. The first use of 'Camelot' as the name for Arthur's court originates with the late twelfth-century poet Chrétien de Troyes. It appears in only one of Chrétien's works, where it seems to have been a literary invention to rhyme with the name Lancelot.

When Martin Keatman and I began our search for the historical King Arthur we decided to ignore these late Cornish and Somerset links and consult the oldest reference to Arthur to place him in a geographical context. We soon discovered that just as the medieval authors had placed him in the wrong historical context, they had also, it appeared, located him in the wrong part of the country. One of the two earliest surviving references to Arthur suggested that he actually ruled the kingdom of Powys – in the Midlands of England and north Wales.

After the Romans left Britain the country fragmented into a number of kingdoms. Powys was the largest and most powerful of these, and covered what is now central England and north Wales. The reference to Arthur, dating from the late seventh century, clearly associates him with this kingdom. In the old British war-poem, *The Song of Llywarch the Old*, now preserved in Oxford's Bodleian Library, the kings of Powys are referred to as 'the heirs of great Arthur'. If they are his heirs, then he must have been thought to be one of them. Why, Martin and I wondered, had no one taken note of this before?

The reason, it seemed, that the poem had previously been dismissed as viable evidence for Arthur as a Powys king was that local historians considered the work to be largely fictitious. The consensus was based on what was thought to be an historical anachronism. The poem concerns Cynddylan, a king of Powys, and his failing struggle against the invading Anglo-Saxons in the mid-seventh century. When he dies he is described as being buried with his shield. The objection was that during the mid-seventh century the Britons of Powys were Christian and, as such, would not have buried their kings in this pagan manner. However, this seemed to us far from being a valid reason to dismiss the poem as fantasy. Many pagan traditions continued in early Christian times. In fact, many have survived to this day, such as the tradition of Easter eggs, derived from the pagan custom of egg-painting to mark the start of summer; and the Christmas tree, originally a pagan custom in which a fir tree was planted indoors during a festival to mark midwinter. Few today, let alone those living thirteen centuries ago, would consider it sacrilegious to continue with these harmless pre-Christian customs. Even if he was a Christian, Cynddylan may still have been buried with his shield.

This ancient reference to Arthur could well be the most important. We knew from the Nennius reference *when* Arthur lived. *The Song of Llywarch the Old* told us *where*. The ruins of the Dark Age capital of Powys, the city of Viroconium, still survive and had recently been excavated. If the war-poem was right, Viroconium was Arthur's capital.

For this reason, Martin and I considered it essential to discover just how accurate the poem really was. Was it a fictitious piece of Dark Age propaganda, as the local historians believed, or was it a ballad accurately commemorating real events? When we studied the text, we discovered that so much in the poem was historically verifiable that it seemed incredible that no one had realized it before.

The first of King Cynddylan's battles referenced in the poem is the battle of Maes Cogwy. Although the location is now unknown, a battle by this very name is recorded in the year 644 in the *Welsh Annals*, a tenth-century history of Dark Age Britain preserved in the British Library. The *Welsh Annals* also include Cynddylan by name in a series of genealogies at the end of the work. Another of his battles to appear in the poem is at Caer Luitcoet (near modern Lichfield), which is also recorded elsewhere: in the ninth-century *Anglo-Saxon Chronicle*, compiled for the English king Alfred the Great. Most importantly of all, the defeat of Cynddylan and the sacking of Powys as described in the poem are recorded in another Anglo-Saxon manuscript, the *Tribal Hidage*. This was compiled in 661, only three years after the event is said to have occurred.

When Martin and I first voiced our opinions on the poem's authenticity to the local historians, they objected on the grounds that it describes the sacking of the Powys capital of Viroconium in 658 which, archaeologists believed, was abandoned over a hundred years before. It was only after our book was published in 1992 that new excavations at Viroconium (just to the east of Shrewsbury) revealed that the city was abandoned far later than anyone had previously thought – at exactly the time the poem says.

As the poem had proved so accurate about so much else,

what reason was there to continue to dismiss it as historical evidence for Arthur as a Powys king? The local historians objected, nevertheless. They hung on to their original argument: Cynddylan would not have been buried with his shield. There was only one way to resolve the matter. The poem actually said where Cynddylan was laid to rest. If we could find his grave perhaps we could discover if he really was buried with his shield. At the very least, if there was a contemporary grave where the poem said there was, it would again demonstrate the poem's historical accuracy.

In one of the monologue verses contained in *The Song of Llywarch the Old* – 'The Lament of Heledd' – the death of Cynddylan is mourned by his sister Heledd. She relates how, after a final battle, his body is taken for burial to the 'Churches of Bassa'. From the poem it is clear that the 'Churches of Bassa' had long been the royal burial site: it also refers to 'the gravemound of Gorwynnion' and other 'green graves' that are there. In fact, in a second elegy on Cynddylan's death within *The Song of Llywarch the Old*, one of Cynddylan's family, Llywarch (after whom the cycle is named), says that he will 'grieve for the death of Cynddylan' until he too is laid to rest there.

Local historians do agree that the 'Churches of Bassa' is today the Shropshire village of Baschurch, some fifteen kilometres to the north-west of Shrewsbury. In secluded countryside on the edge of the village is the Berth, an ancient fortified hillock, surrounded by marshland and linked to the mainland by a gravel causeway. The hill is completely encompassed by Iron Age earth and stone ramparts and joined to a low-lying oval enclosure some 150 metres to the north-east by a second causeway. Until the area was drained to claim arable farmland the Berth would have been surrounded entirely by water, and in the Dark Ages it would have consisted of two islands – Berth Hill itself and a lower-lying, oval-shaped island (now called the Sacred Enclosure), joined by the causeway. All that now remains of this huge lake is Berth Pool, below Berth Hill to the south. As the village itself does not appear to have existed in the Dark Ages, the Berth is the most likely site of the original 'Churches of Bassa'.

Only limited archaeological work had been carried out at the Berth. However, a dig in 1962–3 by Peter Gelling of Birmingham University uncovered fragments of pottery dating from the seventh century – the time that Cynddylan lived. Furthermore, in 1906 a workman cutting turf at the edge of the stream draining from Berth Pool discovered a bronze cauldron, some forty-five centimetres high and thirty wide, which was presented to the British Museum where it was initially dated as a first-century artefact. However, modern examination has dated it much later, to around the sixth or seventh century. Consequently, the Berth does appear to have been in use during the period when Cynddylan died.

Exactly what the Berth had been used for in the Dark Ages was still an archaeological mystery. Its name does suggest that it was a religious, rather than a military or domestic site. The word 'Berth' comes from an Old Welsh word meaning 'sacred', and the oval enclosure was still referred to as the Sacred Enclosure. It was impossible to gauge the degree of sacred associations the Berth may have held during the Dark Ages, since the modern archaeological work had been limited to that of Peter Gelling. However, according to the local historians the plural, 'Churches of Bassa', suggests a group of small Celtic churches. Such a church group, like those more commonly found in Ireland, implies that at some time the Berth supported a monastic or religious community – which lends credence to the Berth being a burial site.

Unfortunately, an archaeological excavation to search for Cynddylan's grave was out of the question for the foreseeable future. Even if we could persuade the county archaeologists that the Berth was the burial site of the Powys kings, there were no funds available in their budget for such a dig. There was, however, the next best thing – a geophysics survey. Put simply, geophysics enables archaeologists to see what lies below the ground without digging. With sophisticated electronic equipment, geophysics constructs a three-dimensional computer-generated image of what is in the soil.

Late in 1995, with the help of Mike Stokes, the curator of Rowley's House Museum in Shrewsbury, and Roger White, the Shropshire archaeologist responsible for commissioning archaeological work in the Baschurch area, a geophysics survey of the relevant part of the Berth was finally conducted. The Berth covered many acres, but *The Song of Llywarch the Old* provided an important series of clues as to the location of Cynddylan's grave. The king's sister Heledd surveys the site as she mourns:

> *The Churches of Bassa are his resting place tonight . . .*
> *I shall mourn till I enter my oaken grave . . .*
> *I shall mourn till I enter my quite oak . . .*
> *I shall mourn till I enter the steadfast earth . . .*
> *I shall mourn till I enter circling staves . . .*
> *I shall mourn till I enter the field's surface . . .*
> *I shall mourn till I enter Travail's Acre . . .*

When Heledd says that she will mourn for her brother till she too enters her 'oaken grave', her 'quite oak' in the 'steadfast earth', she is probably referring to burial in a hollowed oak-trunk coffin, a common practice in post-Roman times. She hopes to one day be buried with her brother, and we are told where this is – within a circle of staves, surrounding a field called Travail's Acre. During the seventh century, when Cynddylan was buried, the smaller Sacred Enclosure was encompassed by defensive earthen ramparts which, judging by what is known of other Dark Age sites, would originally have been topped by a stockade of wooden stakes – 'circling staves'. Within the enclosure is a field, about an acre in size. Travail's Acre, therefore, seems to have been the site now called the Sacred Enclosure.

As there was nothing else within the vicinity of the Berth which so precisely matched the description, we were sure that the oval enclosure was the site of Cynddylan's burial as described in the poem. If Cynddylan's grave remained undisturbed in the soil here, it would certainly be detectable to the equipment of the geophysics team. The team, from Bradford – John Gater, Dr Susan Ovenden, Dr Clare Adam and Clare Stephens – were to use three types of equipment. First, a proton magnetometer, to measure any magnetic anomalies beneath the surface and reveal the presence of objects such as metal artefacts. Second, a resistivity meter: a double-pronged device which sends a current through the ground and measures any change in electrical resistance. It can detect different types of materials beneath the surface. Finally, the most advanced equipment of all: ground-penetrating radar, a scanner which produces a three-dimensional radar picture of what lies deep below the surface.

The procedure took an entire day. As I watched the

geophysics team working in the rain, I began to wonder if it was all a wild-goose chase. At first, none of them seemed particularly thrilled by the findings. However, when I joined them for lunch there was an atmosphere of excitement. Apparently they *had* found something of considerable interest. Frustratingly, though, they would say no more until they had completed the ground-penetrating radar scan later that afternoon and had run the combined data through their computer. By the late afternoon the rain had stopped and the sun came out; as if in response, the team announced that they were ready to reveal their findings.

John, the team's leader, explained that they had found evidence that two wooden buildings had stood on the site, plus a larger stone structure, which might all date from the early Dark Ages. But was it a burial site? Although the type of soil meant that any bones would long ago have decomposed, a circular anomaly had been revealed, right in the middle of the enclosure, some two metres deep and two metres wide. It was completely consistent with a burial ditch of the post-Roman era. More remarkably, at the centre of the ditch was a diamond-shaped piece of metal – most likely the central boss of an ancient shield. It might indeed be the grave of an important seventh-century chieftain.

Was this the grave of Cynddylan? The poem had not only revealed this as the location of his burial, it actually said that he was buried with his shield. Once more, the poem seemed to have been right. It was right about the battles, the historical figures, the abandonment of Viroconium and now the burial of the king. What reason could there be any longer to doubt the accuracy of the poem concerning its contention that Arthur had been a Powys king?

Still the local historians were sceptical. They gave up

trying to discredit the poem, but they argued, instead, that Arthur could not have been a king of Powys because he didn't exist. There was no way to win with these people: except perhaps one – find *his* grave.

According to the poem, Cynddylan's burial site had been the cemetery for many Powys kings. Perhaps Arthur himself was buried here. From the geophysics survey, though, it appeared that there was only one grave in Travail's Acre. Maybe, as the last king to be buried at the Berth before it was abandoned to the Anglo-Saxons, Cynddylan was laid to rest in a part of the site that had previously been reserved for important religious events. The other graves might have been on the larger island, now Berth Hill.

The archaeologists and the local museum, although not wishing to be drawn into the King Arthur debate, were itching to undertake a proper excavation of the Berth. The geophysics survey had given them every reason to believe that this might be an important Dark Age burial site. Funds were made available, and when English Heritage were contacted they initially saw no objection to a team of professional archaeologists, led by Roger White, actually excavating the site. But suddenly, and for no apparent reason, English Heritage changed their minds and refused permission for the dig. To this day, and to my knowledge, their decision has never been explained. It was infuriating: the Shropshire archaeologists had been denied the chance to properly investigate the site, and Martin and I had been denied the chance to put our theory concerning Arthur to the test.

All the same, the geophysics results had gone as far as possible to demonstrate the accuracy of the poem. At least we had shown, yet again, that *The Song of Llywarch the Old* was an accurate Dark Age war-poem: one which described

Arthur as a king of Powys five centuries before anyone placed him in the south of England.

Even without the poem, it was well within the realms of historical feasibility that he had been a Powys king. The archaeological excavations of the Powys capital of Viroconium suggested just that. Viroconium had been the fourth-largest city in Roman Britain, and was without doubt the most important trading centre in the Midlands. Built on the fertile plain overlooking the River Severn, it was originally established as a military base to co-ordinate the Roman conquest of Wales. Sometime around AD 78 the western command of Britain was transferred to the city of Chester, and Viroconium became a thriving civilian town. Although it was to have all the amenities of other provincial capitals, such as cobbled streets, a water supply and a drainage system, the city was far more elaborate and wealthy than most. With its law-courts, market-place and other public facilities, Viroconium became the fourth largest city in Britain. Unlike the other main Roman cities – London, Lincoln and York – all that now remains of Viroconium is its ruined walls, standing in quiet farmland outside the tiny village of Wroxeter, a few kilometres to the east of Shrewsbury.

Standing as they do in the open countryside, the ruins of Viroconium have provided an excellent opportunity for excavation; in the last few decades much archaeological work has been conducted. Today the dig is open to the public and a small museum stands at the site, where some of the excavated material is on display.

Until recently only a fragmentary picture had existed of Viroconium as it was at the end of Roman rule. However, in the late 1960s an extensive excavation was initiated at the site. It was to last for well over a decade, and it brought to light a series of new and almost incredible discoveries. The dig, led by archaeologist Philip Barker, was far more fruitful than any that had preceded it, producing a mass of evidence for the period following the collapse of Roman rule. The results showed that after the Roman army withdrew from Britain, the city was completely rebuilt.

From the excavation of post holes and other tell-tale signs in the foundations and substructure of the city, the new buildings were found to have been made of timber, not bricks and mortar like the earlier Roman town. However, when the evidence emerging from the dig was gradually collated, these new buildings turned out to have been highly sophisticated. They were large and elaborate constructions of classical design, with colonnades and orderly façades, many being at least two storeys high. It appeared, therefore, that when the Roman legions left, Viroconium became Britain's most important city.

Viroconium had assumed a new strategic importance during the early fifth century, a time when the cities of the coastal provinces were suffering constant threat of invasion and pillage. London, for instance, the Roman capital of Britain, was easy prey for the Saxon raiders by route of the Thames; York was continually sacked by the Picts of Scotland, and Lincoln was constantly under threat from the Angles and their repeated incursions inland from the Wash. Although other major cities such as Cirencester, Exeter or Bath could be considered safe from outside attack, they would not have possessed the central expediency of Viroconium. In effect, Viroconium became the capital of early Dark Age Britain.

What about the time when Arthur is said to have lived,

around the year 500, almost a century later? The latest
archaeological excavation of Viroconium took place in the
mid-1990s. What it showed was that, far from being abandoned like other Roman towns of the time for the more
defensible hill-forts, there was yet another major rebuilding
of the city. Not only were new buildings erected and streets
replanned, but the entire infrastructure of the city was repaired. For example, a new drainage system and a fresh
water supply were installed through an elaborate system of
aqueducts. Long stretches of the cobbled Roman roads were
also dug up and completely relayered. In effect, the city was
totally restructured and refortified. And the nerve centre of
this new Viroconium appears to have been a massive winged
building. With its large complex of adjoining outhouses, this
classical mansion appears to have been the palace of an
extremely important chieftain.

The precise date of the rebuilding was determined
through radiocarbon dating. Organic matter – in whatever
form, either animal or vegetable – contains carbon-14, and
once the living organism has died the carbon-14 gradually
decays until, some sixty thousand years later, it disappears
altogether. Through chemical analysis, the amount of
carbon-14 can be measured, enabling dating. Luckily, there
was an abundance of organic matter within the deposit
strata of the final building phase at Viroconium: bones, for
instance, discovered amongst the rubble that had been used
to form the foundations. Radiocarbon dating is only
accurate to within some fifty years, so a number of sample
readings were necessary to gain a more precise date; in this
way, an average core date of around AD 500–50 was obtained
by cross-referencing a series of radiocarbon tests on various
finds.

This remarkable revitalization of the city required considerable wealth and powerful leadership. Who had wielded the influence to organize and motivate such an endeavour, sometime between the years 500 and 550? The work seems to have begun at the very time the Britons defeated the Saxons at the battle of Badon. As this is the only city in the country of the period where such a degree of sophistication has been found, it may well have been the seat of power for the British chieftain who led the Britons at the battle of Badon – in other words, the historical Arthur.

The Song of Llywarch the Old aside, from the archaeological perspective alone, the Powys capital of Viroconium is Arthur's most likely seat of power. So who *did* rule the kingdom of Powys around AD 500? The tenth-century *Welsh Annals* actually provide a name. Although fundamentally of Welsh interest, the annals are also an attempt to catalogue the events of Dark Age Britain as a whole, and are considered a major source for this period of the country's history. Regrettably, they are little more than an incomplete chronology, coupled with brief notations on significant incidents. However, they do include a detailed series of genealogies – the family trees of important Dark Age chieftains. Here we discovered that the king of Powys around AD 500 was named Owain Ddantgwyn.

At first, Martin and I were disappointed. It seemed that the king who rebuilt and refortified Viroconium had not been King Arthur after all. That was, until we discovered that 'Arthur' was not a personal name but a title – a battle-name. The language of the Romano-Britons was Brythonic (a cross between Latin and the native Celtic tongue), and it survives almost intact in modern Welsh – the reason being that many Britons were driven into Wales during the Saxon invasion and thus isolated from Saxon influence. Still preserved in Welsh is the word *arth*, meaning 'bear', and many linguists believe that it derived from the Brythonic *arthur* (a cross between the Celtic and Latin words for 'bear': *arth* and *ursus*). If this was right, then 'Arthur' was actually the king's battle-name – The Bear.

If the warrior who led the Britons in the late sixth century was called The Bear, he would not have been the only such warrior to be named after an animal. It seems to have been a common Celtic practice of the period. Not only are there many examples from Ireland and Gaul, as well as Britain, of various warlords assuming such epithets as The Wolf, The Hound, The Horse and so forth, but the monk Gildas (writing around 545) names a number of British kings by their animal battle-names. This tradition should not be considered as specifically Celtic – the Native Americans, for instance, had titles such as Sitting Bull and White Eagle. The name of an animal, in some way typifying the qualities of the individual, was given to many Dark Age kings as an honorary title. Usually, however, we also know their real names.

There is in fact compelling evidence that Owain Ddantgwyn, the king of Powys around AD 500, had indeed been called The Bear. Many of these battle-names were inherited by the chieftain's eldest son. A whole succession of Welsh kings, for instance, were called The Dragon during the later Dark Ages – which is why there is still such an emblem on the Welsh flag. Indeed, by medieval times the battle-names of warriors from all over the country became heraldic crests, such as the lion device, inherited by the dukes of Cornwall from the title of earlier Cornish kings. Gildas, writing less than half a century after the battle of Badon, actually refers to Owain Ddantgwyn's son, Cuneglasus, as The Bear. If Cuneglasus was called The Bear, then so perhaps was his father. Gildas actually implies as much when he refers to Cuneglasus as the 'driver of the chariot of The Bear's stronghold'. The Bear he refers to here cannot be Cuneglasus himself, but rather, someone who previously held that title: presumably, the man who built the stronghold. As Viroconium was refortified around the year 500 and Owain Ddantgwyn was the king at that time, Owain, it seems, is The Bear.

Surely, then, Owain Ddantgwyn was the warrior who became the legendary King Arthur:

Owain ruled the country's most powerful kingdom at exactly the time Arthur is said to have been Britain's most powerful king.

Owain ruled from Britain's most important city when Arthur is said to have ruled from a splendid capital.

Owain is the most likely candidate for the Britons' leader at the battle of Badon – Arthur is said to have been that leader.

Owain ruled the kingdom of Powys – one of the oldest references to Arthur said that he was a Powys king.

Owain's battle-name seems to have been The Bear – the word 'Arthur' means 'The Bear'.

Regardless of what the local historians continued to think, Martin and I were satisfied that we had found the historical Arthur.

In the search for Avalon, could Owain Ddantgwyn help me find the island? As a king of Powys he was probably buried at the Berth. Unfortunately, the Berth was as unlikely to be Avalon as was Glastonbury. It may have been an island during the Dark Ages, but it in no way matched the description Augustine gave – besides which, if Owain was Arthur, his burial site would be of little help in the search for Avalon. In Geoffrey of Monmouth's account Arthur is not actually buried on the mysterious island. Geoffrey does, however, say that Arthur is taken to Avalon for his injuries to be tended after he is mortally wounded at the battle of Camlan. Presumably – as he is dying – the island cannot be too far from the battlefield. If I could find the site of Owain's last battle, perhaps I could discover Avalon.

Geoffrey tells us that the battle of Camlan was the result of a rebellion led by Arthur's treacherous nephew Modred. At Camlan, their two armies met for the final showdown in which Arthur received his fatal wound. Nennius does not reference this particular battle, presumably as his account concerns only Arthur's victories. However, another Dark Age source does – the *Welsh Annals*. A brief notation for the year 539 records: 'The strife of Camlan in which Arthur and Modred perished'. Unfortunately, we are told nothing further, and no other Dark Age manuscript mentions the battle. Where was Camlan?

According to Gildas, just like Arthur, Owain met his fate at *his* nephew's hands. Also, like the legendary Modred, Owain's nephew defeated his uncle in battle. He does not name the battle site, but I believed I had enough historical information concerning Owain Ddantgwyn to work out where the conflict occurred: at a remote pass in the Welsh mountains that is still called Camlan.

Summary

- The medieval accounts of Joseph of Arimathea's journey to Britain say that he founded his church on the isle of Avalon, and here resided for fifteen years with the Virgin Mary. It was on an island in the west of Britain that Augustine was shown the mysterious church which seemingly housed Mary's mortal remains. It would seem, therefore, that Augustine's island and Avalon were one and the same.

- There is no place in Britain now called Avalon. If ever there was, its whereabouts were apparently forgotten by the twelfth century as none of the medieval Joseph of Arimathea stories say where it is. They do, however, associate it with King Arthur. He is said to have been taken to Avalon for his wounds to be tended after a last battle at a place called Camlan. Arthur and Camlan are perhaps the best leads to rediscover Avalon.

- Although the Arthur in the medieval romances is little more than a fairy-tale king, there does seem to have been an historical figure upon whom he was originally based. Although historical records of the Dark Ages are few and far between, as early as the 830s the Welsh monk Nennius records Arthur as the British leader at the battle of Badon, an historical battle fought between the Britons and the Saxons around AD 500. The battle is recorded by the British monk Gildas, who wrote within living memory of the event, but unfortunately he fails to name its leaders.

- The British leader at Badon was in all probability a warrior named Owain Ddantgwyn, who ruled from the Roman city of Viroconium during the late fifth and early sixth centuries. Recent excavations at Viroconium, a few kilometres to the east of Shrewsbury in the west Midlands, have revealed it to have been Britain's most important city at the time of Badon, indicating that it was the seat of the contemporary British leader.

- Viroconium was the capital of the Dark Age kingdom of Powys. The seventh-century British war poem, *The Song of Llywarch the*

Old – the oldest historical reference to place Arthur in a geographical context – tells us that Arthur was a king of Powys.

- Owain Ddantgwyn may well have been the historical Arthur. Celtic warriors of the period were often given the battle-names of animals. From Gildas we can gather that Owain's battle-name was The Bear, and in Brythonic, the language spoken at the time and still preserved in modern Welsh, the word for 'bear' is *arth*. The name Arthur is believed to have derived from this word, implying that Owain Ddantgwyn and Arthur were one and the same.

VIII

AVALON

Six centuries after Mary's death the native British,
the original Celts, were gradually driven out of what is
now England and reduced to three pockets of resistance –
Wales, Cornwall and Scotland – while others fled across the
English Channel to settle in Brittany. Scotland, however, had
not been a part of the Roman empire and so the Scottish
tribes, the Picts, had little in common with the Celts of Wales
and Cornwall. Ultimately, even Cornwall was conceded to
the Anglo-Saxons, leaving only the area we now call Wales
as the surviving homeland of the Romano-Britons. The
Anglo-Saxons gained so much control over eastern Britain
that they began to refer to the Britons as Welsh, from the
Saxon word *weala* meaning 'foreigners'. The Britons, on
the other hand, began to call themselves *cymru*, 'fellow
countrymen'. From the tenth century onwards it was no
longer a matter of Anglo-Saxon and native Britain but two
separate countries, England ('Anglo-land') and Wales.

During Arthur's time all of Wales and most of central
England were still in British hands. The area was divided
into a number of kingdoms, the largest being Powys which
covered the west Midlands and north Wales. Owain

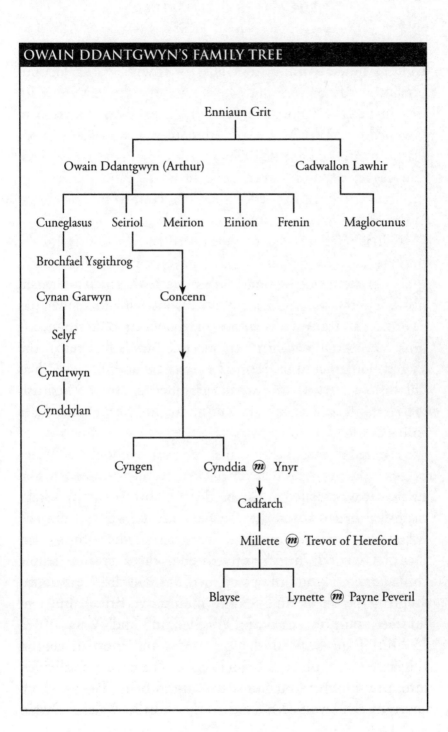

Ddantgwyn had ruled this kingdom from the city of Viro-conium but, according to Gildas, his nephew Maglocunus finally overthrew him and the kingdom split in two. With Owain dead, Maglocunus ruled the breakaway kingdom of Gwynedd in north Wales, and his cousin, Owain's son Cune-glasus, continued to rule the now reduced kingdom of Powys. The legacy of these times can still be seen on the map of modern Britain: Gwynedd is now a county in north-west Wales and Powys is a county in east-central Wales.

Gildas refers to Maglocunus overthrowing Owain but he provides no real details. It must have been in battle rather than a palace coup, though, as we are told that he defeated his 'uncle the king and his brave troops with fire spear and sword'. For the two kingdoms to have formed, the battle must accordingly have taken place somewhere along their shared border. It also occurred shortly before 545, as Gildas talks about it as a recent event. Maglocunus and Cuneglasus are certainly still alive – he addresses them both personally in his work.

Modred's rebellion against Arthur appears to have occurred at precisely this time. Geoffrey of Monmouth tells us that it was settled at the battle of Camlan: an apparently historical event which the *Welsh Annals* record in 539. The most likely site for such a battle is actually along the Powys–Gwynedd border as it existed at the time. In precisely this location is the only place in the British Isles still called Camlan – a bleak and remote mountain pass about eight kilometres to the east of Dolgellau in north-west Wales. Unlike Glastonbury, all that greets the tourist on arriving in this windswept valley is a single signboard telling him or her that this is where Arthur met with defeat. There are no shops or cafés, not even a house. The day I arrived, my only companions were the rain-drenched sheep bleating from the misty hillsides.

Surely Owain's defeat and the battle of Camlan were one and the same. Although the historical Maglocunus did not perish as we are told did Modred, everything else fits. Both battles were fought at the same time and in the same area. Moreover, Arthur's kingdom is said to have fragmented after his death and Owain's kingdom itself broke in two when he died. It seems most improbable that two equally powerful warlords were fighting their nephews in separate battles in the same area at precisely the same time.

What is far more likely is that Modred and Maglocunus were the same man, and that confusion concerning his death arose in the centuries following the battle. Maglocunus actually means 'Mighty Hound'. Welsh manuscripts, such as the genealogies in the *Welsh Annals*, also call him Maelgwyn – 'White Lord'. Perhaps they were both titles for the historical Modred in the same way that Arthur was Owain's battle-name, The Bear, and another 'Mighty Hound' or 'White Lord' died in the battle. Either way, if the historical Arthur was mortally wounded in the valley of Camlan, as Geoffrey of Monmouth suggests, then the isle of Avalon must be somewhere nearby. Augustine provided the only proper description of the island:

> In the western confines of Britain there is a certain royal island of large extent, surrounded by water, abounding in all the beauties of nature and necessaries of life.

There was only one island anywhere near that matched this description – the island of Anglesey, about fifty kilometres to the north-west. It is a large island: the largest in England or Wales, some fifty kilometres from east to west and thirty from north to south. It was a royal island too, which, during Augustine's time, contained the seat of the Dark Age king of Gwynedd. It was also prosperous: the grain basket of northern Wales.

I decided to visit Bangor University, beside the Menai Strait which divides Anglesey from mainland Wales. Here I met with Barry Davis, a research student who had been of invaluable help translating ancient Welsh manuscripts when I was working on my King Arthur book. Barry was not only a Welsh-speaker, he was also an authority on early Welsh literature and the Arthurian legend. He kindly offered to put me up for the night and that evening, with a pile of Arthurian-related material spread out on the table before us, we discussed my theory.

'I've always thought that Anglesey was Avalon,' he said. 'It's the only place that fits with the medieval Grail romances.'

I was quite surprised: I had expected him to shrug the whole thing off. 'Why haven't you said so before?' I asked.

'Because you were convinced that Arthur was buried at the Berth.'

I explained the reasoning behind my belief that Avalon and Arthur's burial site were separate locations. 'In Geoffrey's account Arthur is merely taken to a sanctuary on Avalon for his wounds to be tended. When he died, his body may have been returned home for burial.'

'Anglesey would certainly have been the ideal place to take him for treatment,' said Barry. 'It had a hospice for the sick in the early sixth century. It was founded by St Elen around AD 400.'

'You said it fits with the Grail romances,' I said, intrigued by his earlier statement.

'Yes. Anglesey was in the kingdom of Gwynedd and the romances say Joseph's chapel was in the "White Land". Right?'

I agreed.

'Well, in Brythonic – Old Welsh – "Gwynedd" actually means "White Land".'

In the early 1200s, within a few years of Robert de Boron's original work, a number of other Joseph of Arimathea stories appeared, each author claiming to have consulted authentic source material. Collectively known as the Grail romances, there were four French versions, known as *La Folie Perceval*, *The First Continuation*, *The Vulgate Cycle* and *The Didot Perceval*; an English version known as *Fulk Fitz Warine*, and a Welsh version called *Peredur*. *The First Continuation*, for instance, tells us:

> Joseph and his company prepared their ships and entered without delay, and did not end their voyage till they reached the land which God had promised to Joseph. The name of the country was the White Land.

Here Joseph builds the chapel in which the Grail is secretly kept.

'The Isle of Avalon is a large island in a country called the White Land and Anglesey is a large island in the only kingdom in Britain known to have been called the White Land,' said Barry.

'Sounds pretty convincing.'

'But there's more! Joseph's successor, the man who looks

after the chapel by Arthur's time, has the same name as a legendary lord of Anglesey.'

All the romances associate King Arthur with the Grail and in most of them it is his knight Perceval who eventually finds it, many years after Joseph's time. The guardian of Joseph's chapel is called Bron:

> It happened formerly that the Grail was given to Joseph when he was in prison where Our Lord himself bore it to him. And when he had come from the prison this Joseph entered into a wilderness and many of the people of Judea with him . . . till he came at last to the isle of Britain. Now, in truth, Our Lord made the first chapel, and Joseph made the second . . . So know that the Grail was given into the hands of Joseph, and upon his death he left it to his family and at length to one who was called Bron. (*The Didot Perceval*)

The *Fulk Fitz Warine* romance includes the same character but calls him Bran:

> And his name was Bran, a giant who was wounded sorely in his leg. His wound would not heal, yet by the sustenance of the Grail was he kept alive.

'The description of Bron or Bran in the romances is precisely that of his namesake, Bran, a Dark Age hero in *The Mabinogion*,' said Barry.

The Mabinogion is the most famous collection of early Welsh literature. However, the title is misleading as the works it contains are not by one author, or even from the same period. In reality, it was the title used by the Lincolnshire diarist, Lady Charlotte Guest, for her English translations of twelve early Welsh tales, published in three volumes between 1838 and 1843. They are mainly works from *The Red Book of Hergest*, a collection of documents bound together in one manuscript dating from around 1400. From linguistic analysis, the stories in *The Red Book* (now in the Bodleian Library) range from as early as the seventh century to as late as the fourteenth. The story that includes Bran is called 'The Tale of Branwen' and is thought to date from around the ninth century. It concerns the life of Bran's sister Branwen, but Bran himself appears as a giant of a man who is permanently troubled by a wounded leg.

'In the story Bran is the lord of the Isle of the Mighty,' said Barry. 'The narrative does not specifically identify the location, but it has to be Anglesey as we are told that Branwen is buried beside the River Alaw. Not only is the main river on Anglesey called the Alaw, but Branwen's grave is still to be seen on the river-bank near the village of Elim.'

'So Bran, the lord of Anglesey, and Bran, the Grail guardian of Avalon, probably derive from the same literary source.'

'Yes, and it's the only explanation for the strange story of Bran's head.'

Barry went on to explain that in 'The Tale of Branwen', when Bran dies after a battle with the Irish, his head is cut off and kept as a sacred talisman in 'the White Tower'. When Charlotte Guest translated the work around 1840, she assumed this to be the keep of the Tower of London, which is still called the White Tower. However, the original story does not say where it is. In the medieval *Fulk Fitz Warine* romance the head of the Grail guardian Bran is also cut off when he dies, and it too is kept as a talisman in 'the White Tower', here depicted as a part of Joseph's chapel.

'*The First Continuation* also includes a sacred head in the Grail story,' I said, looking through Barry's copy of the manuscript, 'although here it's depicted as a carved head of Jesus. It was supposedly made by Nicodemus when Christ was crucified.' I read from the narrative:

Nicodemus had carved and fashioned a head in the likeness of the Lord on the day that he had seen him on the cross. But of this I am sure, that the Lord God set his hand to the shaping of it, as they say; for no man ever saw one like it nor could it be made by human hands.

'Do you think there's a connection?' I added.

Barry nodded. 'The Welsh *Peredur* romance, basically a Celtic version of the same story, also has a mysterious carved head in the Grail chapel.'

If we were right, then Bran was being used as a metaphor for Christ's spiritual presence in the chapel. In all the Grail romances, Bran and his twelve brothers regularly share a ritual meal where a mass wafer is eaten and the Grail is drunk from. Surely this was an analogy for Jesus and his disciples at the Last Supper. Bran is taking the part of Christ himself. He is even given the same title as Jesus. In *The Didot Perceval*, Perceval learns that Bran is his grandfather and that he is called the Fisher King:

You have been in the house of the rich Fisher King your grandfather and have seen pass before you the vessel in which is the blood of Our Lord – that which is called the Grail.

In early Christian tradition Jesus was also known as the Fisher King – the reason being that the fish was the secret symbol for Jesus used by the persecuted Christians of Rome. It came from the Greek word for fish – *ichthys* – which was used to convey the first letters in Jesus' Greek title: *Iesos Christos Theou Yios Soster* – 'Jesus Christ, Son of God, Saviour'.

If Bran in the Grail romances and Bran in *The Mabinogion* were one and the same, then Avalon had to be Anglesey. Later that night, as I stood outside looking across the Menai Strait at the moonlit silhouette of the Anglesey hills, I was convinced that I had found Augustine's island. Perhaps out there, somewhere on the other side of the narrow stretch of water, the Virgin Mary had spent her last days.

The more I thought about it, the more it made historical sense: not only that Anglesey was Avalon, but that the earliest Christians had settled on the island.

Anglesey is the English name for the island; the Welsh call it Môn, after the Roman *Mona*. What the ancient Britons called it during the time of Christ is unknown, but it could have been Avalon. The name Avalon comes from the Old Welsh *Afallach*, meaning 'Rich in Apples', and during Roman times Anglesey was a major apple-producing area. Geoffrey of Monmouth also calls it *Insula Pomorum* in his work, which in Latin means 'Isle of Apples'. The main historical consideration supporting the idea that Anglesey was Avalon, however, is that it seems to have been the most important religious centre in Britain during the first century.

The emperor Claudius conquered much of Britain in AD 43, but it was a costly business to continually send troops across the English Channel and his successor Nero decided to abandon the country. But for some unknown reason Nero had a complete change of mind and in AD 61 ordered the military governor, Suetonius Paulinus, to march an army into north Wales and attack the Druid stronghold on Anglesey. The Druids were the priests of the Celtic world and the Roman historian Tacitus, whose grandfather fought with Paulinus, tells us that their chief religious centres were on Anglesey and that Nero had specifically ordered their destruction. It was a foolhardy manoeuvre, and the depletion of troops elsewhere in Britain led to the revolt by the British queen Boudica (Boadacea in the Roman account), who sacked the Roman capital of London. While campaigning on Anglesey, Paulinus learned that Boudica's massive army had left London and was marching north to confront him. Roman rule in Britain would have come to an end if Paulinus had not torn up his emperor's orders and abandoned Anglesey so as to seize the initiative against the warrior-queen. He returned along the newly constructed Watling Street and ambushed Boudica's army at Atherstone in Warwickshire. Although he faced overwhelmingly superior numbers, quick thinking and Roman military tactics secured victory for Paulinus. Her army routed, Boudica fled and took her own life.

Archaeology has confirmed that Anglesey was indeed the centre of Druidism as Tacitus records. In 1942 excavations at the dried-up lake of Llyn Cerrig Bach, at the mouth of the River Alaw, unearthed over 150 precious artefacts that had been thrown into the sacred water as votive offerings to the gods. These artefacts were prized possessions, such as cauldrons, horse trappings and brooches, and as such had clearly not been discarded. Rather, they had been cast into the water as offerings over a period spanning some 250 years until the end of the first century AD. It is by far the largest such cache discovered anywhere in the British Isles, and would appear to confirm Tacitus' account of Anglesey as the country's chief centre for Druidism.

It is as a Druid holy island that Anglesey can be equated with Avalon. Geoffrey of Monmouth portrays Avalon as the home of nine holy virgins who possess magical powers, and the medieval Grail romances portray nine sacred virgins as the Grail maidens. The idea of nine saintly women heading an island religious community is clearly a Druidic concept. The first-century classical geographer Pomponius Mela, for instance, writes of nine priestesses living under a vow of chastity on an island off the coast of Brittany. These women were Druid priestesses from a Celtic tribe similar to the Britons themselves, and were said to have the power to heal the sick and foretell the future. Avalon, it seems, was a Druid island and Anglesey was the most important Druid island in Britain.

A number of Dark Age Welsh manuscripts, such as *The Book of Taliesin* in the National Library of Wales in Aberystwyth, tell us that the Druids were the first British converts to Christianity. If Joseph of Arimathea had come to convert the Britons, then the Druids' most sacred stronghold is exactly where we might expect to find him. Not only does Tacitus record the presence of 'refugees from the Romans' amongst the Druids who fought to protect their sanctuaries, but the Druids of Anglesey having converted to Christianity by Nero's time would make sense of an unsolved historical mystery.

Why did Nero, after deciding to abandon Britain, suddenly change his mind and risk so much to attack the Anglesey Druids? It clearly was not the Druids themselves who so enraged him, as he completely ignored the more troublesome Druids of Gaul. There must have been something specific about the Anglesey Druids. The one people for whom we know Nero had a pathological hatred were the Christians. Was it because Anglesey had become a centre of Christianity that the emperor ordered the attack on the island?

Druidism may also explain the carved-head motif in the Grail romances. A carved stone head, presumably of their chief god, was an important totem for the Celts, and many such artefacts have been uncovered at archaeological excavations throughout Europe. A splendid example was found recently on Anglesey itself and is now on display in the island's museum at Llangefni. When the Celts converted to Christianity during the early years of the Common Era they often retained their own religious practices, which were adopted into a Christian context. The practice of worshipping a stone head may not have been abandoned on Anglesey. Rather, it became the practice of venerating a carved head of Christ.

An early Christian community could well have survived on Anglesey until Augustine's time. Although his legions destroyed some religious centres, Paulinus was forced to abandon his campaign on Anglesey before its completion so as to return to England and confront Boudica. After his narrow victory, the Roman forces were compelled to concentrate their efforts on controlling eastern Britain. Anglesey was left alone for years to come. Although they established a fort overlooking the Menai Strait at Segontium (modern Caernarfon), there is no evidence for a permanent garrison on Anglesey itself until the end of the third century when a naval base was built at Holyhead.

By the time the Romans re-established their presence on the island Nero was long dead and his persecutions of the

The ruins of Viroconium.

Penmon Priory, possibly the nine maidens' sanctuary in the Arthurian romances.
(Jodi Russell)

Above: The first-century stone head from
Anglesey Heritage Museum, Llangefni.
(Oriel Ynys Môn)

Right: Pabo's gravestone from Llanbabo church.
This Dark Age king was once the guardian of
Mary's secret relics. (Welsh Heritage)

Above: The King Catamanus tombstone from Llangadwaladr church. Dating from the very time of Augustine's arrival in Britain, it demonstrates that Anglesey was indeed 'a royal island'.

Right: The Tre-Ysgawen stone. Its sixth-century inscription showed that Augustine's assistant Paulinus had spent time on Anglesey. (Welsh Heritage)

The lead panels from a Christian coffin unearthed at Rhuddgaer. Dating from as early as
the second century, they show that Christianity had become established on Anglesey well
before the foundation of the Roman Catholic Church. (Welsh Heritage)

Right: The tiny chapel in Llanbabo, where the mortal remains of the Virgin Mary may secretly have been hidden when the Vikings invaded Anglesey.

Below: Llangadwaladr Church, said to house the tombs of the Dark Age guardians of the Grail.

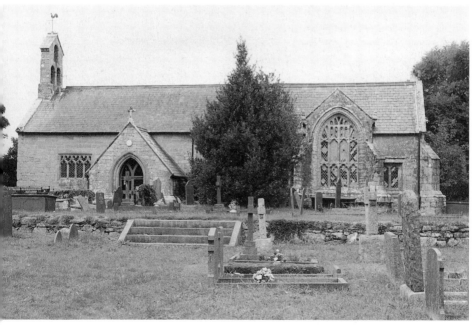

St Mary's Church at Llanerchymedd. It may stand on the site of the oldest church in the world – the Chapel of Joseph of Arimathea.

The sacred spring that may have been the holiest site in Celtic Britain.

The broken 'headstone' lying where we originally found it, just a couple of metres from the well.

The cleaned stone, inscribed with the ancient glyph for Virgo, the virgin. Does it mark the final resting place of the Virgin Mary?

Right: Close-up of the larger stone discovered at the well.

Below: Close-up of the Virgo glyph on the smaller stone discovered at the well.

Christians had ceased. Although sporadic persecutions did occur over the years, these were centred on the major cities of the empire, and outlying areas such as Wales passed fairly unscathed. Indeed, such was the case according to the Alexandrian scholar Origen who, in AD 240, wrote that Christianity was a unifying force amongst the Britons in the west of the island. When Augustine arrived the west of Britain was still practising Christianity.

So where was the mysterious chapel shown to Augustine in AD 597? The answer, it seemed, lay with one of Britain's most enigmatic saints. At the very end of Roman rule, Anglesey actually became the most important centre of Christianity in the whole British Isles. And this was not down to a bishop, a priest or even a monk, but a woman – St Elen, who was none other than the wife of the Roman emperor Magnus Maximus.

Maximus was a British-based general who seized the imperial throne in the closing years of the fourth century. In 376 the emperor Gratianus executed his main rival Theodosius on the charge of high treason. Gratianus was considered by many high-ranking soldiers to be incompetent, and Theodosius had been seen as a possible replacement. The only other threat to Gratianus came from his general Magnus Maximus. Not wanting to risk a civil war, he played safe and ensured that Maximus remained in command of the imperial forces stationed on the far-off island of Britain, posting him to the Segontium garrison at Caernarfon.

It was only a few years before Gratianus made one mistake too many, and the army in the north rebelled. In 383 Maximus was proclaimed emperor by the legions under his command. Taking his troops, he left Britain and sailed for the Continent. He won the support of the legions in Gaul, conquered Italy and marched on Rome. Gratianus was soon assassinated and Maximus took his place. The eastern empire, however, refused to recognize Maximus, instead proclaiming as emperor Theodosius' son, also named Theodosius. In the ensuing civil war Maximus was defeated and killed. However, many in Britain still regarded the Maximus family as the rightful heirs to the imperial throne. Theodosius, on the other hand, did not see them as a threat, and to avoid another campaign he took no action.

According to *The Life of St Elen*, attributed to the eleventh-century monk Lifris from Llancarfan monastery in Glamorgan, Maximus' wife Elen returned to Wales and founded a priory and hospice on Anglesey at Penmon, a peninsula at the extreme south-east of the island. A devout Christian missionary, she became known as St Elen and according to Lifris was considered 'the mother of all Saints' and 'Elen of the Hosts'. She was also called Elen of the Lake, in reference to a purported visitation by an angel at Lake Tegid in Snowdonia. After her death the priory became a centre of pilgrimage for Christians from all over Britain.

So important did Elen become to the Christians of post-Roman Britain that her bloodline was considered an essential element of kingship. From an inscription on the Pillar of Eliseg, a ninth-century monument at Llangollen in central Wales, we learn that Vortigern, the first king of Powys, married Elen's daughter Severa to legitimize his leadership. It records that all the kings of Powys were thereafter descended from her.

According to the *Notitia Dignitatum*, a Roman register of imperial officers compiled around AD 420, the Maximus family emblem, or crest, was a design consisting of two intertwined serpents. The dual-serpent motif occurs in an account concerning Vortigern's successor, Ambrosius, sometime in the mid-fifth century. Ambrosius was an historical figure recorded by Gildas as the leader of the Britons in the period before the battle of Badon. Nennius includes him in an allegorical account of his succession to the throne.

According to Nennius, Vortigern is attempting to construct an impregnable fortress high in the mountains of Snowdonia, but the work is constantly disrupted by a strange series of accidents. The king summons his advisers, who tell him that in order to complete the work he must sacrifice a young boy and sprinkle his blood on the site. Just as the chosen child is about to be killed, he tells Vortigern he knows the cause of the trouble and reveals a cave beneath the fort which contains a pair of serpents. The boy then reveals that he is Ambrosius, the son of a Roman consul. In gratitude, Vortigern names Ambrosius his successor.

The story is quite clearly allegorical. It is only when he reveals the creatures that Ambrosius is accepted as Vortigern's legitimate heir. As the twin serpents are the Maximus family crest, it would seem that Ambrosius has proved himself to be of Elen's bloodline.

King Arthur, too, is linked with Elen's bloodline. Geoffrey of Monmouth provides exactly the same account of Vortigern and the sacrificial boy – with one very significant difference. He calls the child Merlin. In his narrative, this is how Merlin the magician first enters the Arthurian story.

Geoffrey says that Merlin was born in Carmarthen in south Wales and he portrays him as both a magician and a bard. Bards enjoyed considerable influence in Celtic society, being the official court poets whose task it was to compose songs praising the exploits of their kingdom's warriors, and in particular their chieftains. Moreover, they were often thought to possess the gift of second sight, and were generally the most learned men of the tribe. In Carmarthen a bard called Myrddin – the Welsh rendering of Merlin – is actually recorded in the sixth century. Bard to a local warlord called Gwenddolau, he is credited with a number of early Welsh war-poems. He is even recorded in the *Welsh Annals* as losing his mind when his chieftain is defeated in battle.

> The battle of Arfderydd between the sons of Eliffer and Gwenddolau son of Ceidio; in which battle Gwenddolau fell and Myrddin went mad.

This cannot, however, be the man who met with Vortigern as a child in the mid-fifth century; the entry concerns the year 575, over a hundred years later. It would seem that two separate historical figures – Ambrosius and Myrddin – were confused as one in the years before Geoffrey wrote his account.

According to Geoffrey, Merlin acquired Arthur's sword Excalibur from the nine maidens' sanctuary on Avalon. As Merlin is here depicted as the real power behind the throne, this theme is more likely to have originated with a story concerning the king Ambrosius rather than the bard Myrddin. Ambrosius, it would seem, is stepping aside to make way for the younger Arthur. It is not only as Ambrosius' successor that Arthur is associated with Elen's bloodline, but through the sword itself.

The Dream of Rhonabwy, a tenth-century Dark Age war-poem, contains the oldest known description of Arthur's sword. Now in *The Red Book of Hergest*, the work records the sword as having 'a design of two serpents on its golden hilt'. If the historical Arthur's sword really did bear such a device, then it may have been a symbol of the authority of Elen's family. In the later romances Merlin actually receives Excalibur from a mysterious woman known as the Lady of the Lake and, according to Lifris, Elen was herself called Elen of the Lake.

Arthur's sword of kingship originates at the nine maidens' sanctuary on Avalon – a sword that bears Elen's family crest. As Elen was long dead by the time Arthur became king, the story might have been an allusion to the priory she founded at Penmon. Since, at the end of Geoffrey's account, Arthur is again returned to the nine maidens' sanctuary for his wounds to be seen to, this may also allude to the hospice that Elen established at the priory.

If Penmon Priory was the historical setting for Avalon's nine maidens' sanctuary in the Arthurian romances, might it also have been the site of the Grail chapel? After all, nine holy women were also said to watch over the Grail. Had Elen perhaps built her priory on the site of Joseph's original church?

The ruins of Penmon Priory still survive today and I was dying to explore them as soon as possible. However, I had two American friends coming to stay and their plane was due at Manchester Airport early next morning. When I met with Graham and Jodi Russell, a couple from Los Angeles whom I had known for many years, I excitedly told them of my research. Fascinated, they were as eager as I was to see Penmon Priory, so we headed straight back to north Wales. That evening as we sat in the bar of the British Hotel in Bangor, I explained to Graham and Jodi how I believed the authors of the medieval Grail romances actually found out about Joseph's secret chapel.

The only two medieval Grail romances to provide an identifiable source are *La Folie Perceval* and *The Didot Perceval*. According to their anonymous authors, the original Grail story had been taken from a book written by a certain Brother Blayse. A number of modern literary scholars have proposed that the author may have been a monk of that name, recorded at the abbey of St Asaph in north Wales in the late eleventh century. Indeed, St Asaph is the very see of which Geoffrey of Monmouth was bishop when he compiled his *History of the Kings of Britain* around 1135. Some historians have gone so far as to suggest that the book from which Geoffrey claims to have taken his own work – 'a book in the ancient British Language' – was the Blayse original. Interestingly, the St Asaph Blayse was one of Owain Ddantgwyn's direct descendants.

The genealogies in the *Welsh Annals* included the names of Owain Ddantgwyn and his sons Cuneglasus, Seiriol, Meirion, Einion and Frenin. From these family trees I discovered that Cuneglasus' last paternal descendant was Cynddylan, the king whose grave we may have found at the Berth. However, I picked up the trail of Owain's surviving descendants on the Pillar of Eliseg, the monument erected around 850 that bore the inscription celebrating Elen's bloodline. The inscription said that Cynddylan was succeeded by his brother-in-law Concenn, someone who is recorded in an eighth-century manuscript, the Peniarth MS 77, now preserved in the National Library of Wales. The manuscript said that Concenn was the grandson of Owain's second-eldest son Seiriol. The Pillar of Eliseg itself listed

Concenn as the direct ancestor of Cyngen, the man who erected the pillar.

According to a medieval Powys genealogy discovered in St Asaph Abbey by the Welsh antiquarian Edward Lhwyd in 1696, when Cyngen of Powys died without issue about 855, his sister Cynddia married Ynyr, a prince of Gwynedd. His descendants were therefore of the Owain Ddantgwyn surviving bloodline. The same genealogy traces the line directly to a Welsh baron Cadfarch, whose daughter married the Norman baron Trevor, the earl of Hereford, in the late eleventh century. They had a son called Blayse, who seems to have been the St Asaph Blayse. The Shropshire *Feet of Fines*, land-holding documents of the period, show that he was chaplain to the Norman baron Payne Peveril of Whittington in Shropshire from 1101–1114. He appears at Whittington at precisely the time Blayse is last recorded at St Asaph. If this is indeed the same Brother Blayse, then surely it is beyond coincidence that the man who is thought to have composed the first Arthurian Grail romance was a direct descendant of the man whom I had identified as the historical King Arthur.

'That's how I think the medieval romancers got to learn about Joseph's chapel,' I concluded. 'Unfortunately, however, it seems that its location had been forgotten by Blayse's time.'

The Grail romancers are always vague about the chapel's whereabouts. They use terms like the 'White Land' without apparently knowing where or what the White Land is. Robert de Boron, for instance, talks only of the Vale of Avalon, seemingly unaware that Avalon is an island. Even Blayse, quoted in *La Folie Perceval*, while knowing that the chapel is dedicated to the Virgin Mary, admits he has no idea where it is. He tells us only that Perceval discovers the Grail: 'In the chapel of St Mary that is fair, where the holy vessel did bring abundant honey to the bees, in that place now forgotten . . .'

Next afternoon the sun was shining brightly as we arrived at Penmon. Perched on the headland overlooking the sea, the enchanting setting was surrounded by calling birds. Seagulls swooped around the tower of the twelfth-century church, pigeons fluttered from the ruins of the medieval abbey, and crows circled above the remains of the original priory. All that still survives from Elen's time is a circle of stones from a nun's cell and a brick-lined, sunken bath: a holy well into which still trickled the clear, fresh waters of a hillside spring.

Fifteen centuries ago the priory would have consisted of a cluster of beehive huts made of turf and brushwood, a small chapel constructed along similar lines and a preaching cross erected in an open square. It would all have been surrounded by a high wall to protect the monastery from pirate raids from across the Irish Sea.

As Jodi examined the medieval ruins and Graham explored the church, I sat on the wall beside the holy well, looking through the photocopies I had made from Barry's exhaustive collection of books. Interestingly, by the time of the battle of Camlan, when Owain Ddantgwyn may have been brought here for his wounds to be tended, the priory was actually being run by his own son, Seiriol.

The Catholics of Elen's time had separate monasteries for men and women, but the Celtic Church of one and a half centuries later actually had mixed retreats. There were separate quarters for the nuns and monks, but they came together for communal work and worship. Some were even married and lived together on the site. Owain's son Seiriol was one such married priest. According to Peniarth MS 77 and another eighth-century ecclesiastical manuscript known as Mostyn MS 144 also in the National Library of Wales, the original priory founded by Elen was enlarged by its benefactor, Owain's eldest son Cuneglasus. After the war with Maglocunus, Cuneglasus moved to Viroconium but his younger brother Seiriol remained in Gwynedd where he was already the abbot.

In the sixth century, Penmon Priory had been one of the two most important monastic settlements on Anglesey. The other, at Holyhead on the opposite side of the island, had been founded by Seiriol's contemporary, Cybi. According to *The Life of Cybi*, compiled by an anonymous monk from Llancarfan monastery in the tenth century, the two monastic settlements had close ties. Apparently Cybi and Seiriol made a special daily journey to meet at a holy well halfway between the two settlements, somewhere in the middle of the island. Its location, however, has long been forgotten.

I watched a young couple make a wish together as they threw a coin into Penmon's holy well. I wondered if they knew just how old, and significant, this custom really was.

From finds such as the votive offerings at Llyn Cerrig Bach it is known that the Celtic people of Europe revered rivers, lakes and pools; and in particular, springs. They were not only considered portals to the underworld, the realms of gods and spirits, they were especially sacred to Eostre, the goddess of the moon, fertility and healing. It was believed that by making votive offerings – casting their possessions into the water – the goddess would bestow favours, heal the sick or grant wishes. (She was later adopted by the Saxons.)

When they conquered the Celtic realms, the Romans too

began to venerate the goddess Eostre. At her sacred springs they built well-shrines and adopted the native customs. One such shrine has been excavated on Hadrian's Wall in northern England. There, at Coventina's Well, a small wall was built around the spring and a little building erected over it. When the well was excavated it revealed numerous votive offerings, particularly coins. It seems that whereas the Britons had offered their prized possessions such as beads and brooches to the goddess, the Roman soldiers threw coins: a practice that has survived to this day in the tradition of wishing-wells. When the country was Christianized, the shrine was not abandoned. Rather, it was consecrated in the name of a saint, St Coventina, and made into a holy well – a Catholic healing shrine. The same is true of the hundreds of holy wells that still survive throughout the British Isles. Even today devout Catholics make pilgrimages to them in the hope that their waters can heal disease.

It was the holy well that first had me thinking of an altogether different site. I had already begun to doubt whether Penmon Priory was really the site of Joseph's chapel. As I studied a copy of the *Royal Commission Survey* on the ancient monuments of Anglesey that morning, I discovered that there was no archaeological evidence of such early occupation. Despite a number of exhaustive excavations, not one single artefact – not a coin, a statue, or even a piece of broken pottery – had been found anywhere on the site that predated the fifth century. Moreover, it had been worrying me that there was nothing apparently connected with the Virgin Mary. During Augustine's time his mysterious chapel had been dedicated to the Virgin, but this one had been dedicated to St Elen. No matter how important Elen had been, she certainly did not outrank the mother of God.

Penmon Priory might have been the healing sanctuary where the wounded Arthur was brought; it might have been the place where his sword was fashioned; but it was not, it seems, the chapel shown to St Augustine in 597. There had been no chapel here.

However, there was another possible location – the place where Seiriol and Cybi were said to have met. If the well was halfway between the two monasteries, as the account said, then it would have been a forty-kilometre walk there and back: an unlikely daily trek. The story, I decided, might be based on the memory of an important regular pilgrimage. If so, by definition, it would have to have been to a site that was considered more holy than either Holyhead or Penmon. Was that because it was at or near the venerated chapel Augustine saw – the last resting place of the Virgin Mary?

Early Christian churches were invariably built over or near holy wells. Joseph's chapel may therefore have been near one. The chapel may have been destroyed along with so many others on the island when Anglesey was pillaged by the pagan Vikings in the ninth century, but the remains of the holy well might still survive. Ancient holy wells were not really wells at all, but natural springs surrounded by a small stone wall. It was not until later, medieval times that more elaborate structures were built over them, giving them the appearance of little chapels.

'So you think we're looking for the remains of a tiny stone well, somewhere in the centre of this huge island?' said Jodi, after I had explained my theory. 'Even if it still survives it may be completely overgrown. How can we hope to find it?'

'Where was the Druids' most sacred sanctuary?' Graham asked.

'I don't know. Tacitus doesn't say. Why do you ask?'

'If Joseph or Jesus converted the Druids, wouldn't they have built their first church at the locals' most sacred site?'

Certainly, whenever the Christians converted the pagans, the first thing they did was to erect a church on the site most sacred to their previous deity or deities. This served a twofold purpose. Firstly, it was a tangible sign that the Christian God had displaced the old gods, and secondly, it meant that the general populace could continue to worship in familiar surroundings.

'So where do you think the Druids' most sacred site would have been?' asked Jodi.

'Well, the Alaw must have been the most sacred river on the island,' I said, 'as Branwen was buried beside it.'

Branwen was the sister of the lord of the isle. Perhaps the story reflected the river's hallowed status. It was not only that the Alaw was the largest river on Anglesey, it was at its estuary that the myriad votive offerings were unearthed.

'Near the river mouth?' Graham suggested.

'More likely the *source* of the Alaw,' I said. 'The most venerated of all the Celtic water sites were springs. We're looking for Seiriol's well – a spring. It has to be the source of some stream or river.'

Hurriedly, we opened our Ordnance Survey map. The source of the Alaw was indeed in the centre of the island, just as Seiriol's well was said to have been. The problem was that it split into a number of tributaries, and without a larger-scale map there was no way of knowing which was the source proper. We decided that the best thing to do was to visit the island's museum at Llangefni. I had already made an appointment with the museum's technical services officer, John Smith, for later that afternoon. Perhaps he could help us discover the Alaw's source.

Summary

- According to the monk Gildas, just like Arthur, Owain met his fate in battle against his rebellious nephew. In the early sixth century Britain was divided into a number of kingdoms, the largest being Powys which covered the west Midlands and north Wales. Owain Ddantgwyn had ruled this kingdom, but his nephew Maglocunus finally overthrew him and the kingdom split in two. With Owain dead, Maglocunus ruled the breakaway kingdom of Gwynedd in north Wales and his cousin, Owain's son Cuneglasus, continued to rule the now reduced kingdom of Powys.

- Gildas refers to Maglocunus overthrowing Owain, but he provides no geographical details. But for the two kingdoms to have formed, the battle must have taken place somewhere along their shared border.

- The twelfth-century writer Geoffrey of Monmouth tells us that Arthur's final battle was at Camlan. It was an apparently historical event which the Dark Age *Welsh Annals* record in 539. The most likely site for such a battle is actually along the Powys–Gwynedd border as it existed at the time. In precisely this location is the only place in the British Isles still called Camlan – a bleak and remote mountain pass about eight kilometres to the east of Dolgellau in north-west Wales.

- If the historical Arthur was mortally wounded in this particular valley of Camlan, then the isle of Avalon must be somewhere nearby. Augustine provides what seems to be the only proper description of the island in his letter to the then Pope: 'In the western confines of Britain there is a certain royal island of large extent, surrounded by water, abounding in all the beauties of nature and necessaries of life.'

- There is only one island anywhere near Camlan that matches this description – the island of Anglesey, about fifty kilometres to the north-west. It is a large island: the largest in England or Wales. It was a royal island too which, during Augustine's time, contained the seat of the Dark Age kings of Gwynedd. It was also prosperous: the grain basket of northern Wales. Furthermore, it was in the 'White Land', which is where the Grail romances say that Avalon is to be found. In Old Welsh the name Gwynedd actually means 'White Land'.

IX

THE FORGOTTEN CHURCH

ORIEL YNYS MÔN – Anglesey Heritage Gallery – in Llangefni is a new complex of buildings which house many of the archaeological discoveries made on the island. When we arrived the technical officer, John Smith, was in a meeting, so we took the opportunity to look around. In particular, I wanted to see the famous stone head that dated from the very time that Joseph of Arimathea may have come to the island. It had evidently been worshipped by the Druids and just such an artefact could have been behind the legend of Bran's head in the Grail chapel. The head, about half a metre high, depicted a far stranger-looking entity than I had imagined. He had a lantern jaw, a long nose, heavy eyebrows and the most peculiar, mischievous smile. He looked more like the Joker in a pack of playing cards than the traditional image of a Celtic god.

According to a theory proposed by my friend the author Andrew Collins, such a god may have been called Ak. As the Lord of Misrule, his name had become rendered as Jack in such mischievous mythical sprites as Jack Frost, Jack-in-the-box and Spring-heeled Jack. He may have been the equivalent of the Nordic god Loki. Loki was the trickster of

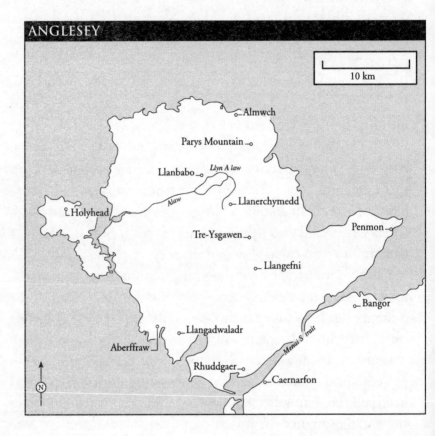

the gods, and an effigy of him was burnt each year at the start of winter to stave off his unruly influence during the cold days ahead. The Celtic Ak may have given rise to the similar custom of 'smoking the fool'. In the Middle Ages an effigy of a fool, or jester, was burnt on a bonfire at the beginning of November in many parts of Britain. In fact, it still is, in the guise of Guy Fawkes. In 1605, after Fawkes was arrested attempting to blow up the Houses of Parliament with a huge stash of gunpowder, it was fool-burning that evolved into 'Guy'-burning.

'If Ak was similar to Loki, he would also have been a wise fool,' I explained to Graham and Jodi. 'He was believed to be beyond the influence of cause and effect. Something like the crazy medicine man of certain Native American tribes – his lunacy was thought to give him a unique perspective on the universe.'

'Is that where the Fool in the Tarot pack came from?' asked Jodi. The Fool in the ancient Tarot pack became the Joker in modern playing cards. The original cards, however, were used for divination and the Fool symbolized both wisdom and chaos.

'It's quite possible, if Ak is somehow related to Bran's head in the Grail romances,' I said. 'The Tarot pack and the Grail romances seem to be based on exactly the same symbolism.'

The *Folie* romance appears to contain the most complete version of the Grail story. It may not be the oldest in its extant form but most literary scholars agree that it was copied from a romance that predated the others as it contains evidence of early Anglo–Norman French, dating from the early 1100s.

The story opens with Perceval's encounter with a

mysterious red knight. The knight tells Perceval that he must defeat him in single combat if he is to pass over the bridge he is guarding: a theme that occurs in many later Arthurian romances, although the protagonists are then portrayed as Arthur and Lancelot. Although he fights bravely, Perceval is beaten. The knight, however, agrees to spare his life for one year, in which time he must acquire the skills to defeat his opponent or die. Once again, this theme occurs in a later romance, *Sir Gawain and the Green Knight* (*circa* 1400), in which the Green Knight offers the same bargain to Gawain.

After the knight leaves, Perceval is met by Merlin, who tells him that the only way to better the red knight is to seek the wisdom of the Grail. Oddly, we are not told what the Grail actually is or what wisdom it might impart. Merlin returns to the forest and Perceval sets out to find the Grail chapel. When he eventually discovers it he is invited to a banquet held in honour of the Fisher King, Bran, and his wife Queen Wenyfair. During the feast a procession enters from a side chamber bearing 'the Grail Hallows' – four separate 'Grails'. The extant *Folie* manuscript includes an illustration of the procession showing a maiden carrying a chalice, followed by a page with a spear and four servants bearing a draped box with a sword on top. Later in the story we are told the significance of the Grail Hallows: the holy chalice contained Christ's blood, the spear pierced his side during the Crucifixion, the sword beheaded John the Baptist and the draped box holds the plate of the Last Supper. The banquet then ends and the Fisher King retires alone to the side chamber to spend the night at prayer.

Later, Perceval decides to follow the king into the chamber, in the hope of examining the Grail Hallows more closely. Inside, he finds the king gone and is confronted instead by a hooded man whom he assumes to be a priest but soon discovers is a Pope. The Pope tells Perceval that he must leave the chapel and, after the hero is temporarily blinded by a brilliant flash of light, he finds himself standing in the forest accompanied by a wise woman. The woman explains that, as the guardian of the Grail Hallows, Bran is immortal and cannot die until he has been replaced by a successor. As in the other Grail romances, Perceval is to be that successor, although he cannot become the new Fisher King until he has discovered the secrets of the Grail.

In order to discover the secrets, Perceval undertakes a series of adventures. He encounters a number of strange characters, each of whom sets him tasks to perform or riddles to solve. He meets two lovers sitting beneath a tree who ask him to retrieve a golden apple from a giant, a charioteer who holds a bleeding spear that seems to be one of the Grail Hallows, and a hermit who reveals to him a vision of the Crucifixion and the cowled figure of death who kills the grass over which he walks.

Eventually Perceval returns to the Grail chapel to find it reduced to ruins by a lightning bolt cast down by the devil. Unable to die, the Fisher King is alone amongst the rubble. Although frail and weak, he invites Perceval to dine with him. This time it is no banquet but a simple meal of bread and wine. When the Fisher King breaks the bread to share it with his guest, the Grail procession again enters the ruined hall. This time Perceval knows the secrets of the Grail. We are not told what they are but it seems to have something to do with the king himself, as he shines like an angel, hands Perceval a copy of a secret gospel and ascends bodily into heaven.

It is then that the red knight returns to tell Perceval that his year is up and it is time to fight for his honour. Perceval accepts the challenge, but is again defeated. The red knight runs him through with his sword but, as the new Fisher King, Perceval cannot die and immediately recovers. The red knight then laughs and announces that honour is satisfied. He removes his helmet to reveal that he is really Merlin. He had set Perceval the year-long quest so that he could learn to become a worthy Fisher King.

The figures that Perceval encounters during his quest to find the chapel appear scattered throughout the other Grail romances. For example, the lovers appear in *The Didot Perceval*, the charioteer features in *The First Continuation* and the grim reaper is found in *The Vulgate Cycle*. As the extant *Folie* only dates from around 1330, the general consensus amongst literary historians is that it is a compilation from these earlier versions. However, as it appears to have been based on Blayse's early twelfth-century version, it could conversely be argued that the other romancers had only a fragmentary knowledge of the story that the *Folie* contained in its entirety. This seemed to me a more likely scenario, as the characters in the story all belong together. Like a medieval *Alice in Wonderland*, they are all the cards of the Tarot pack.

Six of these characters – the Hermit, the Lovers, the Charioteer, Death and the Pope – feature directly in the *Folie*, and the Magician is present in the form of Merlin. They even appear in numerical order. Other Tarot cards also feature more obliquely in the romance. The first character Perceval encounters after he leaves the Grail chapel is a wise woman – the Priestess, perhaps? He meets the king and the queen of the Grail chapel – the Emperor and the Empress? Some of the other cards could also be present. The Falling Tower and the Devil might be related to the devil destroying the Grail chapel with a lightning bolt. The Judgement card might pertain to the Fisher King's ascension into heaven, and Perceval's inheritance of a secret gospel might correlate with the final card, the World. This card shows an angel, a lion, a bull and an eagle. Since early Christian times these four creatures have been used to symbolize the four gospels, Matthew, Mark, Luke and John. Even the suit cards might be linked with the story. There is a king, a queen, a knight and a page in the *Folie*. Furthermore, the symbols for the four suits are remarkably similar to the four Grail Hallows: the sword, the chalice, the lance and the platter. The sword and the chalice are present in the suits of Swords and Cups, while a lance is similar to a Staff. The suit usually described as Coins, or sometimes Pentacles, is represented by a golden disc, possibly a plate. Finally, the unnumbered Fool card, showing a jester journeying with a pack on his back, might relate to Perceval himself. The literal translation of *La Folie Perceval* is 'The Mad Perceval', but a more accurate interpretation is 'Perceval the Fool'. In the story, the foolish and naive young man must learn to become wise in the ways of the world before he can take his rightful place as the guardian of the chapel.

'What the cards originally meant, no one really knows,' I concluded. 'But if they are connected with the mystery of the Grail chapel, then they may contain some important clues.'

'Even though they only date from the Middle Ages?' said Graham.

'The symbolism may date back to the sixth century,' I said.

Perceval is the name given to the Grail hero in nearly all the medieval Arthurian romances, but he seems to have been based on an historical figure named Peredur, who survived as the hero in the Welsh version of the story, *Peredur*. Not only is this Peredur recorded in the *Welsh Annals* as dying in the year 580, the Welsh genealogies include him as Owain Ddantgwyn's grandson.

'So you think Peredur was the original Fool?' asked Graham.

I explained that he might have been just one of them. My suspicions were that the Fool had originated in an important member of the Celtic tribe who would, in a trance or under the influence of some natural narcotic, assume the role of Ak. In this state he would act as an oracle. 'Such a "medicine man" may have become the first priest or guardian of Joseph's chapel,' I said. 'At least a Christianized version of him. He may have been represented by the stone head, as were his successors.'

Jodi looked at the ancient sculpture which was smiling almost knowingly inside its glass case. 'You think there would actually have been a head like this in Joseph's chapel?' she asked.

'Perhaps one depicting Jesus' head – to represent that the priest spoke with the authority of Christ. That may have been what Augustine meant when he wrote about Jesus and the chapel: "He continues to watch over it." '

We moved on to the next exhibit. It concerned the story of Bran himself. Here was a painting showing Bran and his sister Branwen in Celtic costume: she with a tartan cloak and long blue dress, he with cross-tied breeches and a leather tunic. Around the painting were display cabinets, housing various archaeological finds from the Dark Ages, the time of the story's setting, including a number of ceramic urns and a sixth-century bronze brooch.

In *The Red Book of Hergest* Bran is portrayed as fighting the Irish. Accordingly, the scene is probably set sometime shortly after the Roman legions departed. Until the time of Ambrosius, around 470, the Irish were constantly pillaging northern Wales. It was not until Owain Ddantgwyn's time that they were finally driven out. The Irish in Anglesey were the last to go and were expelled by an army led by Owain's brother Cadwallon Lawhir. If Bran, as he is depicted in *The Red Book*, existed as an historical figure, then he may have been a local chieftain who fought the Irish when they first invaded – somewhere around AD 420. Conversely, the Bran portrayed in the Grail romances is a contemporary of Joseph of Arimathea. This would mean that the Bran in these stories might have been the island's 'medicine man' who first converted to Christianity when Joseph arrived. The name Bran actually means 'Crow' in Welsh so, like Arthur, it was probably a title of sorts. The two stories may therefore have concerned two separate figures associated with Joseph's chapel: one who lived shortly before the Romans invaded and the other who lived shortly after they left.

'Like Fisher King, Bran may have been a title for the Grail guardian,' I concluded.

'Why is he doing that?' said Jodi, pointing to a picture in a guide book depicting Bran as a giant lying across a stretch of water while his men walk along his back.

'At one point in the story, Bran is said to make himself into a bridge to enable his soldiers to cross to Ireland. I think it's symbolic for his true role as Grail guardian.'

This particular aspect of the story had had me puzzled for some time. As in many battle-poems, Bran, as chief warrior, is depicted with superhuman prowess. Many who heard the stories may well have believed the hero had incredible strength, but the idea that he could have grown big enough to lay himself across the Irish Sea would have stretched the credibility of the account beyond anyone's imagination. This version must either have been allegorical or had come about through a mistranslation of the original story. It reminded me of the famous story of King Arthur's sword in the stone: another tale that sounded ridiculous – until one realized how it originated.

In the Arthurian romances, the magical sword is set into a huge stone. (It is not, incidentally, Excalibur, as modern misconception has it – that is a separate sword.) According to the story, only the one destined to be king could draw the sword from the stone. Many try and fail until Arthur arrives and succeeds with ease. In the oldest extant stories of King Arthur, such as Geoffrey of Monmouth's account, Merlin predicts that Arthur will 'draw the sword from the Saxons'. In other words, he will take the fight from the enemy and defeat them in battle. Geoffrey wrote in Latin and in that language the word for a large boulder or stone is *saxum*. It is clear that someone who did not fully understand Latin later took 'Saxon' to mean *saxum* and wrongly assumed that Arthur became king by drawing his sword from a stone.

This is in no way an isolated example of a mistranslation leading to a quirky legend. For instance, there is the legend of Stonehenge, where there is a monolith called the Heel Stone which stands in isolation, some metres outside the main circle of stones. A local folktale tells how the stone came to be there and how it got its name. The devil, it is said, once lived in Stonehenge and one day a holy man – a friar – attempted to drive him away. When the friar failed and ran for his life, the devil uprooted one of the enormous stones and hurled it at him. It just missed the fleeing monk but managed to graze him on the heel. From then on the stone was known as the Heel Stone, after the friar's heel. In reality, the Heel Stone marks the position of the midsummer sunrise. It is above this stone, from the vantage point of the centre of Stonehenge, that the midsummer sun is seen to rise. Significantly, in Greek the words for 'rising sun' are *freos heol.* It is clear that some classical Greek author during the time of the Roman occupation referred to the stone as the 'rising sun' stone – the *freos heol* stone – and years later someone who did not understand Greek misinterpreted the words as the similar-sounding 'friar's heel'. Still later, local folklore, to account for the strange name of the stone, came up with the story of the devil.

When I applied similar thinking to the story of Bran it became obvious why he was portrayed as a bridge. The Grail romances represent Joseph of Arimathea's Church in Britain as an alternative apostolic succession. The *Folie,* for instance, is clearly an allegory concerning the Fisher King's spiritual descent from Christ. Just before his earthly life is over, Bran invites Perceval to a simple meal of bread and wine, just as Jesus did with his disciples at the Last Supper. The Fisher King has taken the place of Christ and, like Christ, he ascends bodily into heaven. Perceval then replaces him as Peter does Jesus. The fact that during Perceval's first visit to the chapel the Pope himself is the only person in the chamber in which Bran should have been praying, surely symbolizes that the Fisher King is himself the Pope.

Bran is an alternative Pope, and the Pope is called the pontiff. *Pontiff,* from the Latin word for 'bridge', refers to the Pope's role as the joiner of heaven and earth. The Pope is the 'bridge' and, presumably, so is Bran. 'In the original story, Bran must have been called the bridge and someone later took it literally,' I concluded.

'So the historical Peredur actually became a kind of secret Pope?' asked Graham.

'Yes, and I think that this is what the head ultimately came to represent.'

'Do you think that Arthur, Owain Ddantgwyn, was one of these guardians?' said Jodi.

'No, but his son Seiriol may have been. It would account for why one of Arthur's men became so associated with the Grail story.'

'But if Seiriol was one of the priests or guardians of Joseph's chapel, wouldn't that mean that it was at Penmon?' Jodi said. 'I thought we'd discounted that.'

'I doubt that the guardian, or whatever he was called, spent *all* his time living in the chapel as the Grail romances suggest,' I went on. 'In the earliest stories there is a retinue of "white maidens" – nuns, perhaps – in permanent attendance at the chapel.'

'What makes you think that Seiriol was one of the guardians?' asked Graham.

'In the genealogies he is called Seiriol *Gwasmair* – "Servant of Mary".' I explained what I had discovered from Barry Davis about the Welsh rendering of Mary. In Welsh Mary is *Mair* or *Fair*, depending on its grammatical mutation. After the word *llan* for instance – 'parish' – it appears as *Fair* – Llanfair – St Mary's Parish. 'As we know from Augustine, and also the *Folie*, that the chapel was dedicated to Mary, the title *Gwasmair* may refer to Seiriol's role as the custodian of the chapel or her tomb.'

I had also concluded that Bran's queen in the *Folie* story may have represented Mary herself, or at least her spiritual presence in the chapel. She is called Wenyfair – 'Mary the White'.

'I thought *gwyn* meant "white",' said Jodi, after I had explained. 'You know, as in Gwynedd – "White Land".'

'Welsh is a complex language,' I said. 'The word *wen* means "white" when it is used in a feminine context, such as in Branwen, which means "White Crow". When it is used in a masculine context, such as Maglocunus' title *Maelgwyn* – "White Lord" – it is rendered as *gwyn*.'

'How come the word "white" keeps cropping up?' Graham wondered.

This had struck me before: White Land, White Lord, White Maidens – even the chapel is described as the White Chapel. 'I think it refers to purity,' I said.

'So the queen in the romance is really called Mary the Pure,' said Jodi.

'Right, and Owain Ddantgwyn, which translates as Owain "White Tooth" may have meant Owain Pure Tooth – he only spoke the truth.'

'So we might be looking for a place with *gwyn* or *wen* in its name,' suggested Graham.

'It's a thought,' I said. As Wales had never been conquered by the Anglo-Saxons and was only much later occupied by the Normans, the place-names have remained almost unchanged since Roman times.

'Or *Mair* or *Fair*,' added Jodi.

'Somewhere near Seiriol's well,' said Graham, indicating an exhibit over on the other side of the gallery.

This exhibit concerned the island's Celtic Church period, and a painting depicted Cybi and Seiriol meeting at the well. According to the guidebook there were three local folktales about the location of the well, but its author regarded them as unlikely. They were all in an area roughly halfway between Penmon and Holyhead. The first, *Ffynnon Cybi* – 'Cybi's Well' – in the hamlet of Carmel, was not old enough as it was only dug in 1423 by the parish priest. The second was a pool called the Pandy about five kilometres further north, but that was created by peat workings in the Middle Ages. Finally, there was a holy well, now called *Ffynnon Seiriol* – 'Seiriol's Well' – in the hamlet of Clorach, but that does not appear in records or on maps predating 1800.

We explained to John Smith that we were looking for the source of the Alaw, believing that it might be the real location of Seiriol's well.

'It seems to be right here,' said John, pointing to a map of the island. The spot he indicated was in the centre of the island, about a kilometre to the south of the village of Llanerchymedd. Here, the thin blue line of the stream stopped at the edge of a country lane (OS 412833).

'Is there an old church anywhere in that area?' I asked.

'Yes, in the middle of Llanerchymedd. In fact, it may be the oldest on the island.' John told us that although the building that now stands dates from the mid-nineteenth century, it was erected on the site of a very much earlier church. Some of the medieval stonework still survives around the porch and the lower parts of the tower. 'The original church may even date from early Christian times.'

John explained his reasoning. The Welsh word *llan*, meaning 'church' or 'parish', occurs frequently in place-names such as Llanellian – 'Parish of [St] Ellian'. The word *llanerch*, however, refers to a clearing containing a chapel or monastery. Llanerchymedd is the only village on Anglesey which still retains this original variant in its name, implying that there may have been a church there before any other on the island.

'Do you think the church at Llanerchymedd existed in the first century?' I asked.

'I'm certain there was at least a settlement there in Roman times,' John replied. 'You can see that it appears to have been on the intersection of two Roman roads.' He showed us on the map how one modern road ran down from Parys Mountain in the north-east and terminated in Llanerchymedd, while the other ran across from Din Lligwy in the east to Holyhead in the west. 'An old footpath continues on where the first of these roads stop,' said John. Beyond the village, a little lane and then a public footpath continued in a straight line. 'That's what you would expect to find along the course of an old Roman road. When new roads were built, the old routes often continued to be used as footpaths.'

John had been the first to propose the existence of this Roman road, but some archaeologists who had been working on Anglesey expressed doubts. He had therefore decided to test his theory. The modern road that runs south-west of the village bends around to avoid a marshy area. However, on the map, a footpath carried on in a straight line to rejoin the road about two kilometres outside Llanerchymedd. John described how he had walked the footpath with a metal spike, prodding the ground to see if there was a layer of stones beneath the surface. The instrument revealed that there was, just as should be expected along the course of a Roman road. 'You could actually see the course of the buried stones marked out by a line of molehills,' he said. The animal had evidently been burrowing its way across the field, creating a mound of earth every so many metres to evacuate the soil from its tunnel, when it had reached the stonework.

Here the line of molehills abruptly changed direction and followed the footpath for some way.

John believed that this road might have been the major trade route on Anglesey, running right across the island from the copper mines at Parys Mountain near Amlwch to the Roman port of Aberffraw at the extreme south-west. After we finished tea he took us to a display case, inside which was a plate-sized lump of dark, roughly moulded copper, about seven centimetres thick. 'It's a copper cake,' he said. 'The Romans transported the copper in that way in saddle-bags on pack-horses. Some have been found where they fell, along the route that passes through Llanerchymedd.'

'So you think that Llanerchymedd was a crossroad settle-ment in Roman times,' I said. 'Where did the other road go?'

'East to west, probably connecting the Roman naval base at Holyhead with the fort at Din Lligwy.'

'Was there a settlement there before Roman times?' Jodi asked.

'It's very possible. The roads may already have been here as Iron Age or even Bronze Age trade routes.'

John explained that the Parys Mountain copper mine was enormous: as recently as the eighteenth century it was the biggest in the world. In pre-Roman times it had been heavily mined. He showed us another display case; inside was a large, pointed hammer stone. 'Many of these have been found in old mine workings at Parys Mountain. They were used to pound the ore and date from many centuries before the Romans arrived. There was certainly a pre-Roman settle-ment at Aberffraw and the copper was probably transported there through Llanerchymedd, just as it was in Roman times.'

When I had previously imagined Joseph of Arimathea

arriving on Anglesey I had envisaged it as being a remote centre of pagan worship. In reality, it appears to have been one of the three most important centres of industry in prehistoric Britain: the tin trade in Cornwall, the lead trade in Somerset and the copper trade here on Anglesey. Traders from Gaul and elsewhere in the Roman empire would have been making regular trips to the island at exactly the time Joseph of Arimathea seems to have arrived. Llanerchymedd appears to have been on a major trade route used by these foreigners.

'Was Llanerchymedd in any way connected with honey farming?' I asked, remembering the verse from the *Folie* romance: 'In the chapel of St Mary that is fair, where the holy vessel did bring abundant honey to the bees . . .'

'I think it must have been, in the past,' said John. 'The *medd* in Llanerchymedd actually means "mead". The name of the village, literally translated, would have meant something like "the clearing where a church stands where mead is made". Mead, of course, is made from honey.'

John's answer to our final question seemed to clinch Llanerchymedd as the place we were looking for. 'Do you know what saint the church is dedicated to?' I asked.

'Yes,' he said. 'Saint Mary.'

The Virgin Mary!

When we arrived at the source of the Alaw, later that afternoon, we found the word we had expected to find. The area, on the edge of Llanerchymedd, was called Cilgwyn – 'White Retreat'.

The little stream wound its way across the fields, beginning abruptly in the thick hedgerow that encroached on the narrow country lane. Somewhere below the nettles and bushes the sound of trickling water could be heard: a natural spring – the source of the river that only five kilometres downstream was big enough to create a reservoir which supplied water to every home on the island. A crow flew from the thicket, squawking in protest as we pulled back the brambles. Tiny animals scurried through the undergrowth as we parted the weeds. They had been drinking from the fresh water that bubbled up from below the ground.

What we discovered there must have been hidden from human eyes for years. Around the spring there was a semi-circular wall of roughly cut stones, covered with moss and algae. It was a manmade well about half a metre wide and half a metre deep with an opening to one side for the water to run out. Beside the well was a granite stone about a metre and a half long. It too had been fashioned by human hands. Although now fallen on its side, it must once have stood upright as a pillar and been a mark-stone of some kind. Any inscription, however, had long ago eroded away.

There was no way of telling how old the well actually was but, going by its similarity to other early holy wells, it could have been here for centuries. It had certainly been forgotten and overgrown for so long that it was not marked on the map or included in the official inventory of the island's ancient monuments. Was this the real Seiriol's well, the place where the two saints were said to have met? Everything seemed to fit. It was the source of the sacred River Alaw; it was called White Retreat; and St Mary's Church – perhaps the oldest chapel on the island – stood just across the fields.

Two thousand years ago this may have been a shrine to a Celtic goddess, the most sacred pagan site on the island.

Joseph of Arimathea, or even Jesus himself, might have made it a Christian site. Was the Grail chapel somewhere nearby?

'It would have been difficult for anyone to build a chapel here,' I said, once our initial euphoria on finding the well had subsided. 'It's too marshy. That's about the nearest suitable location,' I said, pointing to the spire of Llanerchymedd church rising above an avenue of trees.

'Joseph's chapel?' said Graham.

'And Mary's tomb?' added Jodi.

As we made our way down the winding lane to the church, which stood in the middle of the village, I told Graham and Jodi how Mary's body may originally have been interred. The tradition amongst the wealthy Jews of her time was to lay the deceased in a tomb, such as the Garden Tomb in Old Jerusalem. A year later the bones would be collected and put into a stone box, to be stored on a shelf in the burial chamber alongside other members of the family. Such boxes, called ossuaries, were often decorated and engraved with the name of the deceased. There were many ossuaries in museums in Jerusalem, and I remembered seeing one which dated from the very time that Jesus was crucified. It was made from white limestone, about sixty centimetres long and forty centimetres high and wide, and was inscribed in Hebrew: 'Shitrath, daughter of Yehohanan'.

'If Mary was buried in the contemporary Jewish fashion,' I said, 'then there may have been a burial chamber: a vault under the chapel which contained her ossuary. Possibly others, such as Joseph of Arimathea's.'

We were itching to look around the church, but we were in for a disappointment. When we arrived we found the entire place boarded up and securely locked and on the door, a 'Danger Keep Out' sign. Apparently, the building had

fallen into such a state of disrepair that it had been abandoned some years ago. What may have been the oldest
church in the world was now a monument to the decline of
Christianity. Instead of a throng of pilgrims or a happy
congregation, a few young people sat on the porch steps,
smoking and drinking beer.

That evening, as we dined in an Indian restaurant back
on the mainland, we looked through a copy of the *Royal
Commission Survey of the Ancient Monuments of Anglesey*. As
far as we could tell, no vault now existed beneath the church.
However, if there had been one in the past it might have
been filled in when the present structure was built around
1850.

'There's only one way to find out if there ever was a vault
beneath the church,' I said. 'With geophysics.' Perhaps the
same techniques that were used at the Berth could reveal
whether there was an infilled tomb under Llanerchymedd
church. It might also reveal the outline of the original foundations.

'I assume that only an archaeological dig could tell for
certain how old it is,' said Jodi.

She was right, and I would need more than circumstantial
evidence if I was to convince the bishop of Bangor, who was
ultimately responsible for the property, to allow a dig in the
dilapidated building. I needed proof that Llanerchymedd
really was the site of the church in Augustine's letter. That
would at least show that the church was ancient and of
considerable historical interest. I could then, perhaps, reveal
what I had discovered without having to mention Mary or
Joseph of Arimathea. And three new strands of evidence did
indeed emerge a few weeks later, thanks to Barry Davis.

'To interest the archaeologists in the church you need

three things,' he said, when he heard of my conundrum. 'Hard evidence that Anglesey precisely matches Augustine's description, that there were Christians on Anglesey very early on, and that Augustine really went there.' I could almost see Barry beaming down the phone as he paused for a moment. 'And I think I have all three.'

When we met a couple of days later at Bangor's University Museum Barry began by telling me how literary, historical and archaeological sources all confirmed that Anglesey was the only British island that fitted Augustine's description. 'Firstly, it was "abounding in all the beauties of nature and necessaries of life",' he quoted, placing a book on the table. It was copy of the *Brut y Tywysogyon* – 'Chronicle of the Princes' – an eighth-century work from St Asaph Abbey. 'It describes all the principalities of Wales as they were in the Dark Ages and it calls Anglesey, Mon nam Cymru – "Anglesey, Nourisher of Wales". Here was a book written within a century of Augustine's visit to Britain which describes Anglesey's cornfields as so plentiful that they can feed the entire country.

'Secondly, there can be no doubt whatsoever that it was a "royal island", just as Augustine says, at precisely the time he visited Britain.' Barry explained that the genealogies in the *Welsh Annals* name Maglocunus' grandson Catamanus as king of Gwynedd around AD 600. In a second book, he showed me a photograph of an inscribed gravestone. It bore the Latin epitaph: *Catamanus Rex sapientisimus opinatismus omnium regum*: 'King Catamanus, wisest and most illustrious of kings'. 'This comes from Llangadwaladr, just outside Aberffraw. It shows conclusively that the area was the seat of the kings of Gwynedd during Augustine's time. There is only one other island anywhere off the coast of Britain that contained the seat of a contemporary king – the Isle of Man – but that was not Christianized until very much later.'

In the museum's post-Roman gallery one of the exhibit cases displayed three sheets of worn and corroded metal. Apparently they were lead plates from the side of a decomposed wooden coffin excavated from farmland at Rhuddgaer on the most southerly point of the island. One of them, about a centimetre thick, a metre long and a quarter of a metre wide, bore the Latin inscription *Camuloris hic ossa iacent*: 'The bones of Camulus the king lie here.'

'It's a Christian coffin,' said Barry. He pointed to the Greek letter alpha at the beginning of the inscription. 'There would have been an omega at the other, damaged end.' He explained that this was early Christian symbolism for Jesus. They were the first and last letters of the Greek alphabet used in the New Testament Book of Revelation to symbolize Christ as the beginning and end of all things. 'It has been dated to the fifth century,' he said. 'In my opinion, wrongly.'

Barry explained how the use of the suffix *ris* to denote a king was very early Brythonic, which had been replaced by the suffix *rix* by the time the Catholic Church was formed in the early fourth century. This particular use of alpha and omega has not been discovered elsewhere in Britain, but in Gaul a very similar practice occurred amongst Christians – no later, however, than the third century.

'The coffin seems to be at least two centuries earlier than previously thought,' said Barry. 'It may not prove that Joseph of Arimathea was here but it does show that an Anglesey chieftain, someone who was defying Rome by claiming to be a king, had converted to Christianity during the first half of the Roman occupation of Britain. The fact that he was a chieftain suggests that the religion was well established on the island. It goes some way towards supporting Augustine's statement that "the first Neophytes of Catholic Law" had come to the island.'

'So you think that Anglesey really was the island Augustine referred to?' I asked.

'I can't actually prove that Augustine came to Anglesey, but Paulinus certainly did,' said Barry. 'Remember, Paulinus is supposed to have helped repair the mysterious church.'

According to his correspondence with Pope Gregory, Augustine had left his assistant Paulinus in charge of the initial attempts to convert the Celtic Church of western Britain. Augustine himself had been installed as archbishop of Canterbury and was busy consolidating his hold over the Anglo-Saxons. We are not told precisely where Paulinus spent this one year, 598, but it must have been during this time that he helped repair the church.

Barry wanted to take me over to the island so that I could see it in person. We drove over the Menai Bridge, through Llangefni and along the B5111 until, at last, we pulled into a narrow track edged on both sides by thick rhododendron bushes. I followed my companion out of the car and watched as he pulled back an overhanging branch to reveal a marker stone, about a metre and a half high and seventy centimetres wide. A number of lines of ancient script were still visible on the weathered surface.

'It's a gravestone dating from around AD 600,' he said. 'The inscription is in Latin.' Barry handed me an archaeological report on Anglesey's early inscribed stones. The inscription was now very faint but it had been copied in detail in 1870. It was translated:

A most holy lady lies here, who was the very beloved wife of Bivatigirnus, servant of God, a bishop, and a disciple of Paulinus by race a [letters eroded] . . . adocian.

I immediately realized why Barry had been so excited by the find. It must be a Catholic rather than a Celtic Church tombstone; there were no bishops in the Celtic Church. This, together with its date of around 600, made the Paulinus in question almost certainly Augustine's assistant. No one other than Augustine's party of clerics would have been empowered or would have had the wish to appoint a bishop of the Roman Catholic Church. Moreover, this Paulinus appeared to come from exactly the same place as Augustine's Paulinus, Cappadocia in what is now Turkey. The first part of the word describing his nationality was no longer visible when the inscription was recorded, but there was no other nationality of the Roman or post-Roman world ending in ' . . . adocian'. It seems very unlikely that there were two Cappadocian missionaries preaching in northern Wales in the late sixth or early seventh century.

'The stone has been known to archaeologists for over a century but no one has taken much interest in it,' said Barry. 'It's only when you consider it in conjunction with Augustine's letter that its significance becomes apparent.'

'It places the man who was said to have repaired the mysterious church right here on Anglesey,' I said.

'Not just on Anglesey,' he responded, opening up the OS map on the car bonnet. 'We're only a couple of miles from Llanerchymedd.' He pointed to our location in the vicinity of Tre-Ysgawen House, four kilometres south-east of the village.

'It might well be enough to get the archaeologists interested in St Mary's Church,' I said.

Barry sighed. 'Unfortunately, there may no longer be anything in the church to find. The place was probably pillaged by the Vikings.'

Barry was right. The *Welsh Annals* record the first Viking raids in 866 and a battle for control of Anglesey in 876. By the late tenth century the Vikings occupied the entire east and much of the north of the island. It is actually from them that we get the present English name, Anglesey. It comes from the words 'Ongull's Isle', after a Norse chieftain who ruled on the island.

'The pagan Vikings raided, burnt and pillaged all the major Christian sites in the area under their control, which included the area around Llanerchymedd,' Barry continued. 'There is no specific reference to Llanerchymedd being sacked, but if it was as important a church as Augustine says it is unlikely to have escaped. However, all may not be lost.'

Barry explained how the south-west of Anglesey remained in Welsh hands and, although the capital of Aberffraw was attacked in 968, a large payment in gold persuaded the Vikings to retreat to their own side of the island. It was to the church at Llangadwaladr, just outside Aberffraw, that the bones of Seiriol and Cybi were moved before Penmon Priory and the monastery at Holyhead were abandoned.

'Surely the relics of the most important saint of all – the Virgin Mary – would have been preserved too,' said Barry.

'You mean her bones may have been moved to Llangadwaladr?' I asked.

'If they existed, as you think. Llangadwaladr church is actually dedicated to the Virgin Mary.'

The heavy, musty smell of ancient woodwork and crumbling masonry hung in the air as we entered the empty church.

There was no one around, but the door was open and a sign above a collection box in the porch asked visitors to give a donation for a booklet that told the history of the church. From it, I learned that the building was originally dedicated to St Cadwaladr – Llangadwaladr actually means 'Parish of Cadwaladr'. It was rededicated to Mary by the eleventh century, although there is no surviving record as to why. Could it have been because her earthly remains had been moved here?

Cadwaladr had been the king of Gwynedd in the mid-seventh century and had become a monk after the death of his wife. He became one of the leading figures in the Celtic Church, and in 664 at the Synod of Whitby in Yorkshire, when the Celtic Church agreed to rejoin the Catholic Church, Cadwaladr had been a chief delegate. However, he was almost alone in refusing to accept the authority of Pope Vitalian as supreme head of the unified religion. He immediately set out for Rome to challenge the Vatican's position, but died mysteriously on reaching the ancient city. His body was brought back to be entombed in Llangadwaladr church.

As noted earlier, until the Middle Ages churches were dedicated to the saints whose bones or tombs they housed. But, as relics became an increasingly lucrative source of revenue for ecclesiastical establishments of all types, bishops, priests and abbots attempted to acquire the bones of as many saints as they could. The buildings would accordingly be rededicated to the most important saint whose bones they housed. Cadwaladr was Anglesey's most venerated native saint. That the priests had decided to abandon the dedication of their church in his name in favour of the Virgin would support Barry's suggestion that Mary's relics might have been moved here sometime in the tenth century.

When I read of Cadwaladr's epithet, I wondered if the saint himself might have had some connection with Joseph's chapel. Apparently, Cadwaladr was known as *Bendigaid* – 'the Blessed'. This is exactly the title given to Bran in the story from *The Red Book of Hergest*. Had Cadwaladr in his day been one of the chapel's guardians? If so, then it would certainly explain why he had so vehemently disputed Vitalian's right to be head of the Catholic Church. Cadwaladr may have regarded himself as Pope. Alternatively, as the historical sources concerning him date only from the period after the Viking occupation of Anglesey, he may have been given this title many years later when the church he founded came to house Mary's remains.

In the hope of finding anything that might link the church to the story of Joseph's chapel, I began to examine its architectural features. The present structure dated only from the fifteenth century, but it was quite possible that repairs and rebuilding had remained true to the original. Local legend or folklore, perhaps, might also have been preserved in some way.

I stopped abruptly at the altar, staring up at the east window. The stained glass depicted Jesus on the cross with the Virgin Mary to his right and 'the beloved disciple' to his left. Of course, the guidebook said the disciple was St John, but from what I had deduced in Ephesus, it was probably Christ's brother Joseph of Arimathea. Here were Mary and Joseph, the very people I was investigating. Was there any connection? Around the cross were four angels, each holding a chalice in which they collected blood from one of Christ's wounds. Four Grails – the Grail Hallows, perhaps? But it was the depiction of Cadwaladr that had me most intrigued. He had a crown on his head and an orb and sceptre in his hands. Behind him was what appeared to be a flat-topped sarcophagus. Was this in some way indicating that he was the guardian of Mary's tomb?

Although we spent some time in the church and called at the rectory to speak to the vicar, we discovered nothing definite to link the area with Mary's remains. There were no unidentified tombs in the church and no record that any saint's bones other than Cadwaladr's, Seiriol's and Cybi's had ever rested there.

When I returned home the next day, I spent the drive back going over the situation in my mind. I was more convinced than ever that Anglesey was Augustine's island and that Llanerchymedd church was the site of Joseph's chapel. It might be worth letting the Gwynedd county archaeologists in on my suspicions in the hope that I could at least get them to organize a geophysics scan of the church. Then again, if Barry was right, there might be nothing left to scan for and I might lose my only chance to get them to take me seriously. I could try to arrange a geophysics scan of Llangadwaladr church, but here I had no hard evidence of anything.

And there was always the disturbing possibility that Mary's tomb or her remains no longer existed anywhere. In the Middle Ages saints' bones were usually kept in reliquaries – ornamented boxes, often made of gold or silver and encrusted with jewels. During the Reformation when Henry VIII severed the English and Welsh Churches from Rome, religious establishments were stripped of such possessions, which were broken up and their contents thrown away. Under Elizabeth and James I, the veneration of saints' bones was prohibited under British law and those that survived were reburied, often in unmarked graves. Anything that still remained in the open would also have been in danger of complete destruction during the Puritan purges of Oliver Cromwell's time.

All the same, I could not help but feel that I was overlooking something. Although I had not yet picked up Giovanni Benedetti's trail on Anglesey, I was sure that his own investigations had ultimately led him there. If he had, as I suspected, investigated the Glastonbury connection he would almost certainly have come across William of Malmesbury's reference to Augustine's letter. Consequently, he would probably have visited Anglesey. Even though he might not have connected Owain Ddantgwyn with King Arthur, there was plenty of other evidence to lead him there. If Benedetti had found Mary's tomb, as I believed, then there must have been some vital clue that I was either missing or had overlooked.

When I arrived home I found a message from John Smith on my answering machine. I had earlier asked him if he could let me know if he came across a record, legend or folktale of anyone important being buried at Llanerchymedd. Apparently, he had been talking about it with his wife Ann when she remembered an old Welsh rhyme from her schooldays on Anglesey:

> *Yn Llanerch'medd ym Mondo*
> *Y claddwyd Brenin Pabo.*
> *A'r frenhines deg ei gwedd*
> *Yn Llanerch'medd mae hono.*

> In Llanerchymedd in Anglesey
> Is buried King Pabo.

The beautiful queen
Is also there in Llanerchymedd.

I immediately returned John's call and he told me that
the rhyme seemed genuinely old. He kindly photocopied all
he could on the verse and sent it to me. It was actually
recorded as an ancient Welsh ditty in the *Allwydd Paradwys*,
a Welsh almanac of 1670. There was no way of knowing
how old the verse was but King Pabo had been an historical
figure, as the *Welsh Annals* mention him in the year 595:
'The death of king Dunod, son of Pabo'.

According to the medieval Welsh manuscript *Iolo MS* in
the National Library of Wales, 'Pabo was king of the North,
and was driven from his country by the Picts and came to
Wales.' This referred to the kingdom of Gododdin, north of
modern Newcastle, which managed to hold out against both
the Anglo-Saxons and the Scottish Picts until the mid- to
late-sixth century. On reaching Anglesey Pabo became a
monk and was venerated as a saint. Nothing more is known
about him, but if he was buried at Llanerchymedd as the
rhyme asserts he may even have been one of the chapel's
guardians, possibly holding the office between Seiriol and
Cadwaladr.

I was intrigued by the reference in the verse to 'the
beautiful queen'. This did not appear to refer to Pabo's own
queen. If so, it would either have named her or referred to
her as '*his* beautiful queen'. Remembering that Mary seems
to have been depicted as the queen in the *Folie* romance and
that by the sixth century she was firmly accepted as Queen
of Heaven, perhaps – I could not help but speculate – *she* was
'the beautiful queen' who was also buried in Llanerchymedd.

Amongst the photocopies I found something really

exciting. If the rhyme was right about Pabo being buried at Llanerchymedd, then his body had indeed been moved. His final resting place had been found. His tomb had been discovered in Llanbabo church, five kilometres to the north-west. While the sexton had been digging a grave in 1730 he struck a buried tombstone about 1·8 metres down. The large sculptured slab bearing a carved figure of a crowned king bore the inscription: *Hic Iacet Pabo Post Prydain* – 'Here lies Pabo the upholder of Britain.' If Pabo had been moved to Llanbabo, so also might Mary have been. Moreover, if *his* tomb survived there, so too might hers.

Summary

- If Joseph of Arimathea's church was on Anglesey and it housed Mary's remains, then it would be the most hallowed shrine on the island. The two most important Christian leaders on Anglesey just prior to Augustine's visit, abbots Seiriol and Cybi, are said to have made a daily pilgrimage to a holy well at the centre of the island. The well, at the village of Llanerchymedd, must therefore have had special significance. Perhaps it was at Llanerchymedd that Augustine had found his church.

- Llanerchymedd church seems to be the oldest on the island. Although the building that now stands dates from the mid-nineteenth century, it was erected on the site of a very much earlier church. The Welsh word *llan* means 'church' or 'parish' and occurs frequently in place-names such as Llanellian – 'Parish of [St] Ellian'. The word comes from the Old Welsh *llanerch*, which referred to a clearing containing a chapel or monastery. Llanerchymedd is the only village on Anglesey which still retains this original variant in its name, implying that there may have been a church there before any other on the island. Like Augustine's church it is also dedicated to the Virgin Mary.

- The village is only a few kilometres from the Parys Mountain copper mine, one of the most important centres of industry in pre-Roman Britain. Traders from Gaul and elsewhere in the Roman empire were making regular trips to the area at exactly the time Joseph of Arimathea may have arrived.

- According to the twelfth-century historian William of Malmesbury, Augustine left his assistant Paulinus behind at the church to help with its repair. Near Tre-Ysgawen House, just four kilometres from Llanerchymedd, is a marker stone dating from the period of Augustine's visit. On it is a contemporary inscription which confirms Paulinus' presence in the area.

- If Mary's remains were once housed in Llanerchymedd church, they would probably have been removed when the Vikings invaded the east of the island in the tenth century. The remains of Pabo, a sixth-century king of Gwynedd, had also seemingly been buried in Llanerchymedd church and had been removed to nearby Llanbabo. Perhaps Mary's bones had been moved to Llanbabo church at the same time.

X

THE SECRET OF THE GRAIL

A FLASH OF light illuminated the windows of the church and bathed the altar in a moment of flickering brilliance. After a few hanging seconds of ghostly silence the crash of thunder shook the building. It had been threatening to rain all morning and the skies had been darkening for some time. Now they had opened and the downpour began.

Llanbabo church is one of the oldest buildings on Anglesey, much of its stonework dating from pre-Norman times. In the north wall of the simple rectangular chapel was the slab from Pabo's tomb, still where it had been set following its discovery in 1730. Carved into its surface in low relief was the figure of the bearded king, wearing a crown and a heavy, long-sleeved robe. In his right hand was a sceptre but the left was damaged, and whatever he was holding could no longer be discerned.

'It was chipped off when the slab was unearthed by the gravedigger,' said Tom Ellis, as we stood before the figure. Tom had lived around Llanbabo for sixty years, and Barry had put me in touch with him as the person most likely to know of any folklore or legends concerning the church. It was already proving a valuable meeting. 'Pabo apparently held a rose in the other hand,' Tom added.

'Why a rose?' I asked.

'It was said to represent his queen.' Tom explained how legend held that Pabo's wife had died after she pricked her finger on a poisonous rose thorn. 'Pabo clutched the rose in honour of her memory,' he said.

Once more, a folktale concerning this mysterious, name-less queen. Could it, again, refer to the Virgin Mary, and to Pabo's role as guardian of her remains? From the earliest years of Christianity, Mary had been symbolized by the rose. The rosary is named after her – the word actually means 'rose garden' – and most strings of rosary beads still have the image of a rose on the reverse side of the crucifix.

'No one seems to know what Pabo's queen was called,' I said.

'I think by "his queen" the story concerns Pabo's devotion to Saint Mary,' said Tom. I was taken aback: I had not even mentioned the Virgin Mary.

'You mean because the rose is her symbol?' I said.

'Because of the Queen of Hearts. Isn't she supposed to have met with the same fate?'

I knew that in the old children's rhyme, 'The Queen of Hearts', the queen is supposed to have pricked her finger on a rose-bush and died, but I had no idea how that tied up with the Virgin Mary. 'I'm sorry, I don't follow you,' I said.

'The Queen of Hearts represents Saint Mary.' I was still no wiser, so he explained.

When Tom was a boy, the Llanbabo vicar would tell the Sunday school children that the four queens of the playing-card deck were a reminder of the Lady Days. These were four religious festivals, halfway between the solstices and equinoxes, when certain female saints were venerated: 1 February, 1 May, 1 August and 1 November. Apparently, the fifty-two cards of the pack represented the weeks of the year, the four suits were the four seasons and the four queens were the festival days of the saints – St Mary, St Bridget, St Joan and St Ann. Each festival occurred in a different season and, as such, Mary was the Queen of Hearts.

Tom could tell me no more about this tradition of the cards, but it appears to have been more than the vicar's invention. In the pre-Christian Celtic calendar these same days were the most important festivals of the year: Imbolc, Beltane, Lughasadh and Samhain. Each of them had been sacred to a goddess: Eostre, Epona, Danna and Briganta. The goddess Briganta became Christianized as St Bridget and Danna as St Ann. Catherine ultimately replaced Epona and the most important of the goddesses, Eostre, was replaced by the most venerated saint, the Virgin Mary. Each goddess had a flower sacred to her which thereafter became the emblem of the saint. Eostre's and later Mary's flower was the rose. The queens of the playing-card pack are each depicted with one of these same flowers, and the Queen of Hearts holds a rose. Tom, it seemed, was right about a link between the Virgin Mary and the Queen of Hearts.

In the Llanbabo legend the rose represented Pabo's queen, someone who is said to have died in the same unusual way as the Queen of Hearts in the folklore of the playing cards. If the Queen of Hearts is the Virgin Mary, so also, perhaps, is Pabo's queen. This possible link with the playing cards brought me back to the Tarot and the Grail romances. The four queens of the playing cards originated with the four queens of the Tarot, each of whom was depicted holding the same flowers. Hearts originated with the suit of Cups, so if Mary is the Queen of Hearts then she is also the Queen of Cups. Might there be some link between this and Robert de Boron's cup of the Last Supper, which also appears to have symbolized the Virgin Mary?

'Is there any legend that associates this church with the Holy Grail?' I asked.

'You mean the story of Madoc,' said Tom.

Tom told me that there was an old story about a Welsh adventurer in the Middle Ages who supposedly discovered the Grail in Llanbabo church. Unfortunately, he could not remember the details of the story or where, precisely, the Grail was said to have been found.

Mary seemed connected to the church, represented as Pabo's queen, and now, remarkably, the Grail too. I now had further reason than the Llanerchymedd rhyme alone to believe that Mary's relics had been moved to Llanbabo church. I had already discovered that Anglesey legends often turned out to be based on oral accounts of genuine historical events. One folktale connected with Llanbedrgoch, in the south-east of the island, told how a Viking called Peter the Red had his palace in the village. The name of the village actually means 'Parish of Red Peter' (*Bedr* is Welsh for Peter and *goch* means 'red'). Historians were sceptical that the area really did contain a Viking palace, until excavations by Cardiff University in 1997 uncovered an entire Viking village, complete with a chieftain's residence.

'Besides Pabo, were any other saints buried here?' I asked.

'He's the only one I know of but an *empty* tomb was found.' Tom led me now to the opposite side of the church. 'A small tomb was here until the eighteen hundreds. Apparently, no body was found in it when it was opened around

1870, so it was filled in when the foundations were repaired. All that had been inside was an empty stone box.' He explained that the box had been much too small for a coffin, and had rather irreverently been used as an umbrella stand until the vicar threw it out in the 1950s. Evidently, it no longer existed – it had been broken up and used along with other stones to level the playground at a nearby school.

'How big was it?' I asked. An intriguing possibility was occurring to me.

Tom held out his hands to indicate about half a metre square.

Was it possible, I wondered, that this had been an ossuary – one that had contained Mary's bones? If so, then her remains had been moved again. I had already, because of the dedication of the church, begun to suspect that she might have been moved a second time. The *Babo* in its name actually means 'Pabo', in its grammatically mutated form. This was St Pabo's church. Mary was a more important saint than Pabo, so if it ever had contained her relics they were now long gone.

Had the bones been moved back to Llanerchymedd or to St Mary's church in Llangadwaladr, perhaps? The first question I needed to answer was *when* they might have been moved. Perhaps, when the church was rededicated to Pabo? Unfortunately, no such records survived. There was, though, another way to date any possible move.

'Was there ever a time when the church was in danger of being looted?' I asked.

'During the late twelfth century,' said Tom, 'when the Normans first tried to invade northern Wales. That's when Madoc was supposed to have discovered the Grail.'

'Madoc was a real person?' When Tom had mentioned him before, I had just assumed he was a fictional character.

'Oh yes. He was a prince of Gwynedd. They say he discovered America.'

Now I knew who he was talking about. Madoc ap Owain – one of the most enigmatic figures in Welsh history. His connection with the Grail legend was a new one to me. Later, I would re-investigate his story.

By the time we left the church the rain was lashing down. The churchyard was awash with mud, and water gushed from the broken guttering of the chapel roof. Repeated flashes of lightning illuminated the glistening gravestones, the thunder following almost at once. I had left my car over on the other side of the little hamlet up the lane and Tom was going in the opposite direction. He bade me farewell, put up his umbrella, and hurried down the path. As I sheltered in the doorway, waiting for the rain to ease, a fork of lightning cut through the sky and touched down in an adjacent field – less than fifty metres away. I had never before been so close to a lightning strike and was surprised that I could actually feel the discharge, as a tingling sensation, a split second before the thunder crack hit. The hair stood up all over my body as the thunder rolled on and the smell of ionized gas filled my nostrils. There really *was* electricity in the air.

Lightning flashed again, followed by another ear-shattering bang. Nervously, I looked up at the solitary tree, its huge, spreading branches dwarfing the tiny chapel. I was standing directly below the highest thing in the area. I covered my head with my jacket and ran.

*

I spent that night at Barry Davis's house in Bangor. Barry knew all about the story of Madoc and we discussed it into the late hours. Madoc's life had been set against the backdrop of the Norman invasion and what must surely be one of the oddest propaganda exercises in history.

When the Normans invaded England in 1066, they began to use the popular Welsh stories of King Arthur to legitimate their rule. The Norman kings of England, of French blood, needed desperately to prove their divine right to govern the Anglo-Saxons. At a time of poor communications, more than just armies were required to maintain order: the monarchy needed the support of the Church. Also, the continental Capetian dynasty was repeatedly laying claim to the English throne, further pressurizing the Normans to legitimate their rule.

Many Saxon noblemen could rightly claim descent from the true kings of England, such as Athelstan and Alfred the Great, so the Normans needed their own heroic and majestic ancestor. Having grounds for claiming succession from the Celtic Britons, many of whom had fled to France and settled in Normandy during the Saxon invasion of the sixth century, it was to them that they looked. In Welsh legend the greatest Briton was the fabled warrior Arthur. Although next to nothing was known of the time that he was said to have lived, Geoffrey of Monmouth's work transformed this legendary Celt into a medieval-style king, complete with castles, knights and the rules of chivalry. He thus made Arthur both attractive and accessible to the Norman elite – they now had the noble ancestor they sought.

Geoffrey's work was actively promoted by the English king Henry I, who effectively utilized it to counter the claims of the Saxon barons. In Celtic Wales, however, his ploy backfired. The Saxons had never succeeded in conquering Wales; here the Celts were free. If Arthur existed, then he belonged to the Welsh. More so than the Normans, the Welsh were the *direct* descendants of the ancient Britons.

For centuries Wales had been divided into many smaller kingdoms, with much distrust of one another. This worked very much to the Normans' advantage when they invaded south Wales and consolidated their hold over the area in the early twelfth century. In north Wales, however, fear of conquest had a unifying effect, and its tiny kingdoms were drawn together by Gruffudd ap Cynan, the king of Gwynedd. Under his leadership the north resisted, ensuring the survival of an independent Wales for decades to come.

After the death of Henry I in 1135, Gruffudd seized the initiative and used the dead king's own propaganda against his Norman successor, King Stephen. He employed the Arthurian story to remind the Welsh of their past greatness and successfully instigated an uprising in the south. After Gruffudd's death in 1137 his son, Owain ap Gruffudd, strengthened his hand by taking the Arthurian initiative one stage further – if the Normans believed that descent from Arthur legitimated their rule over the English, then precisely the opposite applied in the case of the Welsh. Owain should and, he promised, would, reconquer England itself. To this end he claimed descent from Arthur, assumed the title *Penadur* – meaning 'Chief Arthur' – and adopted the red dragon, said to have been Arthur's emblem, as the Welsh national banner. This heyday of Arthurian-inspired nationalism still has echoes in Wales today. The red dragon remains on the Welsh national flag and the word *penadur*, meaning 'sovereign', still survives in modern Welsh.

Although Owain never conquered England, he successfully resisted the English for over thirty years. During this time Wales began to commit to writing many of its own Arthurian stories to counter those in England, and many have survived in Welsh national manuscripts such as those in *The Red Book of Hergest*. Whereas the Arthur of England became ever more Norman, the Welsh Arthur remained firmly Celtic – an ancient warrior surrounded by heroes, demigods and mythical beings from early British folklore.

By the late 1160s Wales was again in trouble. Not only had Owain ap Gruffudd's pledge to reconquer England come to nothing, but the English were once more firmly in control of the south. When he died in 1170, civil war broke out between his sons: his chosen successor Hywel faced an alliance led by his brothers Rhodri and Dafydd. Hywel was soon defeated, but almost immediately Rhodri and Dafydd began to squabble. It was the perfect opportunity for English invasion.

Here begins the strange story of Madoc ap Owain. Madoc, Rhodri and Dafydd's younger brother, tried to reconcile the two, but to no avail. Convinced that the English were about to invade, he decided to seek assistance from the French king Louis VII, who had been at war with the English king Henry II. Unknown to Madoc, Louis had made peace with Henry the previous year and so the trip proved fruitless. Having failed in his objective, Madoc returned to Wales only to find his brothers still at each other's throats.

In historical perspective the Welsh had no reason to fear an English invasion, as Henry II had turned his attentions to Ireland. However, at the time, Madoc was convinced that Wales was finished. He decided to flee Britain altogether and set sail to find the mythical Fortunate Isles, which were supposed to exist across the western seas.

The earliest account of Madoc's voyage comes from the Flemish poet Willem van Hulst, who spent time in north Wales and appears to have written the story around 1200. This is known from the Dutch copyist Jacob van Mearlant who refers to Willem's *Voyage of Madoc* in the year 1255. Although no original copy of Willem's work has survived, it is partly preserved in a fourteenth-century French translation.

In the story, Madoc sets sail using a 'magic stone' – probably a magnetic lodestone – to guide him. He sails out into the Atlantic and apparently reaches an uninhabited 'paradise in the sun, where fruits grew in abundance'. He returns and, although he produces exotic plants that no one has seen before, he fails to convince others that his new-found land is anything but a yarn.

It is not known what land Madoc is supposed to have discovered, but some believe that it was one of the Canary Isles, others that it was one of the West Indies, and still others that it was mainland America. At Mobile Bay in Alabama a plaque on the beach marks the spot where locals believe Madoc came ashore, three centuries before the time of Columbus.

There can be little doubt that, historically, Madoc made some kind of voyage. Around 1200, the Welsh scholar Llywarch ap Llywelyn made reference to his departure. There are two further references in the fifteenth century: around 1450 Ieuan Brechfa, a poet and historian, wrote that Madoc had sailed in search of 'a fair land across the oceans, unknown and unproved', and in 1470 Maredudd ap Rhys, a clergyman from Ruabon, also wrote that Madoc had discovered a mysterious new land. An extant contemporary reference to Madoc reveals both that he was a seaman and that he possessed a ship. The twelfth-century maritime archives known as *The Black Book of Admiralty*, of which only fragments survive, includes amongst its entries for 1171 the ship *Guignon Gorn*, which is recorded as belonging to Madoc. This tends to confirm that Madoc did attempt some kind of voyage, but sheds no light on any new land he may have discovered.

Further credence is afforded Willem's account by discoveries made by two sixteenth-century historians. The first, the Elizabethan scholar Sir George Peckham, in his pamphlet *A True Report* published in 1583, claimed to have found reference to Madoc's discovery of a new land in a fifteenth-century text. The following year another English scholar, Dr David Powel, published his *History of Cambria*, which included an account of Madoc's voyage. He confirms the existence of Peckham's source, which he reveals was a work by Gutyn Owen, a reliable Welsh historian who worked out of Basingwerk monastery near Flint in the 1480s and 90s. Owen was certainly in a position to examine the Madoc story at first hand, as he had access to the annals of Basingwerk monastery, which then contained the surviving records of the medieval princes of north Wales. Although both the annals of Basingwerk and Owen's own work were destroyed during the dissolution of the monasteries, Owen's reference to Madoc's voyage was included verbatim in Peckham's book:

[Madoc] left the land in contention between his brethren and prepared certain ships with men and munitions, and sought adventures by the seas, sailing west, leaving the coast of Ireland so far north, that he came to a land unknown where he saw many strange things . . . After he had returned home, and declared the pleasant and fruitful countries that he had seen without inhabitants, none who heard him would believe and he was shunned by his fellow countrymen.

'This is where the Grail comes into the story,' said Barry. 'According to Peckham, when Madoc returned he was branded a liar and so mocked that he went off to become a monk. He joined the monastery at Penmon and eventually became the priest of Llanbabo church. It was while he was there that, according to Peckham, he discovered the Grail.' Barry read from the account:

> When Madoc was in old age he discovered here the most illustrious Grail and fearing that the English would lay waste to the island returned it to the *Cornu Copia* where the blessed Saint Cybi ascended.

'Peckham does not say where this is but it's certainly a strange statement,' said Barry. 'In Latin *Cornu Copia* means "Horn of Plenty", and refers to the magical drinking horn of the gods. You see, it's not actually a place. Peckham does not elucidate, so I can only assume that he had simply copied what Owen had written.'

'What about the Grail?' I said. 'Was it a chalice?'

'Yes, the cup of the Last Supper.'

'If I'm right about the chalice being a symbol for Mary, then Madoc may have discovered her remains in Llanbabo church,' I said. 'Perhaps in the stone box in the tomb.'

'If he did, she is probably still on Anglesey,' said Barry. 'Whatever the *Cornu Copia* is meant to be, Peckham says that Cybi ascended from there. This presumably refers to Cybi's legendary ascent to heaven which took place at some unnamed site on Anglesey.'

Barry explained that the Latin *Life of Cybi* now exists in a manuscript collection dating from the early thirteenth century in the British Library. Apparently, it was a translation from an older Welsh original. According to the account, Cybi was off praying on his own when 'Our Lady and her multitude of angels came and took the most holy body of Cybi to heaven'. (Cybi was the saint who met Seiriol each day.)

'Unlike Peckham's account, *The Life of Cybi* does not mention the words *Cornu Copia*, but there are at least three places that I know of which local folklore associates with the site of Cybi's ascension.' Barry opened the map and pointed them out. One was Cybi's monastery at Holyhead, another was by a pool called Llyn Hendref on the Cors Bodwrog stream near Gwalchmai, and another was at an ancient earthwork beside the Cors-y-bol stream at Llantriant.

'There must have been some confusion here,' I said. 'The Horn of Plenty is basically an ancient Greek equivalent of Robert de Boron's Grail chalice. The original story of Madoc was written at more or less the same time that Robert wrote his Joseph story. The succession of writers before Peckham may have thought that the *Cornu Copia* was a place when, in reality, it was just another Grail. In other words, Madoc had taken one Grail – Mary's remains – back to the location of another Grail – another holy relic.'

'You mean at Llanerchymedd church?'

'It's my best bet at the moment.'

'That's interesting,' said Barry, flicking through another book. 'I thought I had seen something similar. The *Folie* romance refers to one of the Grail Hallows – the plate of the Last Supper – as the *Cors Cappa*, although it fails to say why. Perhaps we have another mistranslation.' Barry pointed out that in the *Folie* the plate seems to have been the most sacred of the four Grail Hallows because, unlike the others, it is kept in a draped box. The engraving of it in the extant version in the Bibliothèque Nationale in Paris shows a chunky box, large enough to contain many artefacts. 'Surely too much room for just one plate,' he said.

'You think there was meant to be something on the plate?' I said.

'A head? In Old French *Cors Cappa* means literally "Crow Head".'

'The name Bran means "crow",' I said.

'Yes, and in the Welsh *Peredur* romance the hero sees a similar procession in Joseph's chapel to the one Perceval sees in the *Folie*, except that there is only one artefact – a head on a plate – Bran's head.'

'But Bran is still alive when the procession comes in,' I said.

'I know, but it might have been symbolic. Remember your theory about the head representing the alternative apostolic succession? The guardian of the chapel becomes the alternative Pope. Bran may be alive but his head – his office – is something more. It can be inherited by Perceval. "The king is dead. Long live the king." ' Barry went on to suggest that the original author of the Madoc story may have referred to Madoc taking the Grail to the *Cors Cappa* – Bran's head – and someone by Owen's time who did not understand Old French had mistranslated it as *Cornu Copia* – Horn of Plenty. 'It's possible that the original account had Madoc returning the Grail – Mary's bones, let's say – to the alternative Pope.'

'Who by this time, after the Vikings left, may have returned to the original Grail chapel at Llanerchymedd,' I suggested.

I went to bed that night with my mind spinning with the new discoveries. Chalices, severed heads, playing cards and ancient goddesses all floated before my eyes as I lay there half-awake and half-asleep. Half an hour later, I awoke from one of the most vivid dreams I have ever had. I had been confronted by a huge black crow. My subconscious had solved the riddle. I now knew where to look.

It was still way before dawn but I got up, hurried downstairs and opened the map of Anglesey. I immediately found what I had missed. I opened a copy of Barry's Welsh dictionary. I was right.

'It was the name of these streams,' I said to Barry later that morning, as I pointed out the locations associated with Cybi's ascent to heaven. One had been a pool next to a stream called Cors Bodwrog, and another had been at an earthwork beside a stream called Cors-y-bol. 'The name Cors,' I continued. 'When you mentioned *Cors Cappa* last night, I knew it sounded familiar, I just couldn't think why. The reason was, I had just seen the word Cors on the map. In fact, there are streams called Cors all over the place. Unconsciously, in my tired state, I obviously suspected that the word referred to a stream. When I looked it up in your Welsh dictionary, my suspicions were confirmed. In modern Welsh the word *cors* means "marsh" but comes from the Old Welsh where it specifically refers to a stream that flows through a marshy area. If you take the words *Cors Cappa* as a cross between Old Welsh and Old French you get "Stream Head" – head of a stream – its source. I think Mary's remains were taken back to the well at the source of the Alaw.'

Barry thought for a moment. 'You may be on to something. With all the translating and retranslating of these old romances, at some point such a confusion could easily have come about. A Welsh author might have written "stream head" something like *Cors Pen* – *pen* is Welsh for "head" – and the translator rightly transcribed *Pen* for *Cappa* but had failed to see the relevance of a stream and assumed the word was the same as the French for "crow". This would seem to make more sense to him, as Bran's head was firmly associated with the story.'

'Perhaps when Madoc decided to lay Mary to rest at the sacred well,' I suggested, 'it was being wrongly referred to as *Cors Cappa*, and by Peckham's time it had been further corrupted to *Cornu Copia*.'

'The more sense people tried to make of the story, the less sense it actually made,' added Barry.

'Even if I'm wrong about *Cors Cappa* being the stream head, it still makes sense for Mary's remains to have been buried at the well. Peckham says that Madoc took the "Grail" to where Cybi ascended to heaven. What better place to become associated with Cybi's ascension to heaven than the well he supposedly visited each day?'

The more we discussed it, the more it seemed fitting that the well was where Mary's remains were buried. As the source of the Alaw, there could be little doubt that it was a most hallowed site to the pre-Christian Druids. As an important spring, it would have been sacred to the goddess Eostre. She had been the most exalted and widely worshipped of all the Celtic deities. She had even been adopted by the Anglo-Saxons before they converted to Christianity. At some point after the Celts became Christians, Mary assumed the role of Eostre as she had with Artemis in Ephesus. It stood to reason that Eostre's well became sacred to the Virgin Mary. If Madoc had decided finally to commit her bones to the soil, what more appropriate place?

Nevertheless, Barry and I both agreed that we lacked the kind of evidence necessary to persuade archaeologists that the site was worth excavating. To put the theory to the test, we would have to employ geophysics. Barry agreed to contact the Anglesey Highways and Technical Services Department, who were responsible for the roadside verge on which the well was situated, and see if they would grant permission for the scan. I decided to phone James Whitmore, one of the most sympathetic archaeologists I knew. Although he had no jurisdiction in north Wales, he might know how to put me in touch with a geophysics team we could afford.

'It's the ground-penetrating radar that costs all the money,' he said, when I called him later that day. Such a device is generally used to search for geological anomalies deep underground, he explained: rock formations, for example, that help in the exploration for mineral deposits. 'You don't really need that kind of data if you're only looking for a grave.' He told me he knew of a young couple who, although not full-time professionals, had all the equipment we would need. Helen and Simon Bourne were respected in their field and were often called upon to carry out geophysics surveys for the county archaeologists in Somerset. As it turned out, Helen and Simon were happy to help and their rates were good.

Barry, in the meantime, had contacted the highways department who said they had no objection to us conducting a geophysics scan around the well, provided we left no mess and caused no damage. It was OK, though, for us to cut back some of the brambles in the area we had described.

Over the next couple of weeks, while I waited for the

window in Helen and Simon's busy schedule, I attempted to discover all I could about Cilgwyn, the rural district around the well. John Smith from the Anglesey museum generously provided me with all the information I needed. However, nothing new came to light – not so much as a legend. Even a local farmer to whom I showed the well was completely surprised it was there. No one seemed to have known of its existence.

A couple of days before the geophysics scan, I picked up, for the last time, what may have been the trail of Giovanni Benedetti. Or rather, Barry did. After his own discoveries, particularly of Paulinus' name on the Tre-Ysgawen stone, Barry was intrigued to find out whether Benedetti had actually visited Anglesey. But he could find no record of him in any archives connected with Bangor University or the National Library of Wales. He was about to give up searching when he decided to have a look at the visitor books of Llanerchymedd church. Most British churches have a visitor book – a tradition dating back to Victorian times – and many keep them for posterity. There is usually a column for the name, one for the address and one for comments. St Mary's of Llanerchymedd was now closed, but Barry traced the parish records to the ecclesiastical archives of the bishop of Bangor. He was able to examine a copy of the visitor book covering 1950. Although he failed to find the name Giovanni Benedetti, he did discover someone who might have been him. The 4th of October of that year saw a cryptic entry. The address column was left blank but the name column bore the initials G.B. In the comments column were just two Latin words, *Veni Vidi* – 'I came. I saw.' If this *was* Benedetti, he seems to have found what he was looking for.

The weekend of the geophysics scan finally arrived, and

Barry and I joined Simon and Helen in the British Hotel. The couple explained what they intended to do.

'Firstly we will make soil tests,' said Simon. 'These will determine how acidic or waterlogged the ground is. From this, we'll have some idea to what degree any remains might have decomposed. Then we'll use the magnetometer. It should detect any magnetic anomalies, such as metal artefacts. It will also help to determine whether or not the ground has been disturbed in the past and to what depth. inally, the resistivity meter will produce a computer-generated image of whatever, if anything, is down there.'

I took the three of them to the local Indian restaurant and we talked late into the night. Helen was genuinely intrigued by my search for the Virgin Mary, but Simon was somewhat sceptical. I told him of my theory concerning Joseph as the disciple with whom Mary spent her last days. I also told him of the historical accounts of Joseph's voyage to Britain, about the feasibility of such a journey, and about Augustine's letter. I explained why I thought that Llanerchymedd was the site of Augustine's church and how the trail of clues had led to the well. He accepted that it was all quite possible. But, as for most archaeologists, for him 'possible' was light years from 'probable'.

It turned out to be a perfect day for the operation. The sun shone brightly in a cloudless sky as Barry and I cut down the brambles around the well. A few passing locals eyed us suspiciously as Helen and Simon began to take soil samples but, strangely, no one stopped to ask what we were doing. For the remainder of the morning the couple continued taking various readings with their equipment, and by midday they had run all the data through their lap-top computer and an image was beginning to form on the screen.

By the look on Helen's face, I could tell that the initial results were disappointing. 'I was using the magnetometer,' she said. 'But it's come up with nothing more than a few bits of metal close to the surface: probably old tin cans.' When she began to run the resistivity-meter findings through the computer, though, her expression changed. 'It looks like we've got something here,' she said.

A series of dark patches began to form on the screen. To me, it looked as meaningless as the previous results. Then again, I had no idea what I was seeing. 'Here,' she said, indicating a roughly oblong shape to the left of the image. 'That shows that the soil here has been dug out at some point in the past and then replaced. In real terms it's about two metres long and a metre wide.' She explained that by correlating the information with the magnetometer readings they could tell how deep the anomaly was. Evidently, magnetized rocks that they had found on the surface elsewhere along the verge were registering here at a greater depth. This meant they had found their way into the bottom of the trench when it was dug. 'It's a bit less than two metres deep,' she said.

'So we have what is commonly called a six-foot hole,' said Barry, with a smile. 'A grave!'

'It is the sort of reading you might expect to find in connection with a grave,' said Simon, cautiously. 'It's certainly a manmade trench. However, from the geophysics alone we can't determine its purpose.'

'So there's no body in it,' said Barry. He sounded more disappointed than *I* was.

'There might have been,' said Helen. 'Unfortunately, there's no way to know without excavating.' Because of both the type of soil and the waterlogged conditions the bones would long ago have decomposed, she explained. 'Archae-ology might reveal the discolouration in the soil where bones had been, but there'd be no way to date them.'

'What about radiocarbon dating?' I said.

'Unfortunately not. You need clean samples to detect any meaningful carbon-14. With all the moisture in the soil, there would be just too much seepage – contamination from surrounding organic matter.'

'And there's no evidence of artefacts?' I asked.

'I'm afraid not. Nothing that's survived, at any rate.'

I did not know whether to be disappointed or pleased. On the one hand the results did show that what seemed to be a grave lay beside the well. On the other, there was no way, even with a dig, to determine how old it was or whose remains it might contain. It seemed that, once again, I was in the position I had been in at the Berth. The trail of clues had led to what appeared to be a grave, but there was no way to know for sure. I had never expected to prove anything to the archaeological community, but it would have been nice to know for my own satisfaction that I had reached the end of the trail.

'Where exactly is this trench?' I asked.

'Just over there, in front of that stone.' Helen pointed to an area, some three metres to the south-west of the well, just beyond the fallen mark-stone.

The mark-stone!

'Barry, what do you think this is?' I said, ushering him over to the fallen stone.

'I was looking at that earlier,' he said. 'It's probably a boundary stone. They were used to mark the edge of a farmer's property in the Middle Ages.'

Graham, Jodi and I had examined it before. It was grey

granite, about one and a half metres long and rounded at one end. Although it was now on its side, split in two and half covered with turf, it could clearly be seen that it had been shaped by human hands. I had assumed it might have been a mark-stone for the well. Now that I looked at it again, it reminded me very much of another stone I had recently seen.

'Don't you think it looks like the one at Tre-Ysgawen?' I said to Barry.

'Yes, I suppose so – why?'

'That was a gravestone, wasn't it?'

Simon came over to examine it for himself. 'It's what you might expect to find marking an old grave,' he said, in his usual archaeological tone. 'But there's nothing to suggest it is.'

'Except that you've just found a grave-size hole right next to it,' I said.

Simon still remained as scientifically detached as possible, but Helen was already on her way back to their Range Rover. A few seconds later she returned with a crowbar. 'Let's turn it over,' she said. 'See if anything's on the other side.' With all four of us heaving and struggling, we finally managed to turn it over. However, our efforts were in vain. Apart from the largest number of centipedes I had ever seen, the underside was as featureless as the top.

'There's another one here,' said Barry, pointing into the thicket. About two metres away, just visible beneath the brambles, was a second, smaller stone. It was of golden sandstone and had clearly been shaped. It was rectangular, approximately thirty-five centimetres long and just over half as wide. Like the larger stone, it was lying flat and half-buried in the earth.

'One stone might be a coincidence,' said Helen, as she used the crowbar to push back the thorns, 'but two . . .'

Barry agreed. 'You would not have two boundary stones in the same place.'

'An old milestone?' suggested Simon.

'Or a footstone?' said Helen. She added that in the Middle Ages it was common practice to erect both a headstone and a smaller footstone over a grave.

There was nothing discernible on the upper side, so we heaved it over. 'I think we have something,' said Barry, as he scraped off the dirt with a stick. There seemed to be something carved into it.

Helen collected water from the well and began to clean it down. 'There *is* something,' she said. 'Just one letter, quite large. Looks like a letter W.' About three-quarters of the way up the surface there was what appeared to be a rounded letter W, carved into the stone to a depth of about half a centimetre on one side but shallower on the other, where it had worn away. The design was about ten centimetres square and was clearly no natural formation.

Simon twisted his head to look at it upside-down. 'It's a letter M,' he said. 'The Roman numeral for a thousand. A thousand miles, presumably. I told you it was a milestone.'

'A thousand miles to where?' I asked.

'Rome?' he suggested.

'I thought the Romans measured . . .' I was cut off in mid-sentence by Helen, who was still cleaning up the stone.

'Hold it!' she said, excitedly. 'It's not a letter M.' Now she had fully cleaned away the mud, we could see that there was an extra loop on the right-hand side.

'What is it?' asked Barry.

'Its a Greek glyph,' she said. 'The astrological symbol for Virgo.'

'The Virgin,' I said, as we all stared down at the stone.

As unlikely as it might at first sound, was this remote corner of Wales really the final resting place of the Virgin Mary?

The mother of Jesus does indeed seem to have come to Britain. John's gospel tells us that Mary spent her final days with the disciple who was at the foot of the cross. Only two disciples are at the foot of the cross in any of the gospel accounts, and one of them – Joseph of Arimathea – is the only candidate who places the account in an historical context. In Jewish tradition Mary's closest male relative would have been responsible for her welfare, and her son's closest male relative would have been responsible for his burial. Joseph buried Jesus, so he must have been his closest male relative and, by definition, Mary's too. If the Bible is right, Mary must have spent her final days with Joseph of Arimathea.

Joseph of Arimathea seems to have come to Britain. Now in the Vatican Library, the fourth-century *Evangelium Nicodemi* and its contemporary *Vindicta Salvatoris* both record that Joseph fled Palestine and settled outside the Roman empire, somewhere in the far north. The twelfth-century Grail romances all portray the land as Britain. If Joseph really did come to this country, then presumably so did Mary.

In the sixth century it was seemingly believed that Mary was buried here. In 545 the monk Gildas, in the oldest surviving British history book, says that disciples of Jesus came to Britain in AD 37. In 597 St Augustine wrote to the Pope telling him that he had discovered a church built by such disciples on an island in the west of Britain. He says that it was dedicated to the Virgin Mary at a time when such a dedication could only mean that the church was thought to house her tomb or at least her bones.

Augustine describes the church as being on a large, royal island in the west. Anglesey was a large royal island in the west. Aberffraw on Anglesey was the seat of the kings of Gwynedd in Augustine's time, as demonstrated by the Cata-manus inscription in Llangadwaladr church. There was only one other island that would match this description: the Isle of Man. According to the respected historian William of Malmesbury, writing around 1130, Augustine travelled widely along the coast of Wales but never crossed over to Man. Even without the Avalon connections – Gwynedd as the White Land, the link with the historical Arthur and the legend of Bran – these points alone make it almost certain that Augustine's church was on Anglesey.

According to William, Augustine's assistant Paulinus stayed on to help repair the church. There can be little doubt that Paulinus visited Anglesey, as demonstrated by the contemporary inscription on the Tre-Ysgawen stone. Only a couple of kilometres from the stone is Llanerchymedd church, which the research by John Smith, the curator of the Anglesey museum, suggests is the oldest on the island. Like Augustine's church, it is dedicated to the Virgin Mary.

I was convinced that Llanerchymedd church was the one in Augustine's account and was fairly certain that it once contained what were believed to be Mary's remains. Any relics in the church would certainly have been moved when the Vikings invaded in the tenth century, and Llanbabo church is apparently where they were taken, as evidenced by King Pabo's tombstone.

The evidence for the grave beside the well being Mary's ultimate resting place was, however, far more circumstantial, and relied on the accuracy of the Madoc story and, of course, my interpretation of it. Interestingly, though, as if to complete the circle of my investigation, it was Father Rinsonelli who provided a last piece of evidence to support the possibility that the grave was Mary's. A few weeks after the geophysics survey, I phoned him to share our findings. I had expected him to be uncomfortable with the whole idea, but I wanted to hear his comments, all the same. However, although he did not believe that Mary's bones remained on earth, he did accept that in St Augustine's time they might have been thought to be housed in a church on Anglesey. Moreover, he believed that the Virgo sign was an important indicator that we had found where the purported relics might finally have been buried. He explained that in the Middle Ages, at the time that Madoc lived, the Virgo glyph was indeed used to symbolize the Virgin Mary. In fact, the medieval reliquary, the elaborate box used to hold Mary's relics at Calcata – the ones that turned out to be sheep bones – actually has such a symbol in gold relief on its lid.

Whether the person buried at the Llanerchymedd well really was the mother of Christ, I would probably never know. However, it certainly seemed that someone believed so, once.

My quest to discover the historical Mary had begun in the Vatican, had taken me through the ancient land of Israel, the Roman city of Ephesus and ultimately to this remote part of Wales. In my search to uncover the truth about this mysterious woman, I had discovered a Christian history very different from anything I was taught in school. After my conversation with Father Rinsonelli, I paid a final visit to the grave and in my mind went over the most likely scenario for the historical life – and afterlife – of Mary, the mother of Christ.

Around 20 BC, Mary was born in Capernaum. She was the daughter of Matthias, the priest of the Capernaum synagogue, and Anna, a woman who could trace her descent from the royal house of David. Some ten years later Mary moved to Jerusalem, after Matthias was appointed high priest of the great temple. Here, Anna became a prophetess and Mary grew up in the temple precincts.

As the daughter of the most important religious figure in Israel, Mary was married to King Herod's first son, Antipater, the Roman-endorsed heir to the Jewish throne. When the king's sister Salome skilfully poisoned Herod's mind against his eldest son in favour of her nephew Philip, Antipater was arrested and killed. The arrest of Antipater's family was ordered, but Mary escaped and was smuggled out of the palace in the company of the sympathetic Joseph.

In hiding, in humble surroundings in nearby Bethlehem, Mary gave birth to Antipater's son, Jesus, the true heir to the Jewish throne. At the time, a new and mysterious star appeared in the skies which the Essenes of Qumran took as the long-awaited portent of the Messiah's birth. A company of priests were sent to the prophesied town of Bethlehem to seek out a newborn child. Here they discovered Jesus and, learning that he was truly king of the Jews and that his mother was of David's line, accepted him as the divine son of God, the priest-king who, it had been foretold, would unite and free the people of Israel.

In Jerusalem, Matthias was arrested and made to reveal the whereabouts of Mary and her child. The furious Herod ordered the massacre of all the babies in Bethlehem to prevent the heir's escape. Mary and Joseph, however, managed to flee to the safety of Egypt where they were offered sanctuary by Antipater's friend, Antiphilus, a provincial official. When Herod died, shortly after, Mary and the baby returned to Israel but, as it was unsafe for them in Jerusalem or Capernaum, where Mary was known, they settled in the town of Nazareth. Here, Joseph married Mary, raised a family and made a prosperous living as a carpenter.

When he reached his teens, Jesus left Nazareth to enter the Qumran monastery and began his training as the chosen Messiah. By the time he eventually left the monastery at the age of thirty, he had formed his own unique ideas about the Kingdom of God. He returned to Nazareth, but his mother and brothers refused to accept his new philosophy. Instead, he persuaded his cousins in Capernaum to join him.

As pretender to the Jewish throne, Jesus was ultimately executed by Pontius Pilate, but before his death he was reconciled with his immediate family, who came to accept that he truly spoke with the authority of God. On the cross, he gave his widowed mother into the care of Joseph, his eldest brother. Fearing for their lives, Mary and her second son fled the Roman empire and boarded a trading vessel bound for the copper mines of Britain. After arriving on the island of Anglesey, they lived amongst the Druids and converted them to their unique form of Judaism.

Half a century later, Paul's brand of Christianity had established itself in Ephesus where Mary, as Christ's mother, was venerated as the new Artemis. By the time Constantine created the unified Catholic Church in AD 325, Ephesian Christianity had spread throughout the empire and Mary was widely venerated as the Queen of Heaven.

After state Christianity was established in Britain, Marian devotion quickly spread throughout the country and Joseph's chapel acquired a new significance – it housed the tomb of the Mother of God. However, as the empress Helena had already decided that Mary's tomb was really in Ephesus, the Christians of Anglesey were compelled to keep the site a secret from Rome.

When the western empire collapsed, cutting off Britain from the Roman Church, Christianity developed independently here and the church at Llanerchymedd became the holy centre of the Celtic Church. After the British king Owain Ddantgwyn – the historical Arthur – unified the fragmented Britons and defeated the Anglo-Saxons, his nephew and son became the rulers of western Britain. Another son, Seiriol, became a leading figure in the Celtic Church and the custodian of Joseph's chapel.

By this time, the bones of saints were being credited with miraculous properties, and in western Britain Mary's bones were considered the most sacred relics of all. They could heal the sick, bring spiritual salvation and assure a place in heaven. Seiriol's successors, like Pabo, became the guardians of these sacred relics.

When Augustine arrived in Britain as an envoy of the Pope in 597, he discovered that the Celtic Church still survived in the west. He was taken to see Joseph's chapel as evidence of the spiritual authority of the Celtic Church. Not only did it house the most important relics of all, its guardian claimed apostolic succession from Joseph of Arimathea and Christ himself. When Pope Gregory was told of this, unable to accept anyone but himself as absolute head of the Church, he ordered Augustine to convert the Celts. Augustine left his assistant Paulinus to lead the mission, but when this failed the Pope decided to ignore the matter and censored any mention of the chapel, its guardians or its supposed relics.

Over the next three centuries, as the Catholic Church secured its hold over the British people, the devotees of Joseph's chapel became increasingly isolated and fewer in number. After the Vikings invaded Anglesey in the tenth century, the church at Llanerchymedd was abandoned and Mary's relics were moved to Llanbabo.

Throughout the early Middle Ages, the guardians of Mary's relics continued to exist as a mystical order in this new and secret location. Word of their existence gradually seeped out and legends were born. These in turn gave rise to the medieval romances where Mary's relics were depicted as a sacred chalice – the Grail. As time went by many different and often unrelated relics and artefacts were portrayed as the Grail, and the true story became more and more confused. Finally in the late twelfth century, Madoc, the last guardian of Mary's relics, decided to bury the remains for fear that they would fall into Norman hands.

Here, at the Llanerchymedd well, the mortal remains of the mother of Jesus might finally have been laid to rest. Paradoxically, this would have been at the very time that the Mary of faith really came of age. At the beginning of the thirteenth century every Roman Catholic church had a Lady chapel added, where the Virgin Mary alone could hear the prayers of the pious. The mysterious woman from Capernaum had now become the saviour of souls – the co-redeemer of the universe.

Summary

- Romantic literature of the Middle Ages portrayed Joseph of Arimathea as the Grail guardian. Although many different artefacts were depicted as Grails in medieval works, in the Joseph story the 'Holy Grail' was the cup used by Jesus at the Last Supper. It was said to have contained a few drops of Christ's blood, and Joseph had been charged by Jesus himself to care for it after his death.

- In the Bible, Joseph of Arimathea is seemingly charged by Jesus not with the safety of the Grail but with the safety of his mother. In the legend, Joseph flees Palestine with the Holy Grail. It is possible that the Grail was being used to symbolize the Virgin Mary – the vessel that brought Christ into the world.

- There is a Grail legend associated with Llanbabo church, where Mary's bones may have been relocated. According to an account originally compiled by the Flemish writer Willem van Hulst around 1200, Madoc, a prince of Gwynedd, discovered the Grail at Llanbabo church. When the Normans threatened to invade his kingdom he evidently removed it to a new place of safety. It is possible that this tradition of Madoc and the Grail may reflect the fact that he was responsible for finally laying Mary's bones to rest.

- In the story Madoc is said to have rehidden the Grail at the place where the sixth-century abbot Cybi was believed to have ascended to heaven. The Dark Age tradition of Cybi's ascension seems to place the event at a now overgrown holy well at Llanerchymedd – the same well where he and Seiriol are said to have met.

- Beside the well is what appears to be a grave marked with two stones – a head and a foot stone – typical of twelfth-century burials. The smaller of the stones is inscribed with the astrological glyph for Virgo – the Virgin. In the Middle Ages this symbol was often used to represent the Virgin Mary.

CHRONOLOGY

BC/BEFORE THE COMMON ERA

1000   David, king of Israel.

587   Jerusalem seized by Babylonians.

515   Persians defeat Babylonians.

460   Herodotus describes trade with Britain.

331   Alexander the Great seizes Palestine.

169   Antiochus IV plunders Jerusalem temple.

167   Revolt led by Judas Maccabaeus.

130   Qumran monastery built.

63   Pompey takes Jerusalem.

55   Julius Caesar attempts to invade Britain.

37   Herod installed as king of Palestine.

27   Augustus, emperor.

19   Work begins on Herod's temple.

4   Birth of Jesus. Death of Herod.

AD/COMMON ERA

6   Direct Roman rule in Judea. Roman tax census.

14   Tiberius, emperor.

26   Pontius Pilate, governor of Judea

30   Jesus begins his ministry.

33   Crucifixion of Jesus.

37	Caligula, emperor. Mary and Joseph of Arimathea arrive in Britain.
41	Claudius, emperor.
43	Claudius invades Britain.
54	Nero, emperor.
57	Paul imprisoned at Caesarea.
59	Paul appeals to emperor Nero.
61	Suetonius Paulinus campaigns in Anglesey.
62	Death of James, Jesus' brother.
64	Fire of Rome. Nero's persecutions of the Christians.
66	Jewish revolt.
70	Romans sack Jerusalem and destroy temple.
90	Josephus writes his histories of the Jews.
112	Pliny the Younger refers to Christians in Ephesus.
115	Suetonius refers to Christians in Claudius' Rome.
120	Papias of Phrygia refers to Matthew's 'sayings'.
131	Second Jewish revolt.
135	Bar Kokhba defeated at fortress of Bethther.
140	Justin Martyr first to portray Mary as Queen of Heaven.
180	Irenaeus of Lyons writes *Proof of the Apostolic Preaching.*
240	Origen of Alexandria refers to Christianity in Britain.
262	Ephesus sacked by the Goths.
325	Council of Nicaea. Roman Catholic Church formed.
327	Empress Helena visits Holy Land.
350	*Codex Sinaiticus,* oldest surviving copy of New Testament.
357	Athanasius, bishop of Alexandria, first to propose Mary's perpetual virginity.
364	Roman empire divides.
375	Epiphanius proposes Mary is referenced in Book of Revelation.
380	Gregory, bishop of Nyssa, first to propose doctrine of the Assumption.
383	Magnus Maximus proclaimed emperor.
401	Alaric, king of the Visigoths, invades northern Italy.
408	Alaric lays siege to Rome.

410   Rome sacked by Alaric. Roman legions leave Britain.

430   *The Testament of John* compiled.

431   Council of Ephesus.

452   Leo, bishop of Rome, persuades Attila and the Huns to spare city.

455   Vandals sack Rome.

470   Anglo-Saxons take control of eastern Britain.

493   Odoacer defeated by Theodoric, chief of the Ostrogoths.

500   Battle of Badon.

517   Severus, bishop of Antioch, claims to discover Mary's tomb in Jerusalem.

526   Pope Felix becomes political leader of old western empire.

539   Battle of Camlan. Death of Arthur.

540   Seiriol at Penmon.

545   Gildas writes *On the Ruin and Conquest of Britain.*

549   Death of Maglocunus.

580   Death of Peredur.

585   Death of Pabo.

590   Gregory the Great, Pope.

593   Gregory defends Rome against the Lombards.

597   Augustine and Paulinus visit Britain.

598   Paulinus in Anglesey.

658   Powys sacked and Cynddylan buried.

664   Synod of Whitby: Celtic and Catholic Churches unite. Death of Cadwaladr.

830   Nennius writes *The History of Britain.*

866   First Viking raids on Anglesey.

880   *The Anglo-Saxon Chronicle* compiled.

955   *The Welsh Annals* compiled.

968   Llanerchymedd church abandoned. Mary's remains moved to Llanbabo.

1061 Richeldis de Faverches builds house of Mary in Walsingham.

1100 Blayse writes original *Folie.*

1130   William of Malmesbury writes *The Ecclesiastical History of Glastonbury.*

1135   Geoffrey of Monmouth writes *The History of the Kings of Britain.*

1190   Monks of Glastonbury Abbey claim to discover Arthur's grave.

1195   Madoc buries Mary's remains at the Cilgwyn well.

1200   Robert de Boron writes *Joseph d'Arimathie.* Extant *Peredur* composed.

1205   *The First Continuation* and *The Didot Perceval* composed.

1220   *The Vulgate Cycle* composed.

1260   *Fulke Fitz Warine* composed.

1330   Surviving copy of *La Folie Perceval* written.

1400   *Sir Gawain and the Green Knight* composed.

1470   Sir Thomas Malory writes *Le Morte D'Arthur.*

1534   Henry VIII has himself recognized as Supreme Head of the Church in England.

1539   Dissolution of monasteries in England.

1583   George Peckham publishes his *True Report.*

1604   Johannes Kepler observes supernova.

1611   King James Authorized Version of the Bible published.

1810   William Blake stays at Elton Manor.

1835   David Friedrich Strauss publishes *Life of Jesus Critically Examined.*

1854   Pope Pius IX declares Immaculate Conception dogma.

1882   General Gordon finds Garden Tomb.

1891   'Mary's house' in Ephesus discovered by Catherine Emmeric.

1945   Nag-Hamadi gospels found in Egypt.

1947   Discovery of Dead Sea Scrolls.

1950   Assumption declared dogma by Pope Pius XII.

REFERENCES

All Bible quotations are from the James I English translation.

CHAPTER I

pp. 3–5   Constantine and the Church: Smith, J. H., *Constantine the Great*, London, 1971.

CHAPTER II

p. 20   Roman Palestine: Freyne, S., *Galilee from Alexander the Great to Hadrian*, Wilmington, 1980.

pp. 21–2 Ancient Israel: Shanks, H., Deser, W., Baruch, H., and McCarter, P., *The Rise of Ancient Israel*, Washington, 1992.

p. 21   The Messiah: Boslooper, T., *The Virgin Birth*, London, 1962, pp. 38–49.

p. 22   Mary's childhood: Ashe, G., *The Virgin*, London, 1976, pp. 76–7.

p. 22   Mary in Church doctrine: Thurian, M., *Mary: Mother of the Lord, Figure of the Church*, London, 1963.

p. 23   James of Ephesus: Graef, H., *Mary: A History of Doctrine and Devotion*, London, 1965, p. 42.

314

p. 23   The *Protevangelium* in Origen: Menzies, A., trans., *Origen*, London, 1897.

p. 23   Pope Pius IX and the Immaculate Conception: Palmer, P., *Mary in the Documents of the Church*, London, 1958, pp. 24–7.

pp. 24–5   Jewish history: Aharoni, Y., Avi-Yonah, M., Rainey, A. F., and Safrai, Z., *The Macmillan Bible Atlas*, New York, 1993.

pp. 25–6   Herod's temple: Millard, A., *Discoveries from the Time of Jesus*, Oxford, 1990, pp. 88–95.

p. 27   Money-changers: *ibid.*, p. 82.

p. 29   Mary's service in the temple: Patsch, J., *Our Lady in the Gospels*, London, 1958, pp. 8–10.

p. 29   Ephesus: Cotchett, C., *Ephesus*, Florence, 1993.

p. 35   Quirinius' census: Schurer, E., *The History of the Jewish People in the Age of Jesus Christ*, Edinburgh, 1973, pp. 400–25.

pp. 38–9   The New Testament and Jewish law: Charlesworth, J., *Jesus within Judaism*, New York, 1988.

p. 39   Bultmann: Bultmann, R., *Jesus and the Word*, New York, 1958.

pp. 40–41   Eusebius and the birth of Catholicism: Cupitt, D., *The Debate about Christ*, London, 1979, ch. 1.

p. 41   Non-canonical gospels: Wilson, I., *Jesus: The Evidence*, London, 1984, pp. 27–8.

p. 41   Nag-Hamadi gospels: Robinson, J., ed., *The Nag Hammadi Library*, San Francisco, 1988.

pp. 41–2   Gospel fragments: Keeley, R., ed., *Jesus 2000*, Oxford, 1989, pp. 17–20.

p. 42   Gospel dating: Barrett, C. K., *The New Testament Background: Selected Documents*, New York, 1961.

p. 42   Irenaeus: Potter, K. R., trans., *Against the Heresies*, London, 1921.

p. 43   Jesus' name: Williams, D., ed., *New Concise Bible Dictionary*, Oxford, 1989, p. 269.

p. 43   Josephus quotation: Whiston, W., trans., *Jewish Antiquities*, Edinburgh, 1867, bk 3, ch. 3, v. 3.

p. 49   Papias quotation: Williamson, G. A., trans., *The History of the Church from Christ to Constantine*, Harmondsworth, 1965, p. 153.

pp. 49–50 I. Wilson: *Jesus: The Evidence*, pp. 38–9.

Chapter III

p. 55   Helena in the Holy Land: Wohl, B., *The Life of St Helena*, New York, 1967.

p. 56   Sepphoris: Myers, B., *Galilee at the Time of Christ*, New York, 1998, pp. 46–58.

pp. 57–8   Suetonius: Graves, R., trans., *The Twelve Caesars*, Harmondsworth, 1957, p. 197.

p. 59   *Yeshua*: Soferman, J., *The Jewish Dictionary*, New York, 1984, pp. 257–9.

pp. 61–3   Bultmann: Bultmann, R., *The History of the Synoptic Tradition*, Oxford, 1963.

p. 62   *Almah* and *betulah*: Vermes, G., *Jesus the Jew*, Philadelphia, 1973, p. 218.

p. 67   Supernova in 5 BC: Clark, D., Parkinson, J., and Stephenson, R., 'An Astronomical Reappraisal of the Star of Bethlehem. A Nova in 5 BC', *Quarterly Journal of the Royal Astronomical Society*, 18 (1977), p. 443.

pp. 68–9   Antipater as Herod's successor: Josephus, *Antiquities*, bk 17, ch. 3, v. 2.

p. 70   Golden eagle: *ibid.*, bk 17, ch. 6, v. 2.

pp. 74–5   Capernaum: Court, A., *Israel*, New York, 1985, pp. 147–53.

pp. 80–81 Fishermen's houses: *ibid.*, p.152.

p. 81   Peter's name: *ibid.*, p.152.

p. 82   Inscription: *ibid.*, p. 152.

CHAPTER IV

p. 93   Jewish revolt: Aharoni *et al.*, *Bible Atlas*, pp. 141–57.

pp. 94–5   Dead Sea Scrolls: Millard, *Discoveries*, pp. 102–7.

p. 96   'They shall separate . . .': Vermes, G., *The Dead Sea Scrolls in English*, Harmondsworth, 1962.

p. 96   'Before I move . . .': *ibid.*

p. 97   'I shall dress not . . .': *ibid.*

pp. 97–9   John the Baptist: Carter, W., *The Essenes*, New York, 1996, pp. 57–64.

p. 98   Two Messiahs: *ibid.*

pp. 99–101   Essene beliefs: Hershel, S., ed., *Understanding the Dead Sea Scrolls*, New York, 1992.

p. 102   'Antipater was appointed . . .': Josephus, *Antiquities*, bk 17, ch. 3, v. 2.

pp. 102–4   Disgrace of Antipater: *ibid.*, bk 17.

p. 104   Demise of Matthias: *ibid.*, bk 17, ch. 6, vs 2–4.

p. 104   Division of Herod's kingdom: Aharoni *et al.*, *Bible Atlas*, pp. 165–6.

pp. 105–10   Schreiber: Schreiber, J., *The Laws of the Jews*, New York, 1956, pp. 42–84.

p. 107   Tacitus: Grant, M., trans., *The Annals of Imperial Rome*, Harmondsworth, 1956, p. 354.

pp. 107–8   Jewish laws: Brandon, S., *The Trial of Jesus of Nazareth*, London, 1968.

pp. 108–10   Jesus as Antipater's son: see also Graves, R. and Podro, J., *The Nazarene Gospel Restored*, London, 1953, pp. 45–63.

pp. 111–12   Origen: Menzies, *Origen*.

pp. 111–12   Anna and Clement: Smith, M., *Clement of Alexandria and a Secret Gospel of Mark*, New York, 1973.

p. 112   Mary in the temple: Budge, E., *Legends of Our Lady the Perpetual Virgin and her Mother Hanna*, Oxford, 1933.

pp. 113–14   Gregory of Nyssa and the Assumption: Smith, G. D.,

The Teachings of the Catholic Church, London, 1948, pp. 41–2.

pp. 113–15   Mary's tomb in Jerusalem: Adams, L., *The Tomb of the Virgin Mary*, New York, 1978.

pp. 114–15   *The Testament of John*: Graef, *Mary* pp. 134–8.

p. 115   Assumption declared dogma: Palmer, *Mary* pp. 57–67.

pp. 115–16   Mary's name: Patsch, *Our Lady*, p. 31.

pp. 117–18   Archelaus removed from office: Aharoni *et al.*, *Bible Atlas*, p. 116.

p. 119   'There was one . . .': Josephus, *Antiquities*, bk 17, ch. 6, v. 2.

p. 120   Antiphilus: *ibid.*, bk 18, ch. 5, v. 2.

p. 121   '[Herod Antipas] feared . . .': *ibid.*

CHAPTER V

pp. 125–7   The Burnt House: Millard, *Discoveries*, pp. 12–13.

p. 127   Pharisees: Williams, D., ed., *New Concise Bible Dictionary*, Oxford, 1989, p. 428.

p. 127   End of Christianity in Jerusalem: Brandon, S., *The Fall of Jerusalem and the Christian Church*, London, 1951.

p. 127   Jesus in the Talmud: Goldstein, M., *Jesus in the Jewish Tradition*, New York, 1950, pp. 22–51.

p. 129   Clement quotation: Brownrigg, R., *The Twelve Apostles*, London, 1974, p. 94.

p. 130   Josephus quotation: *Antiquities*, bk 20, ch. 9, v. 1.

p. 130   Hegesippus on James: preserved in Eusebius' *History of the Church from Christ to Constantine*, Williamson, G., trans., Harmondsworth, 1965, bk 2, ch. 23, pp. 99–102.

p. 130   Juda and Simon: *ibid.*

p. 130   Jude: Williams, D., ed., *New Concise*, p. 292.

p. 133   'He shall cleanse . . .': Vermes, *Dead Sea Scrolls*.

p. 133   'One thousand men . . .': *ibid.*

p. 134   'Everyone who wishes . . .': *ibid.*

pp. 135–8   Paul complains: Galatians 2 and Corinthians.

p. 137   Irenaeus: *Against Heresies*. See trans. Shotwell, J., and Loomis, L., *The See of Peter*, New York, 1991, pp. 265–72.

p. 139   Paul, a Gentile: Brandon, S., 'Saint Paul, the Problem Figure of Christianity', *History Today*, October 1961.

p. 139   Stoicism: *The Hutchinson Encyclopedic Dictionary*, Oxford, 1994, p. 808.

pp. 141–2   Catacomb paintings: De Rosa, D., *A Guide to the Catacombs of Rome*, New York, 1988, pp. 45–63.

p. 144   Irenaeus: *Against Heresies*.

p. 144   Pliny: Kidd, B., *Documents Illustrative of the History of the Church*, Oxford, 1920.

pp. 144–5   Bar Kokhba revolt: Aharoni *et al.*, *Bible Atlas*, pp. 193–7.

p. 146   Christianity at Ephesus: Coburn, B., *Early Christianity in the Greek World*, New York, 1991.

p. 148   Mary depictions in the Priscilla Catacombs: Cronin, V., *Mary Portrayed*, London, 1968.

p. 148   Mary depictions at Ephesus: Grabar, A., *Christian Iconography*, London, 1969.

p. 148   Artemis depictions: Regan, J., *The Temple of Artemis*, London, 1998.

pp. 148–9   Justin: Hemer, C., 'Justin Martyr', in *The History of Christianity*, Berkhamsted, 1977, p.108.

p. 149   The growth of Marian devotion: Palmer, *Mary*.

p. 150   Athanasius: trans. *ibid*.

p. 150   Athanasius: Ferguson, E., 'Athanasius', in *The History of Christianity*, Berkhamsted, 1977, p. 136.

p. 151   Epiphanius Ashe, *Virgin*, pp. 151–3.

p. 151   Ambrose quotation: *ibid.*, p. 182.

pp. 152–3   Nestorius: *ibid.*, pp. 187–92.

pp. 152–3   Council of Ephesus and aftermath: Graef, *Mary*.

p. 153   'the most superior . . .': 66th Dogmatic Constitution of the Church.

p. 154   *The Testament of John*, Helena's church and Mary's tomb: Brownrigg, *Twelve Apostles*, pp. 105–22.

pp. 154–5   Mary's house: *ibid.*, p. 114; Cotchett, *Ephesus*, p. 56.

p. 155   Eusebius: Brownrigg, *Twelve Apostles*, pp. 115–16.

pp. 155–6   John in Ephesus: *ibid.*, pp. 115–19.

pp. 155–6   Clement quotation: *ibid.*, p. 119.

pp. 155–6   Mary in Ephesus: *ibid.*, pp. 104–5.

pp. 160–62   Jewish burial tradition: Dodd, C. H., *Historical Tradition in the Fourth Gospel*, Cambridge, 1963, p. 48.

p. 162   The Name Joses the same as Joseph: Lessing, G., ed., *Junger seiner Jesu und Vondem Zwecke*, Brunswick, 1778.

p. 163   Holy Grail: Lacy, N., ed., *The Arthurian Encylopedia*, London, 1988, pp. 305–8.

CHAPTER VI

pp. 166–70   Joseph in Britain: O'Gorman, R., *The Prose Version of Robert de Boron's Joseph d'Arimathie*, Oxford, 1970.

pp. 166–8   *Evangelium Nicodemi* and *Vindicta Salvatoris*: Newman, D., trans., *Gospel of Nicodemus*, Cambridge, 1961.

p. 168   Grail origins: Phillips, G., and Keatman, M., *King Arthur: The True Story*, London, 1992, pp. 41–3.

p. 168   'Now hear how . . .': Thompson, M., trans., *Joseph d'Arimathie*, London, 1951, p. 14.

p. 169   Herodotus: De Felincourt, A., trans., *The Histories*, London, 1954.

pp. 169–70   Gildas: Winterbottom, M., trans., *De Excidio Britanniae: History from the Sources*, Vol. 7, Chichester, 1978.

pp. 171–3   Walsingham: Goodman, P., *The Shrine of Walsingham*, Norwich, 1938.

p. 181   Geoffrey of Monmouth: Thorpe, L. trans., *History of the Kings of Britain*, London, 1966.

pp. 182–4   Arthur's grave: Treharne, R. F., *The Glastonbury Legends*, London, 1967.

p. 183   Relics: Bentley, J., *Restless Bones*, London, 1985, pp. 34–62.

p. 184   William of Malmesbury: Marriot, B., trans., *Chronicle of the Kings of England*, London, 1866.

p. 185   'In the western confines . . .': *ibid.*, p. 109. For analysis of the letter and other surviving copies of it, see Dobson, C., *Did Our Lord Visit Britain?*, Glastonbury, 1936, p. 44.

p. 185   Church dedications: Bentley, *Restless Bones*.

pp. 186–7   Decline of the Roman empire: Jones, A. M. J., *The Decline of the Ancient World*, London, 1966.

p. 188   Anglo-Saxons: Hodgkin, R. H., *A History of the Anglo-Saxons*, London, 1952.

p. 188   Alaric and the Visigoths: Todd, R., 'The Fall of the Roman Empire', in *The History of Christianity*, Berkhamsted, 1977, pp. 179–80.

p. 188   Jerome quotation: *ibid.*, p. 179.

p. 189   Attila: Thomson, E. A., *A History of Attila and the Huns*, Oxford, 1948.

p. 189   Leo: Todd, 'The Fall', in *The History of Christianity*, Berkhamsted, 1977, p.182.

p. 190   Irenaeus' list: Duffy, E., *Saints and Sinners*, New York, 1997, p. 11.

pp. 190–91   Early Church: Fredricksen, P., *From Jesus to Christ*, New York, 1988.

p. 191   Damasus: Duffy, *Saints*, pp. 25–7.

pp. 192–3   Gregory the Great: Rosenberg, H., 'The West in Crisis', in *The History of Christianity*, Berkhamsted, 1977, pp. 218–22.

p. 193   William of Malmesbury: Marriot, *Chronicle*.

p. 194   Peter the rock: Matthew 16:18.

p. 195   Arthur mortally wounded: Geoffrey of Monmouth, *History of the Kings of Britain*.

CHAPTER VII

pp. 198–9   Geoffrey: *History of the Kings of Britain.*

p. 199   Nennius quotation: Morris, J., trans., 'Historia Britonum', in *History from the Sources*, vol. 8, Chichester, 1980.

p. 200   Gildas: Winterbottom, *De Excidio.*

p. 200   The historical Arthur: Phillips, G., *The Search for the Grail*, London, 1996.

p. 202   Chrétien: Topsfield, L. T., *Chrétien de Troyes: A Study of the Arthurian Romances*, Cambridge 1981.

p. 202   Malory: Malory, T., *Le Morte D'Arthur*, London, 1972.

pp. 202–5   *Song of Llywarch the Old*: Williams, I., ed., *Canu Llywarch Hen*, Cardiff, 1935.

p. 204   *Welsh Annals*: Morris, J., trans., *The Welsh Annals*, in *History from the Sources.*

p. 204   *Anglo-Saxon Chronicle*: Garmonsway, G. N., trans., *The Anglo-Saxon Chronicle*, London, 1967.

p. 205   'Lament of Heledd': Williams, I., *Canu Llywarch Hen.*

pp. 205–6   Baschurch: *Transcript of the Shropshire Archaeological and Historical Society*, vol. 49, Shrewsbury, 1937.

p. 206   Cauldron: *ibid.*

pp. 206–7   Churches of Bassa: *ibid.*

pp. 207–11   *Song of Llywarch the Old*: Williams, I., *Canu Llywarch Hen.*

pp. 211–14   Viroconium: Phillips and Keatman, *King Arthur*, pp. 135–43.

p. 214   *Welsh Annals*: Morris, in *History from the Sources.*

pp. 214–15   Arthur, name derivation: Phillips and Keatman, *King Arthur*, pp. 127–9.

p. 216   Gildas: Winterbottom, *De Excidio.*

p. 217   Geoffrey: *History of the Kings of Britain.*

p. 217   *Welsh Annals*: Morris, in *History from the Sources.*

p. 217   Gildas: Winterbottom, *De Excidio.*

Chapter VIII

p. 222   Owain's overthrow: Winterbottom, *De Excidio*.

p. 223   Augustine: Marriot, *Chronicle*.

pp. 224–5   Grail romances: Bogdanow, F., *The Romance of the Grail*, Manchester, 1966.

p. 225   *First Continuation* quotation: Roach, W., ed., *The Continuations of the Old French 'Perceval'*, Philadelphia, 1983.

p. 226   *Didot Perceval* quotation: Skeels, D., trans., *The Romance of Perceval in Prose*, Seattle, 1961.

p. 226   *Fulk Fitz Warine* quotation: Wright, T., trans., *Fulke le Fitz Waryn*, London, 1855.

p. 227   'The Tale of Branwen' Jones and Jones, *Mabinogion*.

p. 227   Bran's head: Wright, *Fulke*.

p. 228   *First Continuation* quotation: Roach, *Continuations*.

p. 228   *Peredur*: Jones and Jones, *Mabinogion*.

p. 228   *Didot Perceval* quotation: Skeels, *Romance*.

p. 229   *Ichthys*: Hemer, C., 'Justin Martyr', in *The History of Christianity*, Berkhamsted, 1977, p. 57.

p. 229   The name Avalon: Stephens, *Oxford Companion*, p. 671.

p. 230   Boudica revolt: Wood, M., *In Search of the Dark Ages*, London, 1991, pp. 13–36.

p. 230   Atherstone: *ibid.*, pp. 30–2.

pp. 230–31   Tacitus: *Annals*.

p. 231   *Book of Taliesin*: Williams, T., trans., *The Book of Taliesin*, Cardiff, 1966.

p. 231   Tacitus quotation: *Annals*.

pp. 231–2   Druids on Anglesey: Stephens, *Oxford Companion*, pp. 154–6.

p. 233   Origen: Menzies, *Origen*.

p. 234   *The Life of St Elen*: Driscoll, M., trans., *Elen Luyddog*, Cardiff, 1931.

p. 234   Pillar of Eliseg: Phillips and Keatman, *King Arthur*, p. 92.

pp. 234–5   Maximus crest: *ibid.*, p. 189.

p. 235   Nennius: Morris, in *History from the Sources*.

p. 236   Myrddin: Stephens, *Oxford Companion*, pp. 419–20.

p. 236   *Welsh Annals* quotation: Morris, in *History from the Sources*.

p. 236   Geoffrey: *History of the Kings of Britain*.

pp. 236–7   *Dream of Rhonabwy* quotation: Jones and Jones, *Mabinogion*.

p. 238   *La Folie Perceval*: MS. Fonds français 12577, Bibliothèque Nationale, Paris.

p. 238   *Didot Perceval*: Skeels, *Romance*.

p. 238   Blayse: Phillips, *Search*, pp. 146–8.

pp. 238–9   Owain's genealogies: *ibid.*, pp. 135–45.

p. 239   The historical Fulk: Burns, M., *The History of Shropshire*, London, 1958, pp. 56–67.

p. 239   *Fulk Fitz Warine*: Wright, *Fulke*.

p. 239   *Feet of Fines*: Page, M., ed., *English Historical Documents*, vol. 3, London, 1958, p. 227.

p. 240   *La Folie* quotation: translation from *MS. Fonds français 12577* by Jane Parker.

pp. 240–41 Seiriol: *Lives of the British Saints*, pp. 177–80.

p. 241   Seiriol and Cybi, pilgrimage: *ibid.*, p. 179.

p. 241   Celtic traditions: Chadwick, N. K., *Celtic Britain*, New York, 1963.

pp. 241–2   Eostre: Barnes, J., *The Celts and Christianity*, London, 1968, pp. 54–8.

p. 242   *Royal Commission Survey: Anglesey: A Survey and Inventory by the Royal Commission on Ancient and Historical Monuments in Wales*, London, 1990, pp. 119–28.

p. 244   Jesus as *Sol Invictus*: Wilson, p. 137.

CHAPTER IX

pp. 247–9   Joker and Fool: Benham, W. G., *Playing Cards: Their History and Secrets*, London, 1931.

pp. 249–53   *Folie*: Parker.

p. 250   *Sir Gawain and the Green Knight*: Lacy, *Encyclopedia*, pp. 404–6.

p. 252   *Didot Perceval*: Skeels, *Romance*.

p. 252   *First Continuation*: Roach, *Continuations*.

p. 252   *Vulgate Cycle*: Burns, J. E., *Arthurian Fictions: Re-reading the Vulgate Cycle*, Columbus, 1985.

p. 254   *Peredur*: Jones and Jones, *Mabinogion*.

p. 254   *Welsh Annals*: Morris, in *History from the Sources*.

pp. 255–6   Bran in *The Red Book*: Jones and Jones, *Mabinogion*.

p. 255   Fifth-century Wales: Bowen, E., *The Settlements of the Celtic Saints in Wales*, Aberystwyth, 1956.

p. 255   Cadwallon Lawhir: *Lives*, p. 209.

p. 255   Bran in Grail romances: Loomis, R. S., *Wales and the Arthurian Legend*, Cardiff, 1966.

pp. 257–8   Alternative apostolic succession: Phillips, *Search*, pp. 116–17.

p. 258   Seiriol *Gwasmair*: Peniarth MS. 77, National Library of Wales, Aberystwyth.

pp. 259–60   Cybi's and Seiriol's wells: Jones, R., *The Monuments of Môna*, Bangor, 1997.

pp. 260–61   Meaning of Llanerchymedd: Bowen, *Settlements*, pp. 1–2.

p. 265   Ossuary burials: Millard, *Discoveries*, pp. 124–5.

p. 266   Llanerchymedd church: *Anglesey: A Survey and Inventory by the Royal Commission on Ancient and Historical Monuments in Wales*, London, 1960, p. 61.

p. 267   *Brut y Tywysogyon*: Jones, T., ed., *Brut y Tywysogyon*, Aberystwyth, 1941.

p. 267   Catamanus inscription: *Anglesey: A Survey and Inventory*, pp. civ, cvii, 87; pl. 19.

p. 268   Camuloris's coffin: *Anglesey: A Survey and Inventory*, pp. cvi, cviii; pl. 15.

p. 269   Paulinus in Britain: William of Malmesbury, *Chronicle*.

pp. 269–70 Inscribed stone: *Anglesey: A Survey and Inventory*, pp. cix–cxiii; pl. 20.

p. 271   *Welsh Annals*: Morris, in *History from the Sources*.

pp. 272–4   Llangadwaladr church: *Anglesey: A Survey and Inventory*, pp. 85–7.

pp. 272–3   Cadwaladr: Jones, *Brut y Tywysogyon*.

pp. 275–6   Welsh ditty: *Lives*, p. 39.

p. 276   *Welsh Annals*: Morris, in *History from the Sources*.

p. 276   Pabo: *Lives*, pp. 38–9.

p. 276   *Folie*: Parker.

p. 277   Pabo's tombstone: *Anglesey: A Survey and Inventory*, pp. cxxxiii, cxxxiv, 35.

CHAPTER X

p. 280   Rosary: *Hutchinson Encyclopedic Dictionary*, p. 715.

p. 281   Celtic calendar: Widowson, K., *The Festivals of the Pagan Year*, London, 1969, pp. 23–31.

pp. 281–2   Queen of Hearts: Benham, W. G., *Playing Cards: Their History and Secrets*, London, 1931.

pp. 281–2   Origins of playing cards: *ibid.*

pp. 283–4   Madoc: Evans, R., *The Legend of Prince Madoc*, Cardiff, 1932.

p. 286   Gruffudd ap Cynan: Stephens, *Oxford Companion*, pp. 228–9.

pp. 286–7   Owain ap Gruffudd: *ibid.*, p. 443.

p. 287   Rhodri, Dafydd and Madoc: *ibid.*, pp. 381–2.

pp. 287–8   Willem van Hulst: Owens, P., trans., *The Voyage of Madoc*, London, 1893.

pp. 289–90 Peckham quotations: Evans, *Prince Madoc*, p. 51.

pp. 290–91 *Life of Cybi*: Cotton MS. Vespasian. A.XIV.

pp. 291–2 *Engraving: MS. Fonds français 12577, Bibliothèque Nationale*, Paris.

SELECT BIBLIOGRAPHY

Ackroyd, P. R., and Evans, C. F., eds, *The Cambridge History of the Bible*. Cambridge 1970.

Adams, L., *The Tomb of the Virgin Mary.* New York 1978.

Aharoni, Y., *The Land of the Bible: A Historical Geography.* London 1967.

——, Avi-Yonah, M., Rainey, A. F., and Safrai, Z., *The Macmillan Bible Atlas.* New York 1993.

Albright, W. F., *Archaeology and the Religion of Israel.* New York 1969.

——, *The Archaeology of Palestine.* Harmondsworth 1956.

Alcock, L., *Arthur's Britain: History and Archaeology AD 376–634.* London 1971.

Anderson, G. W., *The History of the Religion of Israel.* Oxford 1966.

Anderson, M., *History and Imagery in Parish Churches.* London 1971.

Ashe, G., *The Quest for Arthur's Britain.* London 1968.

——, *The Virgin.* London 1976.

——, *A Guidebook to Arthurian Britain.* Wellingborough 1983.

——, *The Discovery of King Arthur.* London 1985.

Attwater, D., *The Penguin Dictionary of Saints.* London 1965.

Aune, D., *The New Testament in Its Literary Environment.* Philadelphia 1987.

Avi-Yonah, M., ed., *Encyclopaedia of Archaeological Excavations in the Holy Land.* Oxford 1976.

Bacon, E., ed., *The Great Archaeologists.* London 1976.

Barber, R., *King Arthur in Legend and History.* London 1973.

Barnes, J., *The Celts and Christianity.* London 1968.

Barrett, C. K., *The New Testament Background: Selected Documents.* New York 1961.

Baugh, G. C., and Cox, D. C., *Monastic Shropshire.* Shrewsbury 1982.

Bean, G., *Aegean Turkey: An Archaeological Guide.* London 1966.

Beebe, H. K., *The Old Testament.* London 1970.

Ben-Dov, M., *In the Shadow of the Temple: The Discovery of Ancient Jerusalem.* London 1985.

Benham, W. G., *Playing Cards: Their History and Secrets.* London 1931.

Bentley, J., *Restless Bones.* London 1985.

Boardman, J., *The Greeks Overseas.* Harmondsworth 1964.

Bogdanow, F., *The Romance of the Grail.* Manchester 1966.

Boslooper, T., *The Virgin Birth.* London 1962.

Bowen, E., *The Settlements of the Celtic Saints in Wales.* Aberyswyth 1956.

Brammel, E., and Moule, C., *Jesus and the Politics of His Day.* Cambridge 1984.

Brandon, S., *The Fall of Jerusalem and the Christian Church.* London 1951.

——, *Creation Legends of the Ancient Near East.* London 1963.

——, *The Trial of Jesus of Nazareth.* London, 1968.

Bright, J. A., *History of Israel.* London 1972.

Brooke, R., *Popular Religion in the Middle Ages.* London 1984.

Brotherstone, G., *World Archaeoastronomy.* Cambridge 1989.

Brown, F., *Hebrew and the English Lexicon of the Old Testament.* Oxford 1906.

Brownrigg, R., *The Twelve Apostles.* London 1974.

Budge, E., *Legends of Our Lady the Perpetual Virgin and her Mother Hanna.* Oxford 1933.

Bultmann, R., *Jesus and the Word.* New York 1958.

——, *The History of the Synoptic Tradition.* Oxford 1963.

Burney, C. F., *The Aramaic Origin of the Fourth Gospel.* Oxford 1922.

Burns, J. E., *Arthurian Fictions: Re-reading the Vulgate Cycle.* Columbus 1985.

Burns, M., *The History of Shropshire.* London 1958.

Calvin, J., *A Treatise on Relics.* Edinburgh 1864.

Carlson, J., and Ludwig, R., *Jesus and Faith.* New York 1984.

Carmichael, J., *The Death of Jesus.* London 1963.

Carter, W., *The Essenes.* New York 1996.

Cassuto, U., *A Commentary on the Book of Exodus.* Jerusalem 1961.

Cavendish, R., *King Arthur and the Grail.* London 1978.

Chadwick, N. K., *Celtic Britain.* New York 1963.

——, *The Celts.* Harmondsworth 1970.

——, *The Age of the Saints in the Early Celtic Church.* London 1981.

Chambers, E. K., *English Literature at the Close of the Middle Ages.* Oxford 1945.

Clancy, J., *The Earliest Welsh Poetry.* London 1970.

Coburn, B., *Early Christianity in the Greek World.* New York 1991.

Comfort, W. W., *Arthurian Romances.* New York 1914.

Conran, A., ed., *The Penguin Book of Welsh Verse.* London 1967.

Cotchett, C., *Ephesus.* Florence 1993.

Court, A., *Israel.* New York 1985.

Cronin, V., *Mary Portrayed.* London 1968.

Crossley-Holland, K., *British Folk Tales.* London 1987.

Cupitt, D., *The Debate about Christ.* London 1979.

Davidson, H. E., *Gods and Myths in Northern Europe.* Harmondsworth 1964.

Davidson, R., and Leaney, A. R. C., *The Penguin Guide to Modern Theology.* Harmondsworth 1970.

De Felincourt, A., trans., *The Histories.* London 1954.

De Rosa, D., *A Guide to the Catacombs of Rome.* New York 1988.

Deissmann, A., *St Paul: A Study in Social and Religious History.* London 1912.

Delaney, F., *Legends of the Celts.* London 1989.

Dickinson, O., *The Aegean Bronze Age.* Cambridge 1994.

Dillon, M., and Chadwick, N. K., *The Celtic Realms.* New York 1967.

Dobson, C., *Did Our Lord Visit Britain?* Glastonbury 1936.

Dodd, C. H., *Historical Tradition in the Fourth Gospel.* Cambridge 1963.

Downing, G. F., *Cynics and Christian Origins.* Edinburgh 1992.

Driscoll, M., trans., *Elen Luyddog.* Cardiff 1931.

Duffy, E., *Saints and Sinners.* New York 1997.

Dunning, R., *Arthur: King in the West.* London 1988.

Eusebius (Williamson, G. A., trans.), *The History of the Church from Christ to Constantine.* Harmondsworth 1965.

Evans, G. J., *Poems from the Book of Taliesin.* Llanbedrog 1915.

Evans, R., *The Legend of Prince Madoc.* Cardiff 1932.

Feldman, L., trans. (Josephus), *Jewish Antiquities.* London 1981.

Fife, G., *Arthur the King.* London 1990.

Finegan, J., *The Archaeology of the New Testament.* Princeton 1969.

Ford, P., *The Mabinogion and Other Medieval Welsh Tales.* Los Angeles 1977.

Fox, R. L., *Pagans and Christians.* New York 1968.

Fredricksen, P., *From Jesus to Christ.* New York 1988.

Frere, S., *Britannia.* London 1967.

Freyne, S., *Galilee from Alexander the Great to Hadrian.* Wilmington 1980.

Garmonsway, G. N., trans., *The Anglo-Saxon Chronicle.* London 1967.

Geoffrey of Monmouth (Thorpe, T., trans.), *History of the Kings of Britain.* London 1966.

Gildas (Winterbottom, M., trans.), *De Excidio Britanniae: History from the Sources* Vol. 7. Chichester 1978.

Goetinck, G., *Peredur: A Study of Welsh Tradition in the Grail Legends.* Cardiff 1975.

Goldstein, M., *Jesus in the Jewish Tradition.* New York 1950.

Goodman, P., *The Shrine of Walsingham.* Norwich 1938.

Grabar, A., *Christian Iconography*. London 1969.

Graef, H., *Mary: A History of Doctrine and Devotion*. London 1965.

Grant, M., trans., (Tacitus) *The Annals of Imperial Rome*. Harmondsworth 1956.

Graves, R., trans., *The Twelve Caesars*. Harmondsworth 1957.

——, *The Greek Myths*. Harmondsworth 1960.

——, and Podro, J., *The Nazarene Gospel Restored*. London 1953.

Gray, J., *The Canaanites*. London 1964.

Green, M., *The Gods of the Celts*. Gloucester 1986.

Hargrave, C., *A History of Playing Cards*. New York 1966.

Harker, R., *Digging up the Bible Lands*. London 1972.

Hershel, S., ed., *Understanding the Dead Sea Scrolls*. New York 1992.

Hodgkin, R. H., *A History of the Anglo-Saxons*, vols 1 and 2. London 1952.

James, E., *The Cult of the Mother Goddess*. London 1959.

Jarman, A. O. H., and Hughes, G. R., *A Guide to Welsh Literature*. Swansea 1976.

Jones, A., *The Herods of Judea*. Oxford 1938.

Jones, A. M. H., *The Decline of the Ancient World*. London 1966.

Jones, G., and Jones T., eds, *The Mabinogion*. London 1975.

——, ed., *The Oxford Book of Welsh Verse in English*. Oxford 1977.

Jones, R., *The Monuments of Mona*. Bangor 1997.

Jones, T., ed., *Brut y Tywysogyon*. Aberystwyth 1941.

Josephus (Feldman, L., trans.), *Jewish Antiquities*. London 1981.

——, (Williamson, G. A., trans.), *The Jewish War*. Harmondsworth 1981.

Kee, A., *Constantine versus Christ*. London 1982.

Keeley, R., ed., *Jesus 2000*. Oxford 1989.

Keller, W., *The Bible as History*. London 1974.

Kenyon, K. M., *Archaeology in the Holy Land*. London 1965.

——, *The Bible and Recent Archaeology*. London 1978.

Kidd, B., *Documents Illustrative of the History of the Church*. Oxford 1920.

Klausner, J., *Jesus of Nazareth*. London 1925.

Kopp, C., *The Holy Places of the Gospels*. London 1963.

Lacy, N., ed., *The Arthurian Encyclopedia*. London 1988.

Lessing, G., ed., *Junger seiner Jesu und Vondem Zwecke*. Brunswick 1778.

Livius, T. *The Blessed Virgin*. London 1893.

Loomis, R. S., *Arthurian Literature in the Middle Ages*. Oxford 1959.

——, *Wales and the Arthurian Legend*. Cardiff 1966.

——, *The Grail: From Celtic Myth to Christian Symbol*. London 1993.

Maccoby, H., *Revolution in Judea: Jesus and the Jewish Resistance*. London 1973.

Mackey, J. P., *Jesus: The Man and the Myth*. London 1979.

Magnusson, M., *BC: The Archaeology of the Bible Lands*. London 1977.

Malory, T., *Le Morte D'Arthur*. London 1972.

Marchant, J., *The Madonna: an Anthology*. London 1928.

Marriot, B., trans. (William of Malmesbury), *Chronicle of the Kings of England*. London 1866.

Mascall, E. L., and Box, H. S., *The Blessed Virgin Mary*. London 1963.

May, H. G., ed., *Oxford Bible Atlas*. Oxford 1974.

Menzies, A., trans., *Origen*. London 1897.

Miegge, G., *The Virgin Mary*. Lutterworth 1955.

Millard, A., *Discoveries from the Time of Jesus*. Oxford 1990.

Moorey, P. R. S., *Biblical Lands*. London 1975.

Morris, J., *The Age of Arthur*, vols 1, 2 and 3. Chichester 1977.

——, *History from the Sources* vol. 8. Chichester 1980.

Moule, C., *The Birth of the New Testament*. London 1962.

Myers, B., *Galilee at the Time of Christ*. New York 1998.

Negev, A., ed., *Archaeological Encyclopaedia of the Holy Land*. London 1973.

Nennius (Morris, J., trans.), *Historia Britonum, History from the Sources*, vol. 8, Chichester 1980.

Newman, D., trans., *Gospel of Nicodemus*. Cambridge 1961.

Nitze, W., trans., *Perlesvaus*. Chicago 1937.

Noth, M., *The History of Israel*. London 1960.

O'Gorman, R., *The Prose Version of Robert de Boron's Joseph d'Arimathie*. Oxford 1970.

Olmstead, A. T., *Jesus in the Light of History*. New York 1952.

Owen, D. D. R., *The Evolution of the Grail Legend*. London 1968.

Owens, P., trans., *The Voyage of Madoc*. London 1893.

Page, M., ed., *English Historical Documents*, vol. 3. London 1958.

Palmer, P., *Mary in the Documents of the Church*. London 1958.

Parry, T., *A History of Welsh Literature*. Oxford 1955.

Patsch, J., *Our Lady in the Gospels*. London 1958.

Pattie, T. S., *Manuscripts of the Bible*. London 1979.

Petrie, W. M. F., *Researches in Sinai*. London 1906.

Phillips, G., *The Search for the Grail*. London 1996.

——, and Keatman, M., *King Arthur: The True Story*. London 1992.

Polano, H., *The Talmud: Selections*. London 1876.

Pollard, A., *The Romance of King Arthur*. London 1979.

Potter, K. R., trans., *Against the Heresies*. London 1921.

Prichard, J. B., *Ancient Near Eastern Texts Relating to the Old Testament*. Princeton 1969.

Regan, J., *The Temple of Artemis*. London 1998.

Renfrew, A. C., *Archaeology and Language*. London 1987.

Roach, W., ed., *The Continuations of the Old French 'Perceval'*. Philadelphia 1983.

Robinson, J., *Honest to God*. London 1963.

——, *Can We Trust the New Testament?* London 1977.

Rowley. H. H., *From Joseph to Joshua*. London 1950.

Sacker, H. D., *An Introduction to Wolfram's Parzival*. Cambridge 1963.

Salway, P., *The Frontier People of Roman Britain*. Cambridge 1965.

Schaberg, J., *The Illegitimacy of Jesus*. San Francisco 1987.

Scholem, G., *The Messianic Idea in Judaism*. New York 1971.

Schreiber, J., *The Laws of the Jews*. New York 1956.

Schurer, E., *The History of the Jewish People in the Age of Jesus Christ*. Edinburgh, 1987.

Schweitzer, A., *The Quest for the Historical Jesus*. New York 1968.

Shanks, H., *Understanding the Dead Sea Scrolls*. New York 1992.

——, Deser, W., Baruch, H., and McCarter, P., *The Rise of Ancient Israel.* Washington 1992.

Sharp, M., *The Churches of Rome.* London 1967.

Sherwin-White, A. N., *Roman Society and Roman Law in the New Testament.* Oxford 1963.

Shotwell, J., and Loomis, L., *The See of Peter.* New York 1991.

Skeels, D., trans., *The Romance of Perceval in Prose.* Seattle 1961.

Smallwood, E. M., *The Jews under Roman Rule.* London 1976.

Smith, G. D., *The Teachings of the Catholic Church.* London 1948.

Smith, J. H., *Constantine the Great.* London 1971.

Smith, M., *Clement of Alexandria and a Secret Gospel of Mark.* New York 1973.

Soferman, J., *The Jewish Dictionary.* New York 1984.

Stambaugh, J., and Balch, D., *The Social World of the First Christians.* London 1986.

Stephens, M., ed., *The Oxford Companion to the Literature of Wales.* Oxford 1986.

Strauss, D. F., *The Life of Jesus Critically Examined.* London 1846.

Tacitus (Grant, M., trans.), *The Annals of Imperial Rome.* Harmondsworth 1956.

Thomas, C., *Britain and Ireland in Early Christian Times.* London 1971.

Thomas, D. W., ed., *Documents from Old Testament Times.* London 1958.

Thomas, W., trans., *Life of St Paul Aurelian.* London 1967.

Thomas, W. J., ed., *Early English Prose Romance.* London 1858.

Thompson, M., trans., *Joseph d'Arimathie.* London 1951.

Thomson, E. A., *A History of Attila and the Huns.* Oxford 1948.

Thorpe, T., trans. (Geoffrey of Monmouth), *History of the Kings of Britain.* London 1966.

Thurian, M., *Mary: Mother of the Lord, Figure of the Church.* London 1963.

Topsfield, L. T., *Chrétien de Troyes: A Study of the Arthurian Romances.* Cambridge 1981.

Treharne, R. F., *The Glastonbury Legends.* London 1967.

Vermes, G., *The Dead Sea Scrolls in English*. Harmondsworth 1962.

——, *Jesus the Jew*. Philadelphia 1973.

Ward, B., *Miracles and the Medieval Mind*. London 1983.

Weinstein, D., and Bell, R., *Saints and Society: The Two Worlds of Western Christendom*. Chicago 1983.

Wells, G., *The Historical Evidence for Jesus*. New York 1982.

Westwood, J., *Albion: A Guide to Legendary Britain*. London 1987.

Whiston, W., trans., *Jewish Antiquities*. Edinburgh 1867.

Whitelock, D., ed., *English Historical Documents: 500–1042*. London 1955.

Widowson, K., *The Festivals of the Pagan Year*. London 1969.

Wilkinson, J., *Jerusalem as Jesus Knew It: Archaeology as Evidence*. London 1982.

William of Malmesbury (Marriot, B., trans.), *Chronicle of the Kings of England*. London 1866.

Williams, A. H., *An Introduction to the History of Wales*. Cardiff 1962.

Williams, D., ed., *New Concise Bible Dictionary*. Oxford 1989.

Williams, I., ed., *Canu Llywarch Hen*. Cardiff 1935.

Williams, T., trans., *The Book of Taliesin*. Cardiff 1966.

Williamson, G. A., trans., (Eusebius), *The History of the Church from Christ to Constantine*. Harmondsworth 1965.

——, trans. (Josephus), *The Jewish War*. Harmondsworth 1981.

Wilson, E., *The Scrolls from the Dead Sea*. New York 1955.

Wilson, I., *Jesus: The Evidence*. London 1984.

Wilson, R. M., *The Lost Literature of Medieval England*. London 1952.

Wilson, S., *Saints and Their Cults: Studies in Religious Sociology, Folkore and History*. Cambridge 1983.

Winter, P., *On the Trial of Jesus*. Berlin 1961.

Winterbottom, M., trans. (Gildas), *De Excidio* Britanniae: *History from the Sources*, vol. 7. Chichester 1978.

Wohl, B., *The Life of St Helena*. New York 1967.

Wood, M., *In Search of the Dark Ages.* London 1991.
Wright, T., trans., *Fulke le Fitz Waryn.* London 1855.
Yadin, Y., *The Art of War in Biblical Lands.* London 1963.
——, *Hazor: Great Citadels of the Bible.* London 1975.

INDEX

Historia Brittonum, 199
History of the Kings of Britain,
181, 238
Holy Grail, 1, 2, 3, 9, 12, 162,
163, 166, 168, 170, 181,
182, 184, 195, 196, 224, 225,
226, 227, 228, 229, 231,
232, 237, 238, 239, 240, 246,
247, 249, 250, 251, 252,
253, 254, 255, 257, 258, 265,
273, 281, 282, 283, 284,
290, 291, 292, 294, 302, 308,
309
Holy Inquisition, 11, 15
Holy Office, 11, 14, 163, 173
holy wells, 242, 243, 264
Holyhead, 232, 241, 243, 260,
262, 271, 291
Honorius, 187, 189
Hound Tor, 175
House of Mary, Ephesus, 154
Huns, 186, 188, 189
Hywel, 287

Immaculate Conception, the,
18, 22, 23
Ireland, 207, 215, 255, 287, 289
Irenaeus, 42, 137, 144, 155, 190
Isaiah, 21, 60, 61, 62, 99, 107,
121
Israel, 18, 19, 21, 22, 23, 24,
35, 54, 71, 91, 93, 95, 107,
117, 121, 122, 133, 135, 136,
143, 144, 151, 304, 305
Israel Museum, 35

Italy, 5, 10, 189, 191, 192, 234

Jacob, father of Joseph, 34, 70,
71, 288
James I, 249, 274
James of Ephesus, 23, 28, 29,
35, 50, 111, 112
James the Younger, 83, 84
James Whitmore, 182, 183, 184,
185
James, brother of Jesus, 40, 43,
129, 130, 140, 162
James, son of Zebedee, 47, 76,
77, 83, 84, 158
Jamnia, 142
Jehovah, 21
Jericho, 59, 83
Jerome, 188
Jerusalem, 10, 14, 16, 18, 20,
22, 23, 24, 27, 28, 30, 31,
34, 35, 37, 38, 39, 42, 45,
46, 50, 51, 55, 59, 70, 73,
75, 83, 84, 88, 93, 99, 100,
101, 102, 103, 104, 107, 108,
110, 111, 112, 114, 116, 117,
123, 125, 127, 129, 130,
132, 136, 137, 138, 139, 140,
142, 143, 144, 145, 160,
171, 176, 179, 180, 265, 305
Jerusalem Temple, 20, 22, 23,
24, 25, 26, 27, 28, 29, 34,
39, 42, 44, 51, 54, 70, 73,
79, 93, 100, 101, 102, 104,
106, 107, 111, 112, 116, 122,